THE
GAY REFORMER

MAURITZ A. HALLGREN

THE
GAY REFORMER

Profits before Plenty under

FRANKLIN D. ROOSEVELT

NEW YORK · ALFRED · A · KNOPF

1935

CONTENTS

CONTENTS

PART ONE

~

WARM AND HUMAN WORLD

ᔊ

THAT there ever would arise a pressing need for bread and circuses probably never occurred to the members of the household into which Franklin D. Roosevelt was born. To them it must have seemed unnecessary that any worthy citizen should have to face the rigors of actual want at any time. Rather would honest toil, self-discipline and a civilized way of life always bring to every man, high or low, a fair reward according to his particular station. Nor were the James Roosevelts of Hyde Park content merely to hold such a philosophy. They practiced its virtues. And they sought to apply it concretely in their relations with the persons, the servants and employees, for whose welfare they felt they were responsible.

Doubtless it could not have been otherwise, for it appears that the Roosevelts were in no way concerned with, and most likely not even aware of, the deeper problems of American capitalism. Members of their class were apt to take it for granted, to borrow a phrase from Charles A. Beard, that "the magnificent system of acquisition and enjoyment . . . would last forever." There was no reason why James Roosevelt, who preferred the ease of a country gentleman but had also his banking and business affairs to consider, should have thought differently. At that time, indeed, virtually everybody was convinced that American business enterprise was destined to go on to ever greater triumphs. It was not only the heyday of the robber barons, not only the Gilded Age of American capitalism, but it was also the period that saw the "American dream" at the apex of its alluring glory. Democracy and equal opportunity would bring ever expanding prosperity for all. Few were the Americans who did not believe this, and those few perhaps only the disgruntled workers in the shops and factories and the German Socialists who had but lately arrived in the country.

There were, of course, certain questions and incidents that arose upon occasion, and these had to be pondered and understood, at least to the extent that they might bear upon one's own fortunes. Difficulties of a financial nature would develop in spite of everything. The practices of the money changers and merchants were not always above reproach. Now and then, in fact, they led to protest and scandal. Political discontents nettled the ruling classes abroad quite frequently, and that sometimes happened also at home, though usually to a lesser degree. And it was not always possible to prevent labor unrest from arising in the background.

These matters were of varying interest and importance to James Roosevelt. While they were in essence alien to the secure and peaceful environment of Hyde Park, they seem to have been discussed within the family circle there as well as at the Roosevelt offices in New York City. For the Roosevelts were possessed of a lively and sympathetic, if somewhat lofty, curiosity regarding the world about them, though it appears that the emphasis was more on questions pertaining to business, finance, cultural activities and good neighborliness than upon the broader problems of social or economic morality.

There came a day, however, when the affairs of the outside world held little interest for the Roosevelts. The panic that was sweeping the financial centers of Europe toward the end of January in 1882, the latest political crisis in France, the endless warfare of the American railway kings, the growing labor troubles of the day, the Peruvian Company and Manhattan

4

Elevated scandals, the Congressional debate on the Funding Bill (a "communistic" measure to the conservatives in the Senate) — all these were for the time forgotten. On this day, January 30, 1882, a son, Franklin Delano, was born to the Roosevelts of Hyde Park.

The arrival of a son in any household is usually a matter of no small moment, but it was notably true of the Roosevelt household. One may not attribute this solely to pride of family, though both parents came from well-established native stock and were pleasantly conscious of the fact. Moreover, the head of the house already had a son by a former wife to carry on the family name. Rather does it seem to have been pride of life, the sheer joy of living, which the two parents shared in abundant measure, that made the advent of another human being in the household the supreme occasion that it was.

It was enough for the elder Roosevelts to know that they had a son — he was the first and only child of Mrs. Sara Delano Roosevelt — and that they could provide him with an environment of peace and plenty. At home he would have the companionship of a father and mother of good breeding, balanced culture and unquestioned social standing. He would have neighbors of similar background and position. He would attend schools of the better sort in the company of sons of other gentlemen. He would go out into the world, into banking or one of the professions, a civilized and dignified young man, possessed of the confidence that comes from blood and discipline.

No less important was the fact that their son, the gods permitting, would never have to know want. The Roosevelts did not live in extravagant luxury — ostentation being in any case very much against their code — but they were more than comfortably well off. Not only could essential needs be met without any trace of that gripping fear for the future that haunts less fortunately circumstanced families whose income depends upon wages or crops, but there would always be more than enough left over for private tutors, trips to Europe, riding horses, rare curios, costly hobbies.

This was the fruit of early family industry, prudent investment and unearned increment. Claes van Roosevelt, who settled in the colony of New Amsterdam in 1636, had to work and work hard to escape poverty. But he succeeded well enough in his way to establish his only son, Nicholas, as a cloth merchant. Jacobus, the youngest son of Nicholas, was also a merchant. He invested his savings in real estate in the lower part of Manhattan Island. His son, Isaac, became a sugar refiner and banker. Isaac's son, James, was likewise a prosperous business man. It was he who bought the first estate near Hyde Park, where he settled with his family. By now the Roosevelts had reached the point where the good life was becoming more attractive to them than the continued pursuit of wealth.

The son of James, another Isaac, was to have been a physician. He studied medicine, but soon found the quiet and ease of country life more to his taste. Content to while away his years among his books, he apparently added little or nothing to the Roosevelt investment portfolio or landholdings. A second James, the eldest son of Isaac and the father of Franklin Delano, inherited the Hyde Park estate and greatly increased its size by purchasing adjoining properties. He combined country life with financial activity. Two of the biographers of Franklin Roosevelt report that this son of Isaac, " judiciously investing the considerable wealth he inherited, became a man of large affairs in New York City business. He spent part of each winter there. In summers or when the roads were in good condition, he often drove behind horses from Hyde Park to the city and took great pride in his thoroughbred stable and in the fine vehicles in his carriage house. As a Roosevelt and a financier, he was prominent in society and entertained frequently at his country house and at the New York City residence. The hospitality of the Hyde Park farmstead was noted up and down the Hudson Valley. Well-educated, he enjoyed the company of men of learning. . . . His business interests led him into activities as varied as the guests who thronged to his home during the evenings." [1]

James Roosevelt married twice. His first wife was Rebecca Howland. To them a son, James, was born. This James Roosevelt later married Helen Astor, aunt to Vincent Astor, whose family's vast wealth was and still is invested in New York City real estate. Upon the death of his first wife James Roosevelt married Sara Delano, owner of coal mining properties and real estate in Pennsylvania. When her father died, she inherited a fortune estimated at not quite one million dollars. When her husband died, his property passed to her, to her step-son James, and to her own son, Franklin.

Several of the Roosevelts took civic duty as seriously as they did their responsibilities as bankers, business men and absentee landlords. Nicholas, the son of Claes, was one of the founders of the town of Esopus — later called Kingston — in Ulster County. Isaac, son of Jacobus, helped to organize the first public hospital in New York City. He was a member of the Continental Congress and of the commission that took over the administration of New York City after the War for Independence began. He represented the city at the State constitutional convention at Kingston and was a delegate to the Poughkeepsie convention which ratified the Federal Constitution. Later he served four years in the State Senate. His son, James, was a member of the State Assembly for a time and thereafter an alderman. James, the father of Franklin, was a World's Fair Commissioner in 1893 and a supervisor of the town of Hyde Park. James R., Franklin's half-brother, was in the diplomatic service for several years, appointed to various posts by President Cleveland, who had been a close friend of James, senior.

To all seeming, then, the Roosevelts of Hyde Park were conscientious and doubtless able citizens. They were perhaps not the most typical, but in any case surely the best representatives of a rising acquisitive society. They aspired to riches not alone for the sake of being wealthy, but because wealth made it easier for them to live upon a high cultural and intellectual plane. James Roosevelt, father of Franklin, must have had more than one opportunity to plunge into that mad scramble for money and power in which so many of his contemporaries were engaged. There were more than a few among the robber barons of the period with less wit than he who amassed millions. He was content to let well enough alone.

This restraint in James Roosevelt was characteristic. He was not a self-made man in the vulgar sense, but he believed in self-discipline, self-assurance — qualities essential to a person of his proud breeding and patrician tastes. He had an orderly mind and a strong feeling for authority and responsibility, provided that the responsibility and authority were founded upon reason and intelligently exercised. He appears to have been tolerant toward others, content to let his neighbors live as they pleased, but insisted upon shaping and improving his own environment to suit his own tastes in so far as that lay within his power.

It is probable that Franklin Roosevelt inherited these traits, though, if he had not, he would soon have developed them. There were few companions of his own age living in the vicinity of the farm. Nor did he have the opportunity of associating with other children at school in his earlier years, for he was taught at home by parents and tutors. His mother later mentioned, with a suggestion of regret, " the comparatively quiet, sequestered life " of her son at that period. " Much of his time, until he went to Groton at 14," she said, " was spent with his father and me." [2] Her own influence on the growing boy was not inconsiderable. In her veins ran the blood of the seafaring Delanos, to whom obedience and conformity were essential laws of life. Yet the father's influence seems to have been much greater. As Mrs. James Roosevelt subsequently said, speaking of the importance of fathers in the training of children: "In my own family I feel that my son's father did far more than I did." [3]

The relationship between father and son was inevitably modified by the disparity in their ages. James Roosevelt was 54 when Franklin was born. Had the elder been austere and aloof and unduly stern the younger would probably have come to regard authority as something remote and perhaps something to be feared. Instead he learned to look upon authority as something to be revered and respected, for his father seems to have succeeded in being his " gay companion," in understanding his troubles and sharing his joys, without stooping in any way to do so. The father maintained his position as a person of worldly wisdom and experience, his dignity as the head of the household, without losing any of that intimacy which made of the relationship between the two a living and important thing to the young Franklin.

Equally important was the fact that the Roosevelts provided their son with all of the advantages of an affluent and well-ordered domestic establishment. They were not extravagant, nor did they pamper the boy. He did not even have an allowance of his own, though his mother later explained that this could be attributed to the fact that allowances were not " customary at that time." Besides, she added, he had no need of money, " for there was no dashing off to the village to buy ice cream cones, there were no movies to see, and all his books and toys were provided for him." [4] So, too, were " his nice clothes." Beginning when he was three, he was taken on frequent trips abroad, to London and Paris, to Nauheim where his parents " took the cure." Before he entered Groton he had been to Europe eight times. "The greater part of this time," one biographer has written, " Franklin was under the care of French and German governesses, and later tutors. He took cycling and walking trips. Franklin's early ' education ' was quite as un-American as Theodore Roosevelt's. It fell into

9

the same groove as that of the other 'best families' they met abroad." [5]

At home he was surrounded with servants. There was a governess, a nurse, a "fat, good-natured French cook" in the kitchen, among others. He was also surrounded with concrete examples of orderly living. The estate was efficiently managed, though more with an eye to providing comforts for the household than a profitable income for the owner. Administration of the farm and household showed evidence of the owner's Dutch lineage and humane instincts. There was orderliness without regimentation, and economy without skimping; servants and employees were fairly rewarded for faithful toil and were always sure to be helped in time of need. Everything on the farm had its proper place, each utensil its proper use, each head of livestock its proper care, each servant his or her proper station.

The young Franklin, according to his biographers, came to regard this "homespun life as natural and inevitable. It was simply the way one lived." [6] It was the only world young Franklin knew. And it doubtless was, as he saw it, a warm and comfortable and human world.

2

NOSTALGIA

∽

ALTHOUGH in later life, under the impact of political reality
and personal ambition, Franklin Roosevelt cast off some of
the influence of Hyde Park, his subsequent attitudes were
necessarily conditioned by the experiences of his childhood
and youth. Hyde Park, the village as well as the farm, was to
him an ideal community. A student, seeking a rational ex-
planation of his philosophy as President, was later to write:

Rugged individualism . . . is the individualism of the so-called
Empire Builders, the individualism of unlimited rights — and no
obligations whatever. It is a degradation of individualism which
has today brought the whole concept of individualism into dis-
repute. The individualism of the American tradition is a wholly
different thing; it is the individualism of duty. Its end is the freedom of life, not the accumulation of wealth. And its means are
responsible and independent citizenship as that word has been
understood for a hundred years in the American colonies and
for a hundred and fifty years in the American States.

The American tradition so defined obviously exists only among
a small minority of the population — the small minority of Americans who have lived for a great many generations directly upon
the land. The family of the President is such a family. . . . It
inherited the tradition of the families living in the [Hudson]
Valley. It had a sense of community. It had a habit of citizenship. It was part of the Republic. And that tradition the President
quite naturally and inevitably inherited. He has always been interested in people as only a man living in a small community can

be interested in people. . . . And his mental picture of the country, his primary assumption about American life, is the somewhat questionable assumption that America still is a collection, a congeries, of such small communities as he knows. He becomes almost oracular on the subject. He is certain that the country *is* just that — and that what will be good for the small communities will be good for the nation.[7]

What both the President and the author quoted above overlooked, however, was the substantial difference between this little Dutchess County community and the hundreds of other small and thoroughly American towns which, no less than Hyde Park, were the keepers of the American tradition of individualism and citizenship. These other communities, with very few exceptions, were made up of petit-bourgeois families within the social as well as the economic meaning of that term. Their leading residents were for the most part retired farmers who had had to work for a living, village bankers, small manufacturers, tradesmen, artisans. They were not wealthy and had little hope of attaining to wealth. Nor had they any contact with the cities, which they tended to identify with wealth and vice, nor with modern industry or the banks, for these bore the stamp of the city, nor yet with cosmopolitan culture whether of the sort that arises naturally from good taste coupled with experience or of the kind the rich can buy merely because they are rich.

Compare these small towns with Hyde Park and especially with the world of affairs that revolved about the Roosevelt household. The Roosevelts were not individuals of limited or parochial interests. They lived abroad almost as much as they did at home. They entertained often, and their guests were men of means and men of learning from far beyond the confines of Dutchess County. The father of Franklin Roosevelt was a business man, a financier, a cosmopolite, not a villager. In how many American communities of the time could these circumstances be duplicated? How many country squires had interests so catholic or so deep? Moreover, though there were working farmers and other members of the lower middle class living in the neighborhood, and though many of these persons found a ready welcome in the Roosevelt home, neither the James Roosevelts nor any of their intimate acquaintances and friends belonged to that class. They were a community of estate-owners, not working farmers. While the Roosevelts probably needed only ten thousand a year to run their farm, there were estates nearby that cost as much as a hundred thousand annually.[8] There may have been poorer folk on one side of the Roosevelts, but on the other side there were richer families. Next door, for instance, lived Colonel Archibald Rogers, the Standard Oil millionaire. Hyde Park, in short, was not a remote petit-bourgeois village; it was a metropolitan suburb. Its residents were not merely patriotic citizens; they considered themselves, and to a large extent actually were, members of the ruling class.*

Whatever else Franklin Roosevelt may have carried away with him, however, there was something Hyde Park did not and could not give him. One of his biographers has pointed out that he was "spared, or he unfortunately never had the advantage of, that early illumination that comes to a boy crowded into the gutter as an atom of a teeming city. He knew nothing of the early hardships, the compensating visions of glory and ambition, that come to a boy on the farm." [9] In brief, he was permitted to know nothing of the harsh realities of industrial life, of the bitter struggle for bread, of the piteous conditions among the great mass of the workers, though he grew up during one of the most turbulent periods in American labor history.

Eight years before he was born there had taken place in

---

* The Roosevelt family tree, published in "The Roosevelt Omnibus," edited by Don Wharton (New York, 1934), shows Franklin Roosevelt to be related by direct or collateral descent to eleven Presidents of the United States, to President Jefferson Davis of the Confederate States, to Robert E. Lee, and to other distinguished public men.

New York City the bloody Tompkins Square riots, the product of widespread hunger. The following year had seen the terrorism of the Molly Maguires in the Pennsylvania coal country at its peak. In 1877 had come the Great Riots, when railway strikers had destroyed huge buildings and other property in Baltimore, Pittsburgh and cities in the Middle West. At the same time the Knights of Labor were locked in a death struggle with Samuel Gompers's new organization. When Franklin Roosevelt was two, the country seemed to be overrun with " tramps " — jobless workers — for whom metropolitan editors recommended a relief diet of strychnine. When he was three, ragged mobs stormed through fashionable Prairie Avenue in Chicago, demanding food. When he was four, a bomb was thrown into a crowd of workers assembled on Haymarket square in Chicago, presumably by an agent-provocateur who hoped to break up the eight-hour-day movement, then the chief objective of organized labor. During his boyhood and youth the warfare went on, resulting in occasional major explosions such as the Pullman strike, the riots at the McCormick plant and the murderous battle of Homestead. There was, after all, another world beyond Hyde Park.

It is not intended here to suggest that it would have been either proper or necessary to keep a boy growing up on a manorial estate on the Hudson or in school at Groton and Harvard informed as to working-class conditions and labor strife. Such a suggestion would obviously be ridiculous. No less absurd was the contention later put forward that the same Franklin Roosevelt, because he happened to be President, had a firm and intelligent understanding of the needs of the workers and of the historic forces behind the class struggle. As President, he was to see the labor problem rather through a nostalgic haze.

Even when he went on to Groton and Harvard, Franklin Roosevelt carried his pleasant little world along with him. He needed the formal education these institutions could provide, not so much for the sake of intellectual development, for that did not necessarily follow, as for the purpose of providing the proper setting for a young man of his caste. Groton was distinctly a " class " school. Sons of the humble and low-born did not matriculate there. Harvard, even more so than today, was the college of the aristocracy of the country. The young Roosevelt slipped into the environment of these schools with all of the ease and grace a well-born American can command.

During this period he was to have somewhat greater freedom than he had experienced at home. Before he entered Harvard he had been constantly under the alert and careful guidance of his parents. They had unobtrusively, yet very positively, imposed their will upon him. It was done, his mother has said, " in such a way that Franklin never realized he was following any bent but his own." [10] At Groton conformity and discipline were considered essential to education. But at Harvard these restraints were relaxed. A young man of 18 was expected to stand, more or less, on his own feet. In addition, Franklin Roosevelt had been at Cambridge only a few months when his father died. This event, however sad in its personal implications, removed a psychological tie with his childhood. Thereafter he began to look about him with greater ease.

There was no need, however, for young Roosevelt to extend his inquiry beyond that which came within the ken of personal experience. He still enjoyed almost perfect security of income and there was no hint that this income would ever be endangered. He was generally accepted on the campus and seems to have taken great pleasure in the social life provided by the numerous clubs he was invited to join. He found no flaws in this life and in any case would never have thought of criticizing it. To have done so after having accepted the courtesies of his fellows would have been unmannerly. Nor did academic questions appear to trouble him. He took the conventional courses in the conventional way. He proved neither a poor nor a distinguished scholar, though the pragmatism he studied under William James probably went far to shape his later attitudes.

When, finally, his independence began to assert itself, though it was doubtless genuine enough, it did not lead him into deep social or cultural explorations. And it was not the independence of the rebel, but rather of the righteous conformist. There is nothing to indicate that he ever fought with anyone, at Cambridge or later, over a matter of fundamental principle. When in his last years he became an editor of *The Crimson*, he found fault with the football team and quarreled with the school authorities; but his criticism of the football team had nothing to do with the social aspects or economic waste of intercollegiate sports, but only with the poor quality of the team's performance; and his quarrel with the Harvard Corporation had to do with fire-escapes and boardwalks, not with educational methods or academic standards.

Harvard was followed by a period of six years or so in which Franklin Roosevelt did most of the things other sons of the wealthy do upon leaving college. His marriage to his distant cousin, Anna Eleanor Roosevelt, was one of the brilliant social events of the 1905 season, made doubly so because of the presence at the wedding of the uncle of the bride and the fifth cousin of the groom, President Theodore Roosevelt. After marriage he completed his course in law at Columbia University and, to all appearances, settled down to the business of law as his life's career.

3

REFORMERS ARE ALWAYS POLITE

IN 1910 Franklin Roosevelt made his debut in politics. It has been said that he " embraced politics as the young Oxford man so widely admired in the better American preparatory schools and colleges embraces them – with a mixture of *noblesse oblige*, good sportmanship, and solemn dedication."[11] He was half pushed, half flattered into entering the race for the State Senate on the Democratic ticket. He was a Democrat because his branch of the family had always supported that party. It was an accepted fact like his religion or the mode of life at Hyde Park. The deficiencies of the party meant little or nothing to him, for he had no positive political views of his own. He had, however, an acquired dislike for people who were not " good " – political bosses, for example – and so he made " bossism " the central issue of his campaign.

It may be doubted that this issue alone won the election for him. There were two other important factors at work. First, the ground swell of popular reaction to Republicanism, which was to split the Grand Old Party and elect Woodrow Wilson two years hence, had already set in. Indeed, the Democrats captured control of Congress in the same election that sent Franklin Roosevelt to Albany. Second, the candidate's pleasing personality won him a following that a less favored Democrat, though fighting on the same issue, might not have obtained.

It was fashionable at the time to deride the bosses. Muckraking was at its apex. Franklin Roosevelt could have chosen no more popular issue upon which to make his debut. True, in their years of labor the muck-rakers had turned up many significant facts, which, had they been properly interpreted for public consumption, might have shaken the foundations of the existing order. But the voters did not grasp — and were not permitted to grasp — the deeper meaning of these facts. They remembered only " The Shame of the Cities " and " The Treason of the Senate." They saw the faults and evils of the prevailing political economy as an unholy alliance of business corruption and political jobbery — and nothing else. The solution was simple: Drive the rascals out. Few were the reformers who did not play upon this theme. The chorus was led by Theodore Roosevelt, though with tongue in cheek, for the muck-rakers were thoroughly despised by this cousin of the Hyde Park Roosevelts.

There were some, however, who looked beyond the bosses. They felt that the answer lay elsewhere than in " good government by good people." In 1910 they were advocating numerous farreaching changes that were even then being put into effect in England and had been in operation in Germany for a quarter century. The Populists, and after them the La Follette Progressives, had long been agitating for "a larger state agency and activity " in dealing with the fundamental problems of society. Behind them stood the Socialists, whose influence was growing. The reforms these groups proposed were, however, too radical for the United States of 1910.

This was also to prove true of the relatively mild changes suggested by the kid-glove reformers who stood with the first Roosevelt at Armageddon in 1912. Despite the labor planks in their platform and despite the fairly strong language used by some of them, these opportunist Progressives were in no sense radicals; they were not, either consciously or otherwise, enemies of capitalist society. George W. Perkins, the Wall

Street banker, did not throw his financial support to the Bull
Moose movement because of any unselfish devotion to the
downtrodden or because he wanted to endanger the sources
of his own munificent income. Nor was Donald Richberg
concerned for the broad working masses as such. He was interested in defending the little man, the artisan, the shop-
keeper from excessive exploitation by the bigger bourgeoisie.
Theodore Roosevelt, the leader of the movement, in the main
wanted power for its own sake; one had to have authority to
dispense social justice and maintain social order. He believed,
as Gilson Gardner put it, that " the rich must be fair and
the poor must be contented — or, if not contented, at least
they must be orderly. I will tell them both. No restraining of
trade by the great corporations and no rioting by the toiler.
Give me the power and I will make them behave." [12] Yet even
the Rooseveltian Progressives did manage to show, through
the measures they advocated, their belief that it was not high-
minded gentlemen in public office, but the assurance of bread,
that the people had to have if the social order was not to be
set askew.

Franklin Roosevelt preferred to fight the bosses. When he
entered the State Senate in 1911, Charles F. Murphy, the
Tammany boss, seemed to be in complete control of that
body. The financiers from whom Boss Murphy in turn took
orders wanted William F. Sheehan elected to the United States
Senate. It appeared that Murphy had only to give the word
and Sheehan would be chosen. He sent out his orders and
promptly ran into mutiny. The freshman Senator from Dutchess County would have none of his dictation.* Instead Franklin Roosevelt brought together a group of other Democratic

* There were other financiers, of course, who were just as anxious to
prevent Thomas Fortune Ryan from getting his man Sheehan a seat in the
Senate in Washington. Unfortunately, William Barnes, Jr., the Republican
boss, lacked votes enough to beat Sheehan. Hence Franklin Roosevelt's
rebellion came as a godsend to this group. It is a curious fact that Franklin
Roosevelt, so far as can be determined from the published record, seems to
have been blissfully unaware of this bankers' struggle behind the scenes.

insurgents and, by holding this little band together by sheer force of personality, succeeded in deadlocking the election for more than two months.

Throughout the long struggle Franklin Roosevelt remained the gentleman, not once forgetting his manners. When Robert F. Wagner, then also a member of the State Senate, accused him of being a publicity-seeker, he " entered a modest disclaimer." When he wanted to call Murphy a liar, which the Tammany boss undoubtedly was, he denied " any intention of impugning " the veracity of the Tammany leader, but said he believed " Mr. Murphy had again been grossly misinformed by some unscrupulous person." Nor had Senator Roosevelt any hesitancy in fraternizing with the opposition, for in his heart he bore them no ill will. And in the end he defeated Sheehan, the Tammany candidate — only to compromise his victory by voting for another but perhaps less obnoxious Tammany man.

Apart from this one outburst, Franklin Roosevelt showed none of the fire of rebellion, none of the fervor that marks the true liberal reformer. He occasionally aligned himself with that generation's crop of " New Tammany " men — including Alfred E. Smith and Robert F. Wagner, who somehow managed to balance their urban progressivism against the demands made upon them as loyal lieutenants of Boss Murphy. Senator Roosevelt also took a firm stand against the practice of log-rolling. He displayed a lively interest in farm relief and especially in plans for promoting banks to finance farm co-operatives. But otherwise his record was without distinction.

Moreover, as he later confessed, he was "lonely " in Albany. He was relieved when the change in administrations in Washington afforded him a reasonable excuse for escaping from an environment in which he was not only ignored by the Republicans, but both ignored and often openly opposed by his own party colleagues. In 1912 he had gone to Baltimore for the Democratic convention, where he had worked for the nomination of the Princeton schoolmaster. Recognized as an alert young man of potential talent, he was offered one or two minor positions in the Wilson Administration. Hundreds of other young liberals, seduced by the promises of the " New Freedom," had invaded Washington and were seeking just such opportunities to identify themselves with the Great Uplift. Any one of them would have been overjoyed to have accepted the post of Assistant Secretary of the Treasury, which Franklin Roosevelt spurned. But when Josephus Daniels approached him with the suggestion that he become Assistant Secretary of the Navy, he eagerly accepted. He was an ardent navalist and could not let this opportunity pass him by.

Here his nationalism came at once to the fore, as revealed by his attitude toward Mexico and Haiti and Germany and by his ceaseless propaganda for a bigger and more efficient navy. He was constantly upsetting the admirals and bureaucrats with his unorthodox schemes for improving the fighting strength of the fleet. No rule was too strong, no precedent too holy for him to set it at defiance if he thought that he would thereby more easily reach his objectives. He was in no way rebelling against the things the navy stood for, but on the contrary was merely attempting to convince the admirals that if they would increase their effectiveness they would have to move along with the times.

After the war came a quiet interlude. In 1920 Franklin Roosevelt was the candidate for the Vice-Presidency on the Democratic ticket. In the following year he was stricken with infantile paralysis, and then began the long and courageous fight against the ravages of this dread disease. His physical incapacity forced him more or less into retirement for the next eight years. It did not, however, prevent him from attending the Democratic convention in Madison Square Garden in 1924 or the one at Houston in 1928. His speeches placing Alfred E. Smith in nomination for the Presidency at these conventions reflected little growth or other change in his political outlook. He was still very much the " good man " in politics, possessed of a great yearning to do the right thing by his fellow men, but without any apparent understanding of the social and economic forces that stood in the way of the changes he seemed to favor.

☼ 4 ☼

PROSPERITY EVERLASTING

∽

On January 1, 1929, Franklin Roosevelt became Governor of New York. His election put him in direct line for the Democratic nomination for the Presidency, for party managers are always tempted to go to Now York State for their nominees because of its large electoral college vote. In Governor Roosevelt's case there was an additional reason. He had proved a better vote-getter than the popular Alfred E. Smith. Thinking to strengthen his Presidential candidacy in his own State, Governor Smith had insisted that Franklin Roosevelt be nominated to succeed him at Albany. The sprightly, personable, aristocratic Protestant from semi-rural Dutchess County would, by running on the same ticket, offset many of the popular objections to the no less personable but still homely and often uncouth Catholic from the sidewalks of New York. But when the votes were counted, Al Smith had lost his native State, while Franklin Roosevelt had just managed to squeeze through. Those in charge of the Democratic machine saw at once who their 1932 nominee was likely to be.

The year 1929 opened no less auspiciously for the country as a whole, or at least it was so regarded by brokers, financial publicists, industrialists, politicians and other devotees of the New Economic Era. Wages had been going up, production was expanding, new wealth was apparently being created in ever larger measure. We were, we were told, remarkably free from unemployment and other economic distress. Those few

23

Americans who had no jobs were lazy, stupid or incompetent; the rest were going on to ever higher, ever dizzier peaks of prosperity. There was no cause for protest or complaint. The New Era had come to stay. American business had discovered the secret of providing the working class with "both the leisure and the money to buy all the things it helps to make." [13] In short, the principal problem of capitalism had at long last been solved. Or so it seemed.

The faithful found additional assurance in the knowledge that the White House was about to be occupied by Herbert Hoover, a distinguished engineer, a scholar, withal a sincere humanitarian, as the country was led to believe. A man of his superior intellect and extraordinary technical training could be relied upon to keep the economic machinery running smoothly. If the impossible should happen and the machine need repair or other attention, who would be better fitted for the task? Not since the ascent of Woodrow Wilson to the throne had the country witnessed such an outpouring of panegyric, especially from the liberals.

A few cautious students suggested that the Wall Street market might get out of hand — but with disastrous results to the gamblers only. On January 1 the financial editor of the New York *Times*, Alexander Noyes, said that the boom "might run beyond all possibilities and the bubble burst." But he hastened to add that "as to the underlying strength of the American economic situation, there is only one opinion." On February 7 the stock market broke under the weight of a gentle suggestion from the Federal Reserve Board that the credit situation was not all that it might be. This produced a few momentary shivers among the shrewder minds in the region below Fulton Street, but not the slightest apprehension or loss of confidence elsewhere in the country. Paul Clay, of the United States Share Corporation, likewise drew no public attention with his prediction on March 14 that "a break of 15 to 25 per cent in the stock market, further deflation in credit, and a lull in trade might be expected before Labor Day." Even Mr. Clay, however, seemed not to understand what this would mean, for he added that when the storm was over, " trade and financial conditions would be far more healthy than they are now and another big ' bull ' movement would begin." [14]

While faith in prosperity everlasting appeared to be shared by everyone, there were in fact a few hardy souls who publicly entertained grave doubts. Ferdinand Lundberg, the financial writer, has recalled the sound analyses of some of these unhonored prophets — analyses that in every case were published before October, 1929.[15] He pointed not only to the almost uncanny foresight of liberals like John A. Hobson and radicals like Friederich Engels, who saw what was lying decades ahead. He also dug up the prophetic statements of students of the post-war period — Gustav Cassel, J. Maynard Keynes, Harold Laski, Sir George Paish, H. N. Brailsford, Friedrich Hertz, Sir Arthur Salter, F. W. Pethwick Lawrence, Frederick Soddy and H. Parker Willis among them — who generally believed, as did Paish in 1924, that " disastrous consequences must ensue from the present policies of those responsible for national and international affairs "; and most of whom felt, as Salter put it in 1927, that the economic warfare being waged throughout the world meant that millions of people " will die, other millions will be unemployed, and countless others will be condemned to live in misery and degradation."

Yet one really did not have to be a prophet to foresee what was coming. Sober analysis of the facts of the 1923–29 boom would have shown that it was the product, not of constructive or progressive forces, but of an oversupply of capital that was seeking profitable employment at a time when opportunities for such employment were few and growing fewer. In its distress this capital turned to speculative and non-productive markets in its search for profits, to the stock market with its paper profits. For a time at least the paper profits of Wall Street kept the boom going. They acted as a narcotic, and the resultant glow upon the cheeks of American capitalism was thought to signify ruddy health.

WHILE THE FEVER CLIMBED

∽

ON January 1 of the year which was to see the crisis break with all its fury upon an unsuspecting and unprepared nation, Franklin Roosevelt reentered political life. His inaugural address and his first message to the State Assembly gave him an opportunity to show how much he had changed and how much he had learned about society in general and political economy in particular since he went, an unsophisticated but hopeful youngster, to Albany eighteen years before. In a paragraph of his inaugural address he summed up his political philosophy. It should be the purpose of government, he asserted:

To secure more of life's pleasures for the farmer; to guard the toilers in the factories and to insure them a fair wage and protection from the dangers of their trades; to compensate them by adequate insurance for injuries received while working for us; to open the doors of knowledge to their children more widely; to aid those who are crippled and ill; to pursue with strict justice all evil persons who prey upon their fellow men, and at the same time, by intelligent and helpful sympathy, to lead wrongdoers into right paths.

Farm relief, minimum-wage legislation, workmen's compensation, public education, hospitalization, honest administration of criminal justice — surely there was nothing here to suggest radicalism or bold experimentation.

In one other place Governor Roosevelt touched upon the

possibility of radical change. Commenting upon the subject of water-power sites, he declared that " the title to this power must vest forever in the people of this State. . . . It is also the duty of our legislative bodies to see that this power, which belongs to all the people, is transformed into usable electrical energy and distributed to them at the lowest possible cost." Here the Governor implied that he might seek legislation looking toward the development and distribution of electrical energy by public agencies. Considering the importance of electricity in modern industrial life, this would have been a radical step.

In his first message to the State Assembly the next day he followed an even milder trend. He was encouraged, he said, by the " excellent condition " of the State's finances. He wanted something done " to the end that the unnecessarily high differential between what the farmer receives and what the consumer pays may be materially lowered." He restated his position with regard to water power. Apart from these and a number of minor recommendations, he offered a public-works and a labor program. The former, however, was not devised, so far as one can learn from the message, with existing or potential unemployment in mind. Highways and bridges were to be built " to meet modern traffic requirements." Unused lands were to be put " to some useful purpose." The "constantly growing population, together with the new demands of civilization," made it necessary to erect " still more buildings to house the wards and the business of the State." His labor program called for:

1. A real eight-hour day and forty-eight-hour week for women and children in industry.

2. The establishment for them of an advisory minimum or fair-wage board.

3. The extension of workmen's compensation to give its benefits to all occupational diseases.

4. The prohibiting of the granting of temporary injunctions

in individual disputes without notice of hearing; and provision for trial before a jury of all alleged violations of injunctions.

5. The immediate study by a commission of experts of the subject of old-age security against want.

6. The continuation of such provisions of the emergency rent laws as are necessary.

7. Further elimination of unhealthy living conditions in the congested areas.

8. Declaration by law that the labor of a human being is not a commodity or an article of commerce.

But nowhere in either message or address did Franklin Roosevelt reveal that he had the slightest inkling of the coming storm. The inexorable laws of the profit system, then about to take their frightful toll, would hardly wait upon the studies of expert commissions or upon the advice of fair-wage boards. A declaration by statute that human labor is not a commodity would not alter the fact that under the profit system human labor can be nothing else. Moreover, one searches in vain for any reference to the weaknesses in the banking structure or to the excesses of the money changers who were even then nearing the climax of their saturnalia in Wall Street. Whatever Franklin Roosevelt's attitude toward the money changers was later to be, it must be borne in mind that it was while he was Governor of New York State, in which Wall Street is located, that they were working their evil practices unchallenged and unchecked.

Perhaps it was too late to check the stock market boom. Perhaps no amount of reprimands or legislation would have done any good. Yet it lay within the power of the State, of which Franklin Roosevelt was the Chief Magistrate, to eliminate at least some of the abuses attending the spree through stricter regulation of the security markets, investment trusts, brokerage firms, bank affiliates, holding companies and deceptive " thrift " accounts. Not only was nothing done in that respect, but not once before the crash in October did Governor Roosevelt lift his voice in public reproof or condemnation of the money changers. In one case at least, that involving the Bank of the United States, he and his Superintendent of Banks had before them definite knowledge of questionable practices, if not of actual wrongdoing; yet he refused to act.

He liked none the less to identify himself with other forward-lookers of the time. " We socially-minded people " was a phrase he used more than once, although his social-mindedness — his interest in old-age security, hospitalization, prison reform and the pursuit of evil persons with strict justice — was largely, perhaps wholly, the product of nostalgic emotion. He had been brought up to abhor individual wrongdoing. He who had always lived amid perfect security, who had always seen the servants at home properly provided for, was invariably touched by the sight of suffering or misery.

It appears, for example, that at no time did he visualize the need for old-age security as the direct outgrowth of an industrial system that makes it increasingly difficult for workers to put away savings of their own against old age, that is continually adding to the surplus of labor, and that is accustomed to discard workers still in their prime as being " too old." Instead, as he has himself admitted, he came around to what he calls old-age pensions in consequence of a personal experience.*

* In an address delivered in Detroit on October 2, 1932, he said:
I will tell you what sold me on old-age insurance — old-age pensions. Not so long ago — about ten years — I received a great shock. I had been away from my home town of Hyde Park during the winter and when I came back I found that a tragedy had occurred. One of my farm neighbors had been a splendid old fellow — supervisor of his town, highway commissioner of his town — one of the best of our citizens. And before I left around Christmas time I had seen the old man, who was eighty-nine, and I had seen his old brother, who was eighty-seven, and I had seen his other brother, who was eighty-five, and I had seen his kid sister, who was eighty-three. And they were living on a farm; I knew it was mortgaged. I knew it was mortgaged to the hilt, but I assumed that everything was all right, for they still had a couple of cows and a few chickens, but when I came back in the spring, I found that in the heavy winter that followed there had been a heavy fall of snow and one of the old brothers had fallen down

In political reform, too, sentimentality played no small part. Governor Roosevelt saw the justice of Alfred E. Smith's proposal for eliminating superfluous county governments and combining the functions of others. He undoubtedly knew that the existence of five separate county governments in New York City was unnecessary, wasteful and conducive to political corruption. He seems also to have known that many of the up-State counties could be abolished without loss of efficiency and with considerable saving to the taxpayers. Discussing the subject shortly after he became Governor, however, he declared that Al Smith had " slipped up " in this one particular. The latter's plan he called " a grand little theory, but I hope that it will be some time before Dutchess County is willing to give up its identity. We have historic counties in New York State and we are mighty proud of them." [16]

In the matter of taxation Governor Roosevelt was not even a progressive, but on the side of the tories. On February 6, 1929, speaking at Albany, he declared that while he did " not know very much about the intricate problem of taxation," he would " urge a plan that will do the greatest good to the greatest number." His plan, as it developed, called for a 20 per cent reduction in income-tax rates and for a sales tax on gasoline. This could hardly be reconciled with his desire to " do the greatest good to the greatest number," for the income tax is far more equitable, from this standpoint, than the sales tax. The former taxes a citizen according to his ability to pay, the latter according to his needs.

Governor Roosevelt had asked the State Assembly for very little, and it gave him less than he had asked for. His labor program was put through only in part and then in emasculated

---

on his way out to the barn to milk the cow, and had perished in the snow-drift, and the town authorities had come along and they had taken the two old men and they had put them into the county poorhouse and they had taken the old lady and had sent her down, for want of a better place, to the insane asylum, though she was not insane, she was just old. That sold me on the idea of trying to keep homes intact for old people.

form. The legislature voted a two-cent gasoline tax, but refused to reduce the income-tax rates. Instead it raised the exemptions, thus favoring the little man, whereas the Roosevelt proposal would have favored the wealthier individuals. He did obtain an appropriation of $12,600,000 for the farmers, to be spent on roads, schools and agricultural research. It would not be fair, of course, to judge him solely by this meager record. After all, the State Assembly with its Republican majority was not his to command.*

* According to the Republicans, Governor Roosevelt did in fact attempt to command the Assembly. Speaking in New York City on May 14, 1929, the Republican Attorney General, Hamilton Ward, charged that the Governor had sought to usurp the functions of the legislature. He said that "the Executive tried to do the legislating," and added that the Governor sent twenty-nine messages to the Assembly "in which one or more legislative matters were not only suggested, but demanded."

✿ 6 ✿

A DOCTRINE IS LAID DOWN

ৡ

AFTER the adjournment of the legislature Governor Roosevelt had time to give some thought to national affairs. He found occasion to discuss the close relations between big business and government. It may be that he had previously undertaken a thorough study of the question.* It seems more likely that he was speaking only for the record. He was, after all, the outstanding Democratic candidate for the Presidency. On July 4, 1929, for example, he spoke at Tammany Hall. The New York *Times* account of his speech, published the following morning, deserves to be quoted at some length:

"No period in history has been so rich in social and economic changes as those that have taken place in the last twenty-five years," the Governor said. "We may well ask: Are we in danger of a new caveman's club, of a new feudal system, of the creation in these United States of such a highly centralized industrial control that we may have to bring forth a new Declaration of Independence?

"It is not that these great industrial and economic mergers are necessarily bad from the economic point of view," the Governor continued, "but the fact is that independence in business is a thing

* In a Jefferson Day speech in 1930 Franklin Roosevelt declared that his information regarding the trend toward monopoly in the country had come from "a prominent New York banker, a Republican." He said that his informant had told him that fifty or sixty large corporations, each controlled by two, three or four men, did about 80 per cent of the industrial business of the country, while the remaining 20 per cent was spread among hundreds of thousands of smaller business men.

33

of the past. Can a man today run a drug store, a cigar store, a grocery store as an independent business? "

It is possible, the Governor said, that the questions presented by the ever-growing aggregations of capital and their effect upon the social and political well-being of the people may find a natural solution, but this does not eliminate the danger implied, he warned. This danger, he declared, emanates from the development of a partnership between business and government. Just as at one time this country was faced by the problem of separation of Church and State, so is it now confronted with the equally important task of separation of government and business.

"If you want to see an example of the partnership of government and business, look at the new tariff bill," the Governor said. "The danger lies in Washington, in Albany, here in New York, and in every hamlet and crossroads in the United States. The doctrine of the separation of Church and State has been pretty well laid down and I believe universally accepted in this country. I want to preach a new doctrine: a complete separation of business and government."

No one reading this speech could doubt that Franklin Roosevelt was firmly and forever opposed to " highly centralized industrial control " and to " partnership between business and government" whatever its form or excuse for being.

PART TWO

BEWILDERMENT

~

MEANWHILE the ominous rumblings that had been heard in the stock market in February were repeated in May and again in September. The speculative vertigo with which American capitalism had been seized was moving toward its inevitable climax.

With this unhallowed event but a few months off, Mr. Hoover's distinguished Committee on Recent Economic Changes in the United States published its first voluminous report. It had discovered impressive evidence that the anarchic forces in the national economy were at last being brought under control. The long-sought balance between production and consumption was virtually within reach. And so the Committee held that there was nothing happening in Wall Street or anywhere else to give rise to alarm. Indeed, its report asserted that "we can go on with increasing activity. . . . We seem only to have touched the fringe of our potentialities." [1]

Reporting for New York State about the same time, Governor Roosevelt declared that within his jurisdiction industry was, on the whole, "in a very healthy and prosperous condition." [2]

Yet the omens from the stock market were not without meaning. The country had come out of the World War with its capital immeasurably increased. Since then it had continued to pile up capital. By 1929 it had accumulated an enormous

37

surplus, now largely in the form of bookkeeping or money capital, which it was finding ever more difficult to put to profitable employment in the normal markets. The idle funds were taking refuge in the securities markets, where at least paper profits might be had. But even Wall Street could absorb just so much and no more of this idle capital. What would happen when that point was reached?

It is the law of capitalism that it must engage in a ceaseless struggle against the tendency of the rate of profit to fall. It must at the same time, and in consequence of this very struggle, strengthen the forces that tend to depress the rate of profit. For it is not by profit alone, but also and more particularly by the accumulation of capital, that capitalism lives. That part of the return on invested capital that goes into the purchase of consumption goods is spent, consumed; it earns no profit. It is and can be only that part which is invested in new capital goods upon which future profit can be earned. Hence capitalism must go on endlessly accumulating capital. But as capital is accumulated, as the facilities for turning out goods are improved and enlarged, the greater becomes the productivity of capital; and the more productive it becomes, the greater is the pressure on the rate of profit.

The profit system tries in various ways to overcome this impasse. It seeks to make capital more productive per unit, as well as in the aggregate, through rationalization and the introduction of wage-saving machinery, and it cuts wages either openly or by subterfuge; for by reducing costs it will maintain its profit margin, at least for a time. It is driven also to combine and concentrate, mainly with a view to controlling markets and prices so as to bolster up the sagging rate of profit. And it seeks new markets for its goods by instalment selling and high-pressure salesmanship at home and through colonial exploitation and other forms of imperialism abroad. Yet all of these devices, except that of expanding markets, have the inevitable effect of reducing consumer buying power; that is, they impoverish the domestic market. Wage-saving machinery and rationalization displace workers who might otherwise buy goods with their wages; the tendency toward monopoly, which restricts production, also creates unemployment; wage cuts, when not accompanied by an equivalent fall in the price level, reduce buying power. This reduction in the capacity of the people to consume, whether absolute or only relative to the total output of goods, in turn depresses the rate of profit, thereby forcing capitalism to still further efforts in the same direction.

The relative and increasing impoverishment of the domestic market not only adds to the surplus of goods and of labor, but also to the surplus of capital. Were all of this surplus capital to be put to work in the domestic economy it would tend, under the inexorable law of supply and demand, to force the rate of profit virtually to the vanishing point. For this reason capitalism in each country is compelled in ever greater measure to look abroad for outlets for its surplus capital and for markets for its surplus goods.

Europe had reached this stage long before 1914. The era of primitive accumulation had come to an end. The "workshop nations" of Europe were no longer able to exploit the colonial markets with the freedom they once had enjoyed. The surplus capital they had exported was taking its toll. The colonial countries were being rapidly industrialized and were buying proportionately less of the manufactured wares of Europe, for with the help of the imported capital they could produce more and more of these goods for themselves. Nevertheless, capital, whether at home or abroad, *must* earn a return. Europe, therefore, was compelled to continue to produce goods – and to find markets for them. The spirited and almost desperate struggle for markets that ensued led to the most disastrous economic crisis in history to date – the World War.

The military phase of the struggle was suspended in 1918, but the economic warfare went on. Tariffs and trade barriers were raised higher and still higher. These barriers not only served to protect home industries, but behind them there arose a number of new industries for which there existed, from the standpoint of world economy, no genuine need. Everywhere facilities for producing goods were being enlarged, while simultaneously markets were being closed by states anxious to guard themselves against the onslaught of goods from neighbors and competitors. But markets had to be found, and so capitalist states everywhere were compelled to resort to new and more potent offensive weapons, to export bounties, outright dumping, currency devaluation, though the cost came out of the wage income of the domestic market. The World War, moreover, had added a new disturbing element in the form of an enormous indebtedness. The capital against which the war debts were originally charged had been blown out of existence, or, as in the case of German reparations, had to a great extent never existed at all. Yet these debts, like all capital claims, had to be satisfied, and this could only be done by existing productive capital, which was already carrying an immense burden of its own. It had not only to produce goods to pay for itself, but to produce still other goods to pay for the war debts.

Germany, upon whom the immediate load fell heaviest, rationalized its industries, beat down the real income of its workers, confiscated the savings of its lower middle class. For it had to pay the war indemnity and could do so only by producing goods and selling them abroad at whatever prices they might fetch. Its sales drive gave a fillip to world trade in general; for the Germans had also to buy raw materials out of which to make the goods they were selling. Nevertheless, the competitive pressure from Germany, with its forced sales at bargain prices, cut heavily into the markets — and profits — of other countries, and so further intensified the economic warfare. Moreover, the German boom was largely financed with borrowed capital, which meant that Germany was merely changing creditors without substantially lessening the debt load that was causing it to play havoc in the world market.

American capitalism, the immediate beneficiary of the bloody crusade to save democracy, had again, as in 1861–65, accumulated a vast amount of new capital. This, of course, had to be put to work. In the domestic market it produced the boom of the 1920's. On the surface it appeared that the whole country was prosperous. But this was far from true. Agriculture remained depressed after the slump of 1921. Throughout the 1920's pauper wages were paid in most of the major industries, and even in the most active years the number of jobless ran between three and four million. Studies by orthodox economists showed that 35 per cent of the American people had incomes so small that they were forced to live at or below the border-line of physical and moral security; another 25 per cent were living at the "minimum comfort" level. In short, at least 72,000,000 Americans were in no position to buy all of the things they needed or could have used; the working class did not have "the money to buy all the things it helps to make," as the publicists for the New Economic Era insisted.[3]

However, the increasing impoverishment of the home market was largely disguised. American capitalism set out to correct the deficiency by building an artificial domestic market on the instalment-selling plan. It sought to lend the submerged classes the buying power they did not have, though how they were to repay the loan, except at the expense of future buying power, was not made clear. In any event, instalment selling, supported by high-pressure salesmanship and extravagant advertising, did for a time give a remarkable stimulus to domestic business.

But domestic prosperity, such as it was, was still not sufficient to give profitable employment to all of the accumulated capital. Had the surplus been put to work at home, it might have wrecked the internal market altogether. Much of it had to be and was sent abroad in one form or another, some of it actually being forced upon reluctant borrowers. This helped to relieve the capitalist-entrepreneur class of a part of its goods surplus — the product of the deficiency in domestic buying power — for most of the exported capital moved out of the country in the form of goods. They were in the main capital goods, of course — a point upon which Secretary of Commerce Hoover, for one, strongly insisted — for only thus could a return on the foreign investments be earned. Yet the capital exported could earn the requisite profits only by producing still more goods, and the production of these goods inevitably increased the competition which American domestic business was already meeting in the world market.

Service on the foreign investments complicated matters. Payments, whether of interest or principal, could only be made in goods or gold. But American business hindered payment in goods by insisting that the high and rigid tariff walls be maintained. Gold came into the country in unprecedented volume, but as it was used to a large extent as the basis for still more bookkeeping capital — bank credit — it added to the problem instead of helping to solve it. The commodities and gold that were brought in had not only to meet the service on the foreign loans, but were also needed to pay for American commodity exports. Indeed, the gold served primarily to balance the commodity account, while the return on the foreign loans was mainly reinvested abroad. Thus, even the profits that were sought through foreign investment of surplus capital went almost wholly into the making of still more capital upon which still more profits had to be earned; and this additional capital, piled atop the existing supply, augmented the ever expanding volume of goods flowing into the world market.

Both in connection with the abnormal increase of American competition and in the case of Germany — for a considerable part of that country's post-war sales drive was financed by American lenders — the war profits of American capitalism helped for a few years, by temporarily stimulating international trade, to hide the fact that markets that could be profitably exploited were still rapidly diminishing. But it should have been obvious that this could not go on forever, that it was not possible — within the limitations of the profit system — to keep pouring out an ever greater volume of goods. Eventually the relative shrinkage of domestic buying power and the narrowing of foreign markets would bring the whole structure toppling down. Yet the spiral did continue upward for some time. When the normal markets for commodities and capital, despite all the pressure and artifices that could be brought to bear upon them, were nearing the saturation point, idle funds turned elsewhere in their restless search for profits. They were attracted to the securities markets in quantities far in excess of normal needs. Besides, the very fact of a feverish industrial activity and a lively foreign trade gave rise to a boom psychology. People believed that prosperity would not only continue, but would expand in geometric ratio, and they began to back their convictions with wagers in the stock market. At first slowly, but then with increasing tempo, Wall Street sucked in the savings and bookkeeping capital of America and to a certain degree that of Europe as well.

Ultimately came the black days of October — for even the paper profits of Wall Street could not go on distending themselves world without end on a diet of nothing but air and black ink. The turn in the economic cycle could no longer be concealed. Now would come the slump, the period of retrenchment. Production would be checked, for the opportunities for making profits had dwindled and would decrease further with prices falling. This would result in unemployment, which in turn would cut into buying power and consumer demand, thereby adding to the strain on prices and profits. New reductions in output would follow, more workers would be put on the streets, demand and prices would continue to fall. Capitalists would seek to save what they could by trimming costs, i.e., wages, for the charges on fixed capital could not arbitrarily be reduced without violating the sanctity of contract, one of the main pillars of capitalism. Wage cuts would mean further contraction of purchasing power, consumer demand, prices — and profits. The uncertainty thus engendered would make even those consumers not directly or immediately affected more cautious and sparing in their buying. The deflation would feed upon itself, voraciously, relentlessly.

More than that, this would not be a crisis of growth, as were the cyclical depressions of earlier days, but a crisis of survival. When capitalism was in the ascendancy, the periodic crises, or so it seemed, acted only to prevent the machine from growing too fast. Then new markets, or the fact that prices had fallen so low that consumption was again stimulated, could always start the productive machine on another spree. But by 1929 there were no new markets to be had and all of the existing markets were preempted or being rapidly closed. Nor would prices be permitted to fall far enough to stimulate consumption. Monopolism had reached the point where prices of numerous commodities were being artificially held up. Meantime, too, the volume of capital claims (usually called debts), which had attended the accumulation of capital, had grown tremendously. These claims were in the form of bonds, stocks, mortgages, loans, bank deposits and the like. They were held not only by industrialists and bankers, but by public and private institutions and by countless private individuals. Indeed, the whole economic system rested upon this capital structure. Any curtailment of the production of goods would necessarily affect not the factory owners and their employees alone, but virtually the whole of society, for only by producing goods to be exchanged at a profit in the market could these claims be satisfied. A price deflation carried far enough to bring about an automatic cure would likewise menace the capital structure. If the capital structure were to come down as the result of a thorough deflation, the capitalist state would come tumbling after it. Hence the state would be increasingly disposed to step in and check the fall of prices and pump new life into industrial activity, although in consequence of this intervention the crisis would tend to become interminable. The causes would be perpetuated, not eliminated.

For a long time the worshippers at the altar of prosperity everlasting refused to believe that the inevitable had happened. No sooner had the brokers' tickers carried the bad tidings from Wall Street than there began one of the most astonishing attempts at self-hypnotism to be found in history. The country's leaders, as with one voice, rose up to declare that "business is fundamentally sound, all we need is confidence, let no one lose his head." The refrain was repeated over and over, until it almost, but not quite, drowned out the ominous crackling from the underlying economic structure. Herbert Hoover, Julius Klein, Charles E. Mitchell and a few other devotees of the New Economic Era were loudest in trying to shout down the rumblings. They were accompanied by a host of lesser soothsayers, business men, bankers and politicians; by college professors and economists, including some, like Stuart Chase, who had previously cast doubt upon the virtuousness of the *status quo;* and by journalists and editors ranging in the color of their political prejudices from reactionary black to petticoat pink. For instance, *The Nation,* though it was later to give the "happiness boys" many a hearty thwack, said in its issue of November 27, 1929:

. . . Not a single important banking or brokerage house has failed, industry as a whole shows as yet little more than a normal seasonal recession, and some unexpectedly good reports have been made even by steel and automobile corporations. Foreign trade remains good, corporation surpluses are still large, and corporations that have not paid dividends before or that have not paid any for some time are preparing to pay them now. Paper values in many cases have evaporated, but real values remain intact.

The great task of the next few months is the restoration of

confidence — confidence in the fundamental strength of the financial structure notwithstanding the strain that has been put upon it, confidence in the essential soundness of legitimate industry and trade. Criticism of Wall Street will not help much, and neither great banking establishments nor well-heeled investors are sufficient for the need. The public that has allowed itself to be drawn into the stock market at unprecedented cost to its pocket must recover its good sense, and the best service that the average man can render to that end is to keep his head and cheerfully shoulder his own share of the blame.

Herbert Hoover could not have stated the case for the beneficiaries of the Coolidge-Mellon-Hoover era in more convincing fashion.

AMID GROWING HUNGER

∽

LET it be said that Franklin Roosevelt did not lend his voice to this Greek chorus. However, he did comment upon the Wall Street debacle in a manner suggesting that to his mind it was no more than a passing affair, of importance mostly to the few misguided beings who had had their fingers burnt. "Much of the activity of the stock market is legitimate and proper," he said at Poughkeepsie on October 25, "but in some cases improper schemes and questionable methods have been used in stock promotion and many investors have lost sight of the real purpose of the Exchange in a fever of old-fashioned speculation." *

A month later, still seemingly unaware that a crisis was actually at hand, he responded in a perfunctory manner to President Hoover's request for cooperation by the State Governments in launching public-works programs as a means of preventing the disturbance in the stock market from resulting in industrial depression. New York would cooperate, Governor Roosevelt replied by telegram from Warm Springs, Georgia, with plans for building hospitals and prisons. Its cooperation would be limited "only by estimated receipts from revenues without increasing taxation." ⁴ In other words, it would go to no extra expense in meeting the emergency.

* State Senator John A. Hastings suggested in a communication to the Governor on November 24 that the State take action to check stock-market abuses and excesses in the future. There is no record of any reply to this suggestion, nor, apparently, was anything done in this connection.

THE GAY REFORMER

In the Governor's annual message to the State Assembly the following January there was still no recognition of the fact that the country had entered upon a period of depression. The message was largely a rehash of its predecessor, which had been delivered amid the glamor and ballyhoo of feverish prosperity. Reading the document today it is difficult to believe that it was written after and not before October, 1929.

The storm, alas, did not blow over. Two months later the Governor was telling an audience in Albany: "Everyone knows that we have left the peak of . . . prosperity behind, for how long I do not attempt to guess." [5] Yet it seemed quite unimportant to do more than state the fact. The meeting had been called to consider the problem of taxation. One might have supposed that the Governor would use the opportunity to discuss ways and means of financing the cost of the depression through higher taxes, for unemployment relief, public works and the like would in the last analysis have to be met out of taxes. Instead he talked about tax "reform." *

* One must not overlook the fact that on April 10, 1930, the existing Public Welfare Law was amended in certain particulars with a view to "providing security against old age want." This amendment was not part of a program to meet the economic emergency, for no such program existed or was contemplated at that date. The amendment was in fact the product of the commission that had been mentioned by Governor Roosevelt in his first message to the State Assembly in January, 1929, and had been appointed by him some time before the stock market collapse.

On November 14, 1934, President Roosevelt had reference to this law when he said: "As Governor of New York, it was my pleasure to recommend passage of the old-age pension act which, I am told, is still generally regarded as the most liberal in the country." In point of fact, neither this nor any other law ever enacted in New York State provides for old-age *pensions*.

A comparison of the act of April 10, 1930, with the Public Welfare Law which it was designed to amend would suggest that the latter was rather more liberal than the former. Under the amendment aged persons desiring relief were required to be at least seventy years old, American citizens, residents of the State for at least ten years immediately preceding their application for relief, and so forth. But the poor law gave an old person qualified to receive relief under the amended law, precisely the same relief without any of these qualifications and requirements. Under either act pauperism had to be established before relief was forthcoming.

It was asserted by sponsors of the amendment that it would do away with

48

By June he was expounding before the Governors' Conference in Salt Lake City his views with respect to the need for unemployment insurance, but even this he did not consider a matter of pressing importance. "Careful planning, shorter hours, more complete facts, public works and a dozen other palliatives," he said, " will in the future reduce unemployment, especially in times of industrial depression, but all of these will not eliminate unemployment." That could only be done through unemployment insurance. But haste was unwise. The problem would have to be carefully worked out so that the insurance scheme would not " by any chance become a mere dole — a handout from local or State governing agencies — which encourages idleness and defeats its own purpose." [6] In his opposition to direct relief for the jobless he was in agreement with other spokesmen of the capitalist-entrepreneur class who likewise were fearful of the " character destroying " aspects of the dole.

In August Governor Roosevelt amplified his position with regard to unemployment insurance in a speech before the State Federation of Labor in which he said that whatever plan was adopted must be based on " sound insurance lines." He pointed out that General Electric and other large corporations had their own insurance systems and asked, " if they are doing it, is it radical or communistic or bolshevistic for us to do it as part of a humanitarian movement? " [7] Again he was the humanitarian in politics, the benevolent patron of labor. He did not bother to inquire into the basic causes of unemploy-

---

the necessity of confining dependent old people in almshouses or other institutions in that it provided for the maintenance of such persons in their own or other private homes. The existing law made exactly the same provision. It said, *inter alia*, that " as far as possible families shall be kept together, and they shall not be separated for reasons of poverty alone. Whenever practicable, relief and service shall be given to a poor person in his own home."

The best that can be said of this amendment is that it was nothing more than a modernized poor law. It did nothing that had not already been achieved toward meeting the need for social security.

ment. Instead it appeared to him morally wrong that the job-less should be left to shift for themselves. Humanity required that something be done for them. But at the same time class-interest demanded that this " something " be financially sound.

Through 1930 the deflation pressed ruthlessly on, dragging down prices, profits and jobs. Occasionally this index or that hesitated for a moment, or even rose a point or two, and each time this occurred the "happiness boys" predicted that the turn had come and prosperity was on its way back. The press associations and newspapers scurried about to find statistical evidence of the upturn — and they always managed to fill a column or so with reports of men being hired, for even in times of depression the labor turnover is fairly large. These predictions and reports undoubtedly helped to bolster the confidence, if not of the public, then certainly of many public men.

Actually the crisis was deepening. Throughout 1930 there was not a single interruption to the deflationary trend. In October, 1929, the country had exported merchandise to the value of $528,500,000; by January, 1930, the value had fallen to $410,800,000; by August to $297,800,000, and by the following December to $274,900,000. In the domestic market the same thing was happening. The index for manufacturing production, which stood at 105 in January, fell to 89 in August and to 82 in December. The wholesale-prices index, placed at 94.6 for the year 1929, dropped to 83.7 in August, 1930, and to 77.7 in January, 1931. The employment index, fixed at 103.3 in October, 1929, fell off to 93.2 in the following January, 85.1 in August and 76.4 in January, 1931. The pay-roll index, an even more certain measure of available purchasing power, stood at 110.9 in October, 1929, and at 94.4 in January, 1930. By August it had dropped to 81.7 and in January, 1931, stood at 68.4.[8]

Governor Roosevelt did not appear particularly disturbed or even impressed by the ominous speed of the deflationary process. His campaign for reelection in the autumn of 1930 turned mainly upon other and more conventional issues. In the middle of November, after he had been reelected, he announced that he was inviting the Governors of six neighboring States to join with him in working out a common program to meet the unemployment situation. He suggested that they extend the free employment-exchange systems in their States, spread public building over the whole of each year, set up public reserve funds in good years to tide them over bad years, study the question of unemployment insurance, and standardize labor laws, compensations laws and taxes affecting industry. He designated Henry Bruere, a New York banker, to look after the details. There was surely little in this program to indicate that an emergency was at hand.

Nor could one gather from Governor Roosevelt's second inaugural address on January 1, 1931, that the country was in the fifteenth month of a depression that had already taken a frightful toll. His annual message to the legislature did refer to unemployment, but it was done in such a way as to leave the impression that the situation was well under control. For the rest the message was much like those that had gone before. Its labor program was little changed from that which he had first put forward in January, 1929.

Referring to unemployment in his message, he reported that "public works are being speeded; all available funds are being used to provide employment; wherever the State can find a place for a man to work it has provided a job. . . . It has been possible for the Administration to take farreaching steps both to mitigate and relieve the emergency, and also to plan for the future." By these and other means much unemployment that might otherwise have developed had been "prevented."

Nevertheless, unemployment and mass misery continued to spread, practically without let or hindrance, through the next twelve months. In January the employment index for New York State stood at 75.4; by December it had fallen to 67.7.[9]

In the meantime there had been serious financial troubles in New York City. On December 11, 1930, the Bank of the United States had been closed by the State Superintendent of Banks. This was the first important American banking house to fail during the crisis. Its collapse injured or ruined some 350,000 small depositors. The failure might have been prevented by intelligent, or at least energetic, action on the part of the Governor of New York. The plight of the bank was a matter of common gossip for months before Superintendent Broderick finally closed its doors.

The money changers in charge of the bank, two of whom later went to jail for their criminal mishandling of other people's money, rode high, wide and handsome during the frenzied days of 1928 and 1929. The practices of their kind were overlooked by those in authority. Seemingly nobody wanted to embarrass financiers who were making possible our everlasting prosperity. Governor Roosevelt himself sat silent, as has been noted, while these and other bankers plied their trade in the temple.

There had been a forewarning in the City Trust scandal — which in time sent Bank Superintendent Warder to prison. As a result of this affair, Acting Governor Lehman had appointed Robert Moses to conduct an investigation of the State Banking Department. Upon concluding his inquiry Mr. Moses recommended that " thrift " accounts be given the same legal protection as that accorded similar accounts in savings banks. The New York law required the funds of savings banks to be invested in any of a limited number of securities whose worth and soundness had been established by rigid test. This was done to give the most adequate protection possible to the savings of small depositors. But many of the commercial banks circumvented the law by soliciting " thrift " accounts, which they held were not savings accounts and therefore not subject to the restrictions of this law. Mr. Moses also denounced the practice of creating bank affiliates, mostly on paper, which were financed with depositors' funds and used mainly to facilitate gambling in securities and real estate to the greater profit of the bank officers. He said that unless these practices were checked other banks would follow the City Trust, and in this connection, while appearing before a legislative committee, he mentioned the Bank of the United States.

Governor Roosevelt was not satisfied with the Moses report. He created a commission of his own to study it. It was understood at first that he intended to put Mr. Moses on this commission. In the end he omitted the name of Robert Moses, but did appoint Henry Pollak, who was not only a director of, but also counsel for, the Bank of the United States! It is not surprising that the Governor's commission, as well as the legislative investigating committee, in the words of Norman Thomas, "almost completely disregarded the Moses report and solemnly concluded that everything would be all right if everybody would put his money in a sound bank." [10] And not long thereafter, as Robert Moses had indicated, the Bank of the United States failed, the small depositors lost their money, and Messrs. Marcus and Singer went to the penitentiary.

Three months after the failure Governor Roosevelt insisted that it lay with the State Assembly to restore confidence in the banks, confidence which he himself had done so much to weaken. A New York *Times* dispatch from Albany on March 21 reported that his attitude was " said to be that the closing of the Bank of the United States at a time of severe economic depression has shaken the faith of many people in the State banking system, and that the legislature should take some action at this time to restore public confidence." In a special message to the Assembly on the 24th he declared: " The responsibility for strengthening the banking law rests with you." He asked for a statute, somewhat belatedly, that would extend the same protection to " thrift " accounts as that given to savings accounts. Ignoring his own part in the drama, he sought to blame " the Federal Government " for the rise of " thrift " accounts. The Republican opposition, recalling that the Governor, or at least his Superintendent of Banks, had known of the condition of the Bank of the United States for months, simply snorted at this transparent attempt at whitewash and declared that the Governor already had plenty of power to deal with the banks.

✵ 3 ✵

PANIC BEGETS ACTION—
OF A SORT

ᔋ

FINALLY, on August 28, 1931, Governor Roosevelt formally
and publicly acknowledged not only that an emergency had
arisen but that something would have to be done about it. He
told the Assembly, convened in extraordinary session, that
"the time for platitudes as to the necessities of the situation has
passed. The time for immediate action is at hand."

The country then had almost two years of depression behind it. It was soon to enter a third winter of increasing distress. The summer of 1931 had been especially severe. Europe
was in the grip of panic. The Creditanstalt of Vienna had
failed in May, deliberately wrecked in the course of the economic warfare that had been sweeping the world since long
before 1929. Because of this bank's close relations with finance
capitalism in neighboring countries, its failure had instant repercussions throughout Central and Southeastern Europe. By
the first week of June it appeared that the German financial
structure was about to be dissolved in chaos. Germany's banks
and politicians flashed appeals for help to London, New York,
Washington. President Hoover responded with his moratorium
of June 20, but this — thanks mainly to French intransigence;
the French had not wrecked the Creditanstalt for nothing —
did not prevent the virtual collapse of the German banking
system in the first week of July. Before the end of the summer
the panic was to sweep England, the Scandinavian countries

and many lesser nations off the gold standard. It was to hasten the course of deflation in the United States. Stock market prices, which, according to *The Annalist*, averaged $237.52 in March, fell to $190.59 in August, to $156.80 in September, and to $119.96 in December. Wholesale prices in the same period dropped from 75.5 to 68.1, while the pay-roll index went down from 74.9 to 55.8.[11] Purchasing power and profits were rapidly dwindling.

One could perhaps ignore the ancient prognostications of a Marx, an Engels, or a John Hobson. One might dismiss the more recent warnings of a Sir George Paish or a Gustav Cassel. One could even overlook the fact that there had already been nearly two years of depression, two years of growing misery which all of one's platitudes about public works and unemployment insurance (in the future) and all of one's "far-reaching steps" had utterly failed to check. Now certainly "the time for platitudes as to the necessities of the situation" had passed. Now — finally — "the time for immediate action" was at hand. With one's familiar and well-ordered world crumbling all about one, with destitution increasing on every side, the inevitable could no longer be put off. It is of such unerring foresight that statesmanship is made.

In addressing the State Assembly on August 28, however, Governor Roosevelt did not acknowledge that he himself had failed to read the signs correctly. He did not admit to any shortcomings in his own platitudinous recommendations for meeting the emergency during the past two years. Instead he said:

I would not be appearing before you today if these were normal times. When, however, a condition arises which calls for measures of relief over and beyond the ability of private and local assistance to meet, even with the usual aid added by the State, it is time for the State itself to do its additional share.

As my constitutional duty to communicate to your honorable

bodies the condition of the State, I report to you what is a matter of common knowledge — that the economic depression of the last two years has created social conditions resulting in great physical suffering on the part of many hundreds of thousands of men, women and children. Unless conditions immediately and greatly change, this will, we fear, be aggravated by cold and hunger during the coming winter . . . the number of our citizens who, this coming winter, will be in need will, so far as it is possible to estimate, be nearly, if not quite, twice as many as during the winter of 1930–31.

There are many causes. Many individuals and families, because of prolonged unemployment, have exhausted their savings and their credit. Many who were at work last winter and were enabled to take care of their relatives and friends are now themselves out of work. In the same way, many employers who up to recently, with fine public spirit, have continued to use their resources to prevent the laying-off of workers, are finding that they can no longer do so.

Last winter the distress was to a great extent alleviated along three distinct lines: First, through the recommendations of the Commission on Stabilization of Employment, which pointed out the method of staggering employment in order to provide work for more people [in short, a share-the-work scheme that transferred most of the burden of the depression to the shoulders of the working class], and was largely instrumental in bringing about the coordination of relief work of the various municipalities and private agencies throughout the State; second, by the authorization and construction of large additions to public works on the part of the State and the political subdivisions thereof; third, by generous response by private individuals in the form of contributions for relief.

We could proceed in accordance with the same program and policy used last winter were it not for the facts which, according to the best information obtainable, seem incontrovertible. The first is that the amount of relief needed will of necessity be vastly greater this coming winter; secondly, the resources hitherto used will not be adequate to meet the additional needs.

In specific terms, the Governor urged that the income-tax rates (which the State Assembly two years before had inconsiderately refused to lower at his demand) be now increased by about 50 per cent and that the additional revenue thus provided, to the sum of $20,000,000, be set aside as an unemployment relief fund. He wanted the money spent for the most part on public works, and he especially emphasized that none of it should under any circumstances be paid out " in the form of a dole." The State Assembly a few days later voted its approval of this program.

Since it was estimated that there were at that time " in excess of 1,500,000 people out of work and more or less in need " in the State, the $20,000,000 appropriation worked out at the rate of $13.33 (before deducting administrative and other costs) for each of these needy persons and their families. Moreover, since most of it was to be spent on public works, a large part of the fund would be drained off to meet the customary capitalist charges — contractors' profits and the like — leaving much less than $13.33 for each needy person. This surely was not a munificent contribution with which to supplement the charity of the cities and counties and the private agencies. Indeed, as matters turned out, not all of the $20,000,-000 was spent by the end of winter, bureaucracy and political contracting being what they are.

Franklin Roosevelt's conservatism with respect to money matters was one hindrance to a more adequate relief program. Throughout this period he was always safely orthodox on the question of governmental financing. He believed in the balanced budget. In his relief message of August 28 he made it clear that the cost of relief should be met out of current taxation and not by borrowing. " It is the duty," he said, " of those who have benefited by our industrial and economic system to come to the front in such a grave emergency and assist in relieving those who, under the same industrial and economic order, are the losers and sufferers."

Ten days later he made more precise his views with regard to government spending. He vigorously criticized the plan of the Republican Administration in Washington to borrow the money it believed it had to have to finance its program for dealing with the depression and unemployment relief. In a speech at Syracuse, as reported by the New York *Times,* he said:

There is current toward public expenditures and public affairs an attitude that sometimes passes for optimism and faith in the future, but which really amounts to nothing more than the rationalization of a spendthrift. Now, I believe firmly in planning for the future. I believe in anticipating the needs of the coming generation and in building with a view to expansion, but I don't believe in saddling on a future generation the financial obligations that belong to the present.

The future will have its own problems and its own demands. . . .

I don't believe in banking on fools' luck as applied to the public finances in spite of the fact that it has come to the rescue of some communities and some divisions of government in this nation at times in the past. . . .

Right now we have to consider how to meet . . . an emergency. Shall we meet it according to the example of our Federal Government, which feels itself obliged to put out $800,000,000 of long-time bonds to cure the defects of a budget whose revenues have not come up to expectations?

I think we should be very foolish and recreant to our trust if we should follow any such precedent. We don't know what the future holds for us. This depression is today's problem. . . .

I think most of us are agreed . . . that we cannot and must not borrow against the future to meet it. We must share now out of what we have, not out of what we expect to have some day in the future. We must distribute fairly among those who are able to pay, the burden of aiding those who cannot exist without help. The funds that we must have for unemployment relief should be raised by the speediest possible method of current taxation that will result in such an equitable assessment.

Here again, as in the case of his opposition to " partnership between business and government," he employed language that rang with unmistakable conviction. No one reading his Syracuse speech could doubt that he was an unyielding advocate of a balanced budget and that he truly believed the attempts to justify government borrowing to meet an emergency was " nothing more than the rationalization of a spendthrift." Here again he appeared to be laying down a doctrine, not for the moment after the manner of a self-seeking opportunist, but a doctrine that he clearly meant to be accepted as a permanent and integral part of his own political philosophy.

4

THE FLESH IS WEAK

∽

FRANKLIN ROOSEVELT was slowly but inevitably won over to
the need of doing something for the jobless. The *mores* of
Hyde Park required it. Yet recognition of the moral need for
relief did not carry with it recognition of the fundamentals of
the economic problem. Two years and three months after the
bursting of the prosperity bubble, he was still of the belief that
the crisis was mainly the product of understandable human
error. Men had themselves to blame for what had happened;
men — but the right kind of men — would repair the damage
and set the house in order again. There was need for economic
change, but not for fundamental reconstruction. It was primarily a question of replacing " unsound materials with new."
In his message to the State Assembly on January 6, 1932, he
said:

We face the necessity of employing new measures of value, for
the good reason that many old values have disappeared; new com-
parisons of property and of man's remuneration for his work, for
the good reason that many of the old proportions have proved
false.

It would be useless as well as ungracious to place the blame for
our present situation on individuals, or groups, or on any specific
acts. What we can do is to learn from the recent years in a spirit
of humility and of generosity what to avoid in the process of re-
building our economic and social structure upon a surer foundation. . . . We know that many of those who ran after false gods

are heartily sorry for their sins of omission and commission; that many of the leaders of American thought in government and in business appreciate the errors of their teaching. That is well; and nothing is to be gained by making them the scapegoats.

Nevertheless, more than two years have gone by and these leaders have as yet shown us few plans for the reconstruction of a better-ordered civilization in which the economic freedom of the individual will be restored. . . .

Thoroughly unsound, even if wholly legal [sic], banking practices have been growing for a generation. Many banks became mere bond-selling houses. Many bankers forgot that it was of doubtful ethics to sell their own securities to their depositors and to trust funds for which they themselves were trustees. Many billions of securities were sold to the public at prices unjustified even by the expectation that we had reached an immutable millennium, a permanent Utopia. Consolidations, mergers, holding companies, investment trusts were touted in every corner of the land, a pyramiding unequalled since the days of the Mississippi Bubble. . . .

Today we recognize the unsoundness and the danger. The bubble has burst with all its rainbow glory. The public has burned its fingers in the flame of wild speculation and has learned now to fear the fire. . . .

We should not seek in any way to destroy or tear down — except in order to replace unsound materials with new. The American system of economics and government is everlasting. Rather should we seek to eliminate those methods which have proved mistaken. . . .

Again on May 22, speaking before the graduating class of Oglethorpe University in Atlanta, Governor Roosevelt emphasized the moral and personal equation. He spoke of the mirage of prosperity that had entranced the country in 1928 and 1929 — a mirage that he himself had not seen fit to question. " Many who were called and are still pleased to call themselves the leaders of finance," he said, " celebrated and assured us of an eternal future for this easy-chair mode of living. And to the stimulation of belief in this dazzling chimera was lent not only the voices of some of our public men in high office, but their influence and the material aid of the very instruments of government which they controlled. . . . Beneath all the happy optimism of those days there existed lack of plan and a great waste. This failure to measure true values and to look ahead extended to almost every industry, every profession, every walk of life."

Some of the results of this lack of foresight were apparent. The Governor went on to say:

. . . we cannot review carefully the history of our industrial advance without being struck with its haphazardness, with the gigantic waste with which it has been accomplished, with the superfluous duplication of productive facilities, the continual scrapping of still useful equipment, the tremendous mortality in industrial and commercial undertakings, the thousands of dead-end trails into which enterprise has been lured, the profligate waste of natural resources.

He conceded that " our basic trouble was not an insufficiency of capital." He declared that it was rather " an insufficient distribution of buying power coupled with an over-sufficient speculation in production." He added that " we accumulated such a superabundance of capital that our great bankers were vying with each other, some of them employing questionable methods in their efforts to lend this capital at home and abroad." True, but not the whole truth. Why was there an insufficient distribution of buying power? Why did not wages rise " proportionately to the reward to capital "? Why were the bankers seeking to lend our surplus capital at home and abroad, even employing questionable methods to that end? It is not enough to accuse the money-changers and industrialists of being " selfish " and " opportunists," for this is to imply that capitalism has no laws of its own, or at any rate that such laws are subordinate to selfishness and greed. Yet capitalism does have its own laws, and these, while they undoubtedly encourage greed and selfishness, even without the help of such qualities must lead to maldistribution of buying power and creation of surplus capital.

Nevertheless, Franklin Roosevelt persisted in his belief that human weaknesses were at bottom mainly responsible for the country's plight. This became dogma with him in the Presidential campaign in the autumn. He set aside his suggestion of January 6 that "it would be useless as well as ungracious to place the blame for our present situation on individuals, or groups, or on any specific acts" and that "nothing is to be gained by making them the scapegoats." There was, of course, something to be gained. If he could convince the electorate of the necessity of accepting Herbert Hoover as the scapegoat for the depression, then he would himself become President. Again and again during the campaign, therefore, he "ungraciously" heaped the blame upon this hapless individual and his specific acts. He went so far as to say, without equivocation, that Herbert Hoover and his colleagues were personally responsible for the depression.

At Sioux City, Iowa, on September 29, he declared that the Republicans " have adopted the boldest alibi in the history of politics. *Having brought this trouble on the world,* they now seek to avoid all responsibility for the mismanagement of the affairs of this nation by blaming the foreign victims for their own economic blundering. They say that all of our troubles come from abroad — that the Administration is not in the least to be held to answer. This excuse is a classic of impertinence. *If ever a condition was more clearly traceable to two specific American-made causes, it is the depression of this country and the world.*" Again at Indianapolis on October 20 he said: " The American people, conservative and peace-loving, have had an experience under the present Republican leadership that they do not wish to continue. The unsound and unintelligent venturing into economic policies that this Administration, and that the present candidate for President, sponsored has brought a terrible retribution. His economic heresies have all ' come home to roost,' and *this Administration stands convicted of having produced this brood of disaster-producing gambles with national prosperity.*" And again in Baltimore on October 25: " The White House and the Treasury Department issued statements that definitely encouraged and stimulated this speculative boom. They led the people on to certain and disastrous destruction. There is the record. No partisan words will ever wipe it out. It stands, and the lost savings of millions bid us remember. The destruction came likewise from the false policy of lending money to backward and crippled countries. The Administration encouraged the policy that sought to open markets in foreign lands through the lending of American money to these countries. This was definitely sponsored by the Republican candidate for President in 1928, and for a time it became a cardinal factor in the policy of his Administration. That it was utterly and entirely unsound I have demonstrated many times. It brought a terrible retribution. This charge, which I have made repeatedly in this campaign, has never been answered."

It must be remembered, of course, that these absurd statements were made in the heat of a bitter political campaign. Franklin Roosevelt could not afford to be too gracious to the man whom he hoped to succeed in one of the most powerful political offices in the world. Nevertheless, though he might have employed more temperate language at another time, his campaign utterances on the whole reflected his actual judgment as to the principal causes of the depression. At no time did he indicate that he held any views substantially in conflict with them. Men — politicians, bankers, speculators, " the lone wolf, the unethical competitor, the reckless promoter, the Ishmael or Insull whose hand is against every man's " — were solely to blame for what had happened.

5

AUDACITY AND DIVIDENDS

∽

EVEN before 1929 Franklin Roosevelt had lectured on the need for " radicalism and experimentation " in government.[12] Precisely what he meant by this he had never made clear. He had risked no experiments in his two terms in Albany. The somewhat timid advances in the field of social legislation that he proposed had all been tried elsewhere.

In his Atlanta speech of May 22 he returned to the subject when he declared that the way out of the depression could only be found through trial and error. He confessed to a lack of understanding of the laws of capitalism; they mystified him. He held, nevertheless, that it was within the power of men to prevent these laws from following their normal course and taking their usual toll. In his exact words:

Some hold to the theory that the periodic slowing down of our economic machine is one of its inherent peculiarities — a peculiarity at which we must grin, if we can, and bear because if we attempt to tamper with it we shall cause even worse ailments.

According to this theory, as I see it, if we grin and bear long enough, the economic machine will eventually begin to pick up speed and in the course of an indefinite number of years will again attain that maximum number of revolutions which signifies what we have been wont to miscall prosperity, but which, alas, is but a last ostentatious twirl of the economic machine before it again succumbs to that mysterious impulse to slow down again.

This attitude toward our economic machine requires not only

66

greater stoicism but greater faith in immutable economic law and less faith in the ability of man to control what he has created than I, for one, have. Whatever elements of truth lie in it, it is an invitation to sit back and do nothing. . . .

He was convinced that man could control, "by adequate planning, the creation and distribution of those products which our vast economic machine is capable of yielding. . . . It is well within the inventive capacity of man, who has built up this great social and economic machine capable of satisfying the wants of all, to insure that all who are willing and able to work receive from it at least the necessities of life."

But of plans of his own he had none. Indeed, he continued:

Let us not confuse purpose with method. Too many so-called leaders of the nation fail to see the forest because of the trees. Too many of them fail to recognize the vital necessity of planning for definite objectives. True leadership calls for the setting forth of the objectives and the rallying of public opinion in support of these objectives.

Do not confuse objectives with methods. When the nation becomes substantially united in favor of planning the broad objectives of civilization, then true leadership must unite behind definite methods.

The country needs and, unless I mistake its temper, the country demands bold, persistent experimentation. It is common sense to take a method and try it; if it fails, admit it frankly and try another. But above all, try something.

Here he had obviously jumped, without benefit of logic, to the conclusion that mankind can set up its own economic laws and should do so through something variously called "experimentation" and "planning." Not that this conclusion was necessarily unsound, but he had established no premise upon which to base it. He could not, therefore, logically demonstrate how his "objectives" were to be attained. To cover his confusion he had perforce to relegate method to a subordinate position. In truth, he had no method, but believed that if we tried enough ways we should eventually find one that worked. He was implicitly conceding not only that he did not know why the economic system had run amok, but also that he did not know how to set it right again.

Had he followed a process of deductive reasoning he would have discovered that the experimental method is not suitable to a liberal democracy. If the experimentation were to be truly scientific and not merely a cloak for opportunism or dilettanteism, the task would have to be left to trained political economists. Certainly, except in the rarest instances, the ordinary politician or office-holder, though he may be versed in the subtle art of catching votes, has no more than superficial knowledge of political economy as a science. More than that, since political phenomena, in the words of John Stuart Mill, exist "in almost boundless excess" and since the results of political measures are conditioned "by nearly every fact which exists, or event which occurs, in human society," [13] it would clearly be necessary to attempt to control these phenomena. And it is just as clear that this could not be done if political authority were diffused through democratic or representative institutions. The authority would have to be centered in the hands of the experts. To follow any other course, to leave the task in the hands of politicians dependent upon popular vote for their authority, or to leave it to untrained political economists who would not know what they were about, would be nothing less than reckless speculation with the lives and welfare of human beings. The necessary measure of scientific control might be approached under a dictatorship, but surely never under Franklin Roosevelt's "everlasting" American system.

While granting that it is possible for mankind to control, "by adequate planning, the creation and distribution of those products which our vast economic machine is capable of yielding," it does not follow that this is possible in an economic system based upon production for private profit. If the planning were to have real meaning, and not merely to consist in lofty statements of desirable objectives, it would have to depend upon complete or practically complete control of all the factors entering into the national economy. The primary purpose of economic planning would be to establish a balance between production and consumption. But this objective could not be attained by deliberate method except as it might be achieved through the imposition of a control over prices, profits, wages, savings and investments so exacting that it would destroy the existing profit system.

No doubt the President's emphasis on " experimentation " and particularly " planning " — terms which he used interchangeably, though they are essentially antithetical — can be partly ascribed to the objective requirements of the political situation. These phrases promised action where action appeared to be wanting. Herbert Hoover seemed to many people to be remaining passive in the face of multiplying calamity. They were ready to oust him in favor of a man who dared to act, to take a chance. " Experimentation " spoke both of action and of risk. Besides, " planning " was then politically popular, especially among the petit bourgeoisie, the chief sufferers from the depression.

It would be unfair to suggest that Franklin Roosevelt was bent only on catching votes. He certainly intended to try new methods of dealing with the economic problem. Every candidate for the presidency must and does promise new measures and new methods. Indeed, since the national economy is not static but dynamic and forever changing, every President in office, whatever his name or political faith or whatever he may have promised in his campaign, must and does propose measures and methods that are untried and therefore " experimental." The degree of such experimentation varies, how-

THE GAY REFORMER

ever, from President to President according to his particular theory of the state and his interpretation of the powers of the office.

Before the advent of the second Roosevelt in the White House there were two schools of thought regarding the extent to which a President ought to go in having recourse to political experimentation; that is to say, how far the power of the state should be used in dealing with economic and social problems. The *laissez faire* school, which included Presidents McKinley, Taft, Harding, Coolidge and Hoover, spoke for the upper bourgeoisie. It preached the doctrine that the state should hold its intervention in such matters to a minimum. While this doctrine did not prevent aid and comfort from being extended in many ways to finance and monopoly capitalism, it served as an excuse for not extending state aid to the petit bourgeoisie and proletariat.

The progressive school, which included Senator La Follette the elder, Theodore Roosevelt, Woodrow Wilson and the latter-day Republican insurgents, spoke or pretended to speak for the lower middle class. The progressives held that the machinery of the state should be used as freely and extensively as might be necessary to help other classes besides the upper bourgeoisie. (Theodore Roosevelt even contended that there reposed in the President an undefined residuum of power to do anything he considered socially necessary or desirable that was not specifically forbidden him to do.[14])

Basically, the conflict was between two opposed economic interests. The petty capitalists, farmers and skilled artisans had no real economic power, for the effective economic power rested with the monopoly and finance capitalists. Yet they had the ballot and they were numerically superior to the capitalist class. Hence they had potential political power, which they could use, and occasionally sought to use, to modify the economic power of the upper bourgeoisie. This had to be done through the machinery of the state, and so the progressive school sought always to expand the authority of the state. By the same token the *laissez faire* school resisted every effort to enlarge the power of the state over economic affairs.*

Franklin Roosevelt's talk of " planning " and " experimentation " — forms of state intervention which the advocates of *laissez faire* would avoid at all costs — indicated that he would take the progressive side. Moreover, if he were to win the election, it would be largely by the votes of the most dissatisfied elements in the lower middle class, the principal victims of the crisis of monopoly capitalism. Socially and economically, however, he had little in common with the petit bourgeoisie. On the other hand, neither his social background nor his personal economic interests nor yet his political training would seem to have placed him among the monopolists. Rather was he a member of the *rentier* class. Though political accident or opportunism might lead him astray, he would tend to see the economic problem through the eyes of the *rentier*.

This class, no less than any other, is interested in protecting the sources of its income.† Its income is derived from invest-

* At no time from the rise of monopolism until 1933 did the progressives completely control the state. At no time did they even approach such control, although at least two Presidents had identified themselves with the progressive school. The failure of the numerically superior lower middle class to take advantage of its political power to capture the state outright in its own interest may be ascribed largely to the tenacious hold of the " American dream," which was responsible for the belief that *laissez faire*, that is, democratic liberalism, served equally the interests of all sections of the middle class. Had the petit bourgeoisie ever captured the state, the reaction of the monopolists would have been interesting to observe, for history shows no exception to the rule that the ruling class will always fight to retain its power.

† Strictly speaking, this class includes only those whose income is derived chiefly from investments. Actually, however, it includes many other individuals and institutions who have other and more important interests, but who also own shares, bonds, mortgages and the like. These persons are frequently inclined to place their interests as *rentiers* before their other interests. This is all too often true of the small merchant, professional worker, or wage-earner who has a few shares of stock in a big corporation. He can usually be persuaded to oppose a political measure designed to restrict a corporation in which he has money invested, even though the proposed measure might help him as a wage-earner or petty capitalist.

ments. Its investments form that great capital-claims structure upon which modern capitalism rests. More than that, its investments are to a large extent the very life's-blood of the giant monopolies. By the same token the *rentier* class prospers only as monopoly prospers. It should be obvious that this class would not want to see the great industrial and financial combinations taken over by the state or broken up for the benefit of the small capitalists. It would want the state to intervene only to the extent that might be necessary to ensure more honest and efficient management of these combinations. It would want the sources of its income safeguarded, perhaps even underwritten by the state, but certainly not destroyed.

Franklin Roosevelt might be expected, then, to follow neither the progressive nor the *laissez faire* formula. He would in all likelihood take a third path. He would be audacious, would compromise the principles of democracy, would enhance the power of the state, not in the interest of the petit bourgeoisie, not to restrict or unduly embarrass the monopolists, but to make honest men and efficient managers out of the latter. He would show that honesty pays dividends.

6

RENDER UNTO CAESAR

∽

IT was not only their incompetence or dishonesty or lack of foresight Franklin Roosevelt held against the bankers, industrialists and Republican politicians who in his view were to blame for the country's distress. He also accused them of neglecting the responsibilities of leadership. They were leaders, he contended, who were unwilling or unable to lead. Hence their failure; for the one solution he laid before the country, apart from his advocacy of "experimentation," was active and intelligent leadership. The people, he declared, demand "that they be given a new leadership. . . . The complete solving of these economic problems which are national in scope is an impossibility without leadership. . . . The times and the present needs call for leadership . . . leadership broad enough to understand the problems not only of our nation but of their relationship to other nations . . . a leadership practical, sound, courageous and alert."

He had long thought and talked in terms of leadership. And he had always sought to assert himself in this capacity when and where he could. He was the leader of the rebellion against Boss Murphy in 1911. He was the man who took the lead, gave orders, kept the naval machine running smoothly and efficiently (if we may take the word of his several biographers) while he was Assistant Secretary of the Navy. He was very much the man who stood above politics and commanded the State Government in the name of the people rather than

73

in behalf of any party during his four years in the Governor's chair in Albany. Indeed, leadership, in this sense, came naturally to the man. He gave directions and issued commands with the air of one who is born to rule and has not the slightest doubt that his ruling is wise and beneficial. His great confidence in himself made it difficult, if not quite impossible, for him ever to question his own attitudes and decisions. What he did would always be good.

His conception of leadership was a heritage from Hyde Park. It was an unusually positive example of what some psychologists call father-authority. This he had clearly derived from his intimate contact with his own father, whom he respected and revered and who must have seemed to him in his childhood the fount of all wisdom and authority. The elder Roosevelt was the active head of a healthy and intelligently organized household. He directed the affairs of the family and farm humanely, even joyously, and yet firmly. His authority made life for the boy, Franklin, run along happily and efficiently. There was nothing of compulsion or coercion about it. Rather did it take the form of confident and friendly leadership. And the sole objective of this leadership was the common good of the household. What the father did was always good.

Franklin Roosevelt's sense of father-authority was superimposed upon two distinct Rooseveltian traits, self-confidence and self-assertiveness. That he possessed these traits in abundance he revealed early in boyhood. Mrs. James Roosevelt, his mother, has related several incidents touching upon this side of the boy's character. For example:

I usually read aloud to him as he puttered. On one particular evening when he seemed less interested in the sound of my voice than usual, I put down the book of stories, and said:

"Franklin, I don't think there is any point in my reading to you any more. You don't hear me anyway."

Franklin looked up, a whimsical smile on his face, and, much to my surprise, quoted verbatim the whole last paragraph of the essay I had been reading.

When I expressed what I felt was a very natural surprise at his ability to do so, he replied:

" Why, Mom, I would be ashamed of myself if I couldn't do at least two things at once." [15]

His self-assertiveness and his precocious sense of leadership were even more strikingly reflected in another incident:

Franklin had a great habit of ordering his playmates around, and for reasons which I have never been able to fathom, was generally permitted to have his way. I know that I, overhearing him in conversation one day with a little boy on the place with whom he was digging a fort, said to him:

" My son, don't give the orders all the time. Let the other boy give them sometimes."

" Mummie," he said to me quite without guile, lifting a soil-streaked face, " if I didn't give the orders, nothing would happen! " [16]

One other quality — personal courage, the will to conquer in the face of personal danger — was essential to the man. Although he had by then become set in his outward characteristics, until he was nearly 40 he had had to undergo no real test of personal courage. There had developed no convincing evidence that he possessed that indefinable quality which induces mankind to follow individuals who have it and to ignore those who do not. The test came, or rather began, in the summer of 1921. The year before Franklin Roosevelt had gone through an unusually strenuous campaign as the Democratic nominee for the Vice-Presidency. He was apparently run down in consequence of the exertion. Yet he did not stop to rest, but after the campaign proceeded immediately to other activities. It was not until late in the following summer that he finally went to Campobello, the family summer home in New Brunswick, for a brief vacation. He was feeling none too well. One afternoon he went for a long run with the eldest of his children to shake off a chill. Tired and doubtless overheated, he plunged into the icy waters of the Bay of Fundy. Two days later infantile paralysis had laid him low.

Among those who survive this devastating malady there is usually to be found a tendency toward chronic invalidism, spiritual defeatism. In this particular case the doctors were pessimistic. Family and friends wavered between fear and hope. But Franklin Roosevelt refused to concede defeat. He called up all of that self-assertiveness which was his birthright. He decided for himself that he would not permit this " childish " disease to break him, dash all his hopes and aspirations, and put a period to his career. He would win through. And he did, though for several years he appeared to make no progress toward physical rehabilitation.

It has been said that he set out to learn everything he could about the disease, to conquer it with knowledge. It is to be doubted, however, that what he learned was of any considerable help compared with the indomitable will he brought into play. It might be said, too, that men in less fortunate financial circumstances would perforce have had to surrender because they could not buy the medical services Franklin Roosevelt had at his disposal. It cannot be denied that his checkbook gave him an added advantage. But this does not alter the fact that his triumph was psychological to a far greater extent than it was physical. He was still to be deprived of the use of his legs, to be compelled to get about only with the aid of canes and braces and friendly arms, to be consigned to a life of comparative physical inactivity, a torture in itself for a man of his lively disposition.

This magnificent fight against what appeared to be insuperable odds suggests something more than brute courage. It speaks also of a will to conquer. And it was this quality in Franklin Roosevelt that made of him a leader of men, albeit of weaker men, for in him they seemed to sense that stability of purpose and determination to succeed which they themselves lacked but felt they ought to have. That this characteristic might fail their hero in times of stress would not matter; indeed, it would never occur to them. Just as in the case of his fifth cousin, Theodore, who likewise overcame physical disability by sheer determination, Franklin Roosevelt might lose most of his purely political following (for, despite the common belief, his leadership was not to be built upon political shrewdness), but so long as he lived he would retain a large and devoted personal following.

Franklin Roosevelt's attitude toward leadership was, then, not wholly an accident of political opportunity. It had real substance. He was himself a leader of men. He was, moreover, conscious of the fact. But leadership is impotent unless it has a means of expressing itself. In politics it can only express itself in terms of power. A William Jennings Bryan may by personal magnetism or oratorical fervor arouse the emotions of millions of downtrodden souls, but unless he can attain to a position where he can satisfy their demands, his leadership is ineffective and comes to naught. Franklin Roosevelt understood this. Throughout his political career he had reached out for ever more power. And this power he sought for himself alone. He knew how to share duties, to obtain the cooperation of subordinates, but was ever reluctant to share authority. Party organization was to him hardly more than a stepping stone to power, a necessary means of acquiring and holding the votes of the people. Legislative bodies had to be dealt with since the forms of democracy required it, but the legislative, in his judgment, was more efficient when it yielded precedence to the executive. Constitutions and statutory laws he looked upon as flexible and subject to interpretation; they could always be stretched or amended or replaced. What really counted was the philosophy and good motives of the man — the leader — who was directing affairs. In him should be centered the effective political authority.

77

While he was Governor of New York, Franklin Roosevelt inevitably placed himself firmly on the side of those who believe in States' rights and against those who thought the ends of society would be better served by a centralization of authority in Washington. Indeed, he felt that the trend toward concentration of power in the Federal Government would, if continued, lead to division and ruin. He had no hesitation in speaking out on the subject, though in airing his views he laid down another of his hard-and-fast doctrines which he was lightly to discard the moment it no longer served his political ambitions. For example, in a radio broadcast on March 2, 1930, he declared:

The preservation of this home rule by the States is not a cry of jealous commonwealths seeking their own aggrandizement at the expense of sister States. It is a fundamental necessity if we are to remain a united country. . . .

The doctrine of regulation and legislation by " master minds," in whose judgment and will all the people may gladly and quietly acquiesce, has been too glaringly apparent in Washington during these last ten years. Were it possible to find " master minds " so unselfish, so willing to decide unhesitatingly against their own personal interests or private prejudices, men almost god-like in their ability to hold the scales of justice with an even hand — such a government might be to the interests of the country, but there are none such on our political horizon, and we cannot expect a complete reversal of the teachings of history.

Now, to bring about government by oligarchy masquerading as democracy, it is fundamentally essential that practically all authority and control be centralized in our national government. The individual sovereignty of our States must first be destroyed, except in mere minor matters of legislation. We are safe from the danger of any such departure from the principles upon which this country was founded just so long as the individual home rule of the States is scrupulously preserved and fought for whenever they seem in danger.

It doubtless did not occur to Governor Roosevelt that within three years or so he would himself be endangering the individual home rule of the States by the adoption of a sweeping program which speeded up the concentration of authority and control in the Federal Government. It seems not to have occurred to him that he might soon be defending, rather than condemning, regulation and legislation by " master minds," that he would, indeed, being going much further than any of the Republican Administrations in Washington in this respect. Nor, perhaps, did it dawn upon him that it was he himself who would carry out the surprisingly accurate prediction, stated elsewhere in the same broadcast, that if the usurpation of States' rights and tendency toward centralization in Washington went on, we should soon be spending many billions of dollars in excess of the normal Federal budget, which in 1930 he thought had already reached extravagant proportions on a basis of exceedingly thin constitutional sanction.

For it was apparent that the broader was the political jurisdiction of the States the more authority he would have as Governor of a State. During his first two or three years in Albany he considered the question of States' rights a fighting issue. While returning from the Governors' Conference in Salt Lake City later in 1930, he suggested that the question ought to be fought out at the polls in the forthcoming Congressional elections and in the national election in 1932. He felt, in the words of a newspaper correspondent accompanying him, that " the widespread protest against Federal interference in State affairs, voiced at the Governors' Conference, could not fail to arouse countrywide interest and response." [17] It was high time, in his opinion, for a revolt against the increasing power of the Federal Government.

But Franklin Roosevelt was not content merely to defend the political authority of the States. He was equally zealous in endeavoring to enhance his own prestige and authority at the expense of the legislative. He bombarded the State Assembly with messages in which he did not simply suggest or recommend laws he desired, but virtually demanded such legislation. He sought to surround himself with " master minds " of his own choosing to deal with agriculture, milk, old-age relief and the like. It is arguable that had he been inclined to take the attitude that the Governor is no more than an administrative or executive officer, he would have obtained even less than he did from the Assembly, for he was faced with a hostile majority. But it would have been entirely out of keeping with his character had he not sought to dominate the State Government and had he not sought to reduce the legislative to a position subordinate, in effect, to that of the executive.

He usually managed to find sanction in constitutional prerogative or in traditionalism for his authority. What "we learned in our school books about the American form of government " [18] was to him the only safe criterion — at least where his personal power was concerned. Later he was to endow this school-book interpretation of the American form of government with an exceedingly generous flexibility to the attainment of the same end, but so long as the letter of the basic law suited his purpose he would depend upon it. This was true in the famous budget case. The New York State Constitution holds the Governor responsible for the expenditure of funds appropriated by the Assembly. Governor Smith, however, had allowed the Assembly to assume a certain measure of control over such funds. He had learned that by this concession he could obtain legislative approval for numerous reforms which the Republican majority might otherwise have blocked. Governor Roosevelt acknowledged the merits of such political bargaining, but held, nevertheless, that he alone should control and supervise the expenditure of all State funds. This was provided in the Constitution and there could be no compromise with that document. It was a question, as two of his biographers subsequently put it,[19] of adhering strictly " to the constitutional plan as established by the Founders. No careless or general abiding would suffice. The obedience to fundamental law must be real, in word and in spirit, in intent as well as in phrase." *

In other words, though it cost him a part of his legislative program — and it did — he would insist upon holding the purse strings and the power they gave him. In a strict legal sense, of course, he was right, as the Court of Appeals finally ruled, but the implications of his attitude are not without interest. Whereas Alfred Smith had been willing to compromise, to yield on questions of prestige and power for the sake of practical gains, Franklin Roosevelt preferred to forego accomplishment for the sake of protecting and enhancing his own authority.

* As a matter of fact, the Budget Amendment to the New York State Constitution was of comparatively recent date. The "Founders" had nothing to do with it. It may be said, indeed, that the executive budget actually transfers from the legislative to the executive a power over public finances which the "Founders," still living in fear of executive tyranny, intended to keep securely in the hands of the legislative. This is not to condone log-rolling or pork-barrel legislation nor to deny the technical superiority of the budget over former methods, but is stated here merely to keep the historical record straight.

7

THE GOOD MAN IN POLITICS

∽

FRANKLIN ROOSEVELT had never wallowed in the gutter with the professional politicians and doubtless never would. Indeed, he regarded politics as lofty public service and, therefore, a field which people of the "better sort" should dominate. He made this clear in a statement to the Yale *Daily News*, in which he said:

Politics is not and ought not to be a specific career such as medicine or the law. Politics, in the true realization of the sense of the term, is public service, and public service of one sort or another ought to enter into the life of every college man and should by no means be considered a separate profession. . . .

Every man ought to have enough social consciousness to realize that at least a portion of his time should be devoted to public service. If these principles are followed, two desirable results will be accomplished: First, politicians will be eliminated as a class in the community and, second, a type of person will be brought into public life who is needed there and who is now, unfortunately, rarely found in control of our government.

His "good man in politics" would naturally be actuated by only the best of motives. He would be public-spirited in a self-denying sense. He would not only be above gutter politics, but above personal prejudice. Most assuredly would he place himself above class interest. This was precisely the view Franklin Roosevelt had always taken of himself. From the beginning of his political career he had striven — at any rate, when speaking for the record — not for partisan advantage or private gain, but always for " the public good." Thus, when he was launching his fight against Boss Murphy in 1911, which marked his debut in politics, he had occasion to state that although he differed with his cousin Theodore " on a great many questions," these were only " differences between men who are both seeking to do their best for the public good." [20]

True, he was really making a virtue of political necessity. Every politician knows that what he does, or promises to do, must be advertised as being intended to benefit all and not just a single group or class and certainly not his party alone. Yet, where the average politician might only pretend to non-partisanship merely as a means of winning votes or gaining favors for his party or for special-interest groups dominating his party, it would appear that Franklin Roosevelt actually believed he was working solely for " the public good." He enjoyed complete economic security and so could have had little, if any, thought of personal aggrandizement. He did not need the dubious social distinction that the prestige of a political job might offer. And his philosophy of life was built around the well-ordered community, in which those responsible for the welfare of the community were really obligated to assume the burdens as well as the benefits of leadership.

In any event, he had little difficulty in publicly donning the role of the " good man in politics." He could at times take on a disarming air of superiority and disinterestedness. And he rarely lost an opportunity to strike this attitude. For example, in his annual message to the State Assembly in January 1930, he declared:

In concluding my message last year I said that it is of small importance who first points out the road to progress, and expressed the hope that all measures affecting the welfare of the State would be discussed frankly and fully between us, with no consideration on either side of partisan advantage. Possibly the idea was too novel to be carried out as fully as I suggested.

But while he could thus pose as the devoted servant of the people in January, he had no hesitancy in taking a frankly partisan position in the following autumn when seeking votes for reelection. For instance, in a campaign speech in Buffalo on October 20 he asserted:

I need not point out to you who initiated and started these reforms. It is true, of course, that both Republicans and Democrats in the legislature voted for them. But although the Republican Party has been in control of the legislature absolutely for twenty years, nothing was done to relieve the counties of the State from this staggering burden of taxation until I became Governor and until I pointed out the way.

For the truth of the matter is that, despite his lofty ideals and his extraordinary concept of his powers of leadership, he reacted in a manner no different from that of ordinary politicians whenever he was put to the test. He doubtless was sincere in his idealism and he certainly believed in himself, but he also realized that he could not hope to attain to office on the strength of his goodness alone. He fully appreciated the value of party politics and of the party machine.

Occasionally he found those who tended the machine rather ungentlemanly and even noisome. None the less, after his abortive effort at revolt in 1911 he always managed to hold his nose whenever the stench of the gutter became too strong for his sense of political ethics. For he soon came to understand that the party's strength rested in the last analysis upon the day-to-day activities of the petty and not always scrupulous guardsmen in the wards and precincts. He was a rebel, independent in spirit, and righteous, but he was also and at all times a conformist. His sense of conformity never permitted his righteousness to carry him to the point where he might impair the prestige of the party or weaken its vote-getting power. He was, as he said during his fight against Boss Murphy, "a Democrat first, last, and all the time." [21]

Even as early as 1911, indeed, he was far from opposed to an alliance with Tammany Hall, but felt that nothing was to be gained "through an alliance between Tammany Hall and the up-State Democrats until the character of leadership in the Tammany organization has been changed." [22] Stated otherwise, it was not the principles upon which the Wigwam had always operated to which he objected, but the character of some of its leaders. In time, he not only swallowed the tiger, but bossism and all its other evils, real and fancied, as well.

Never, while he was Governor, did he unnecessarily or consciously alienate the machine politicians who on election day might produce much-needed votes. In his 1932 legislative message he declared that "year after year legislatures have completely and brazenly ignored recommendations by the Governor and demands from the public for safeguarding and improving our election machinery." But two years before he had vetoed, at Tammany's behest, a sound and sane bill that would have gone far toward eliminating election frauds. Again, the Hewitt reclassification bill, passed at the 1932 session of the Assembly, would have removed some of the inequities then found in the civil service and would have made it difficult for the party machine to manipulate many of the lesser State jobs. Although Governor Roosevelt "looked with great favor on this serious effort to reclassify the State employees," he deemed it expedient to return the bill without his approval. Why? Simply bcause it promised to do the job it set out to do. [23] Every liberal and reform organization favored it. Tammany and the other municipal rings were opposed. After deliberating over the measure for twenty-nine days, Governor Roosevelt finally accepted the Tammany position.

In his 1932 message he asserted that "local government has in most communities been guilty of great waste and duplication, of unnecessary improvements, and of thoroughly unbusiness-like practices." But not a word did he have to say about the scandalous situation within the local government of New York City which the Seabury investigation was then unearthing. In 1930, when the smell of corruption in the New York City courts had begun to upset even the more complacent members of the community and caused them to join the reformers in complaining, the Governor balked at supporting or initiating an inquiry. He wrote that he could not act " until it becomes apparent that the local officials charged with prosecuting crime within their respective jurisdictions have refused or failed to carry out the duties imposed upon them by law." But it was just these local officials who were to be investigated. He was asking Tammany to investigate itself.

Ultimately the stink became so noticeable that he was moved to ask the Appellate Division of the State Supreme Court to undertake an inquiry. In much the same manner public opinion prodded and pushed him into supporting the legislature when that body voted a sweeping investigation into the affairs of the municipal government. But his heart was not in the job. The only heat or indignation he showed at any time during the city investigation was directed not at Tammany, but at John Haynes Holmes and Stephen Wise of the City Affairs Committee for their zealousness in demanding that men of established guilt be removed from office. Messrs. Holmes and Wise got for their pains the retort that " if they would serve their God as they seek to serve themselves, the people of the city of New York would be the gainers." [24] At another time Samuel Seabury, counsel for the investigating committee, complained that, although the facts in the case of Sheriff Farley of New York County had long been known, it was not until " I myself filed charges before the Governor and after two months' delay [that] we got some action." [25] And while Governor Roosevelt finally removed the sheriff, he did nothing about other members of the sheriff's staff, though the investigation proved that they pocketed even more of the people's money with no more regard for the law.

Nor did Franklin Roosevelt go out of his way to annoy the

McCooey ring, Tammany's counterpart in Brooklyn. On the contrary, it was just at this time that he gave his official approval to the shameless "bipartisan judiciary deal." Brooklyn probably needed four new courts. The Republicans at Albany refused to support the necessary legislation because they knew the political spoils involved would go exclusively to the McCooey Democratic machine. And the Democrats lacked the requisite votes in the State Assembly. A deal was arranged whereby twelve instead of four courts would be established, seven of the new judgeships going to the Democrats, the remaining five to the Republicans. Governor Roosevelt knew of this deal. Prominent citizens and civic leaders of Brooklyn warned him of it. It was a matter of general comment among the people. Nevertheless, with all of the scandalous facts before him, he signed the bill creating the twelve judicial plums for Boss McCooey and his Republican allies. Later he declared that if the voters of Brooklyn did not like the judges the bosses had picked for them, they could vote for other candidates — but everyone knew that Boss McCooey's candidates always won in Brooklyn.

There can be no doubt that in the Walker case Franklin Roosevelt appeared exceptionally shrewd and skillful and that here, moreover, he was seemingly on the side of law and order — and clean politics — which meant, as many believed, that he was publicly challenging and defying Tammany Hall. The reformers and liberals of New York City especially thought that he was virtually taking his political life into his hands when he finally got around to Jimmie Walker. Actually he was doing nothing of the kind. His political life was safe enough, as he doubtless knew. Tammany, loyal to Alfred E. Smith, had stood against him at the Chicago convention, but he had captured the Democratic nomination for the Presidency notwithstanding; and since it was clear by then that the Democratic nominee would win the election no matter what Boss Curry and his henchmen might do, he obviously had nothing further to fear from Tammany Hall. And once in the White House he could, with the help of the titanic patronage machine at the disposal of every President, virtually dictate his renomination.

In putting the Walker hearing over until after the convention he gained an added advantage, for in the meantime the playboy of Tammany, squirming with self-conscious embarrassment under the onslaught of the civic reformers, was making himself daily more ridiculous with his explanations. Most of the facts in the case had been known long before the convention, but now the facts had become such that Franklin Roosevelt could safely consider them incontrovertible. Not only did Jimmie Walker stand convicted in public opinion, but even Tammany had come to regard him as a liability. It was ready to throw him to the wolves in order to save itself. The Governor handled the hearing in impressive fashion. He brought into play all of that poise and wit and " charming " personality which he knows so well how to call up when occasion demands. By his skillful questioning he quickly reduced Mayor Walker to his true proportions. Jimmie could not stomach the polite but biting ridicule and so hurriedly resigned to save himself from further punishment.

8

THE MAN WHO MADE
THE KING

৶

AMONG the pretty legends adorning American life is that which holds Franklin Roosevelt to be an exceptionally astute politician. He does without doubt make a pleasing appearance in public. He seems always to be saying the right thing at the right time and in the right place. He knows how to keep people interested in what he is doing. He has a knack for winning devoted personal followers. And he knows most of the tricks of the political trade. For instance, he is especially adept, to an extent beyond the ability of the average American politician, in appearing simultaneously on both sides of every public question. Yet all of these qualities together are not enough to assure victory at the polls and certainly not enough to assure success in a party convention.

There is a secondary legend, now rapidly losing ground, which holds that Louis McHenry Howe, Franklin Roosevelt's sour little Man Friday, has been the real political sorcerer behind the throne. It is asserted that years ago Colonel Howe recognized the extraordinary stature of his friend and determined to make him President. Thereafter he guided his every public move and watched over every syllable of his public utterances with a view to keeping him eternally pointed toward the one goal. This fable has an intriguing aspect and doubtless also some factual substance. But Presidents, alas, are never made quite in this romantic fashion.

Political success is built neither upon lofty aspirations nor upon good intentions nor yet upon personalities however pleasing. It is built upon organization; in the case of national elections, upon that complex network of local, State and national committees so ably described by Lord Bryce and which he called " an army kept on war footing, always ready for action when each election comes around." This " army kept on war footing " is composed of political specialists — the despised professional politicians — who give their full time to the one job of producing votes and putting men into office. They furnish the liaison between business and government on the one hand and between the voters and government on the other. Nor could it perhaps be otherwise in a democratic society as extensive and complicated as our own. So many are the offices to be filled, so varied their duties, so involved and confusing the everchanging political questions that the layman — to say nothing of the " type of person " Franklin Roosevelt would like to see in " control " of the government — is virtually compelled to leave his political conscience largely in the safekeeping of the specialist. And because of the complexity and intricate legalism of government the business man finds that he can get things done better and quicker by dealing through the professional politician — with the help of campaign contributions — than by using a more direct approach. The arrangement is mutually profitable — except, it may be, for the voter.

Since the professional politicians constitute the permanent party organization, they invariably dominate the party conventions. Most of the delegates are usually small office-holders, while the leaders are the larger office-holders or the party bosses. No amount of winsome manners, or of artful publicity, or of skillful juggling of political issues will win a nomination for the candidate who does not have the support of these professional party workers. However much he might pretend to have been above trafficking with precinct captains and their bosses, it was their support, acquired in his behalf by one of the ablest of political specialists, that won for Franklin Roosevelt the Presidential nomination of the Democratic Party in 1932.

James A. Farley — "call me Jim" — was the specialist employed for this purpose. He was a mixer and back-slapper of the first order. Alva Johnston has called him " probably America's fastest contacter" because of his extraordinary ability to get acquainted with people and hold their friendship. He was no less able as an organizer. After fifteen years as a gypsum salesman, he organized a building materials firm of his own and within a short while he had established what practically amounted to a monopoly in the sale of building materials in New York City. His political standing — for he was also State Boxing Commissioner and was on his way to the chairmanship of the Democratic State Committee — helped him in this respect. " Smart metropolitan building projects," Mr. Johnston wrote, " know that they commit no error of judgment if they get themselves built of Jim Farley bricks, Jim Farley cement, Jim Farley plaster, and Jim Farley terra cotta." As boxing commissioner, he cleverly mixed pugilism with politics and both with his "contacting." As Democratic State chairman, he soon became the New York party boss. In fact, he quickly took over most of the work of the national committee, though John J. Raskob was still nominally the national chairman. He began as an Al Smith man, but after the Roosevelt victory in the same 1928 election that saw Al Smith decisively defeated he transferred his allegiance to the newly elected Governor. " The enormous plurality of Roosevelt in 1930," said Mr. Johnston, " was due in part to Farley's industry, personality, and passes, and to personal and literary contacting." [26]

About this time Jim Farley set out to win the Democratic Presidential nomination for Franklin Roosevelt. During the summer of 1931 he visited nineteen States and talked the Roosevelt cause to leading Democrats, i.e., professional party workers who would run the Chicago convention. He made other trips and wrote thousands of letters, warm personal notes. At the end of the year Mr. Johnston said of him that "he has reached a stage where it is difficult to keep track of his legion of pals and he dares not send out form letters for fear of wounding some temporarily forgotten old buddy to the heart. Today his political correspondence extends to every State and often keeps him in his office until two and three a.m." When the party convened in Chicago toward the end of June, 1932, Farley had obtained Roosevelt pledges from a majority of the delegates.

But these were not enough; a two-thirds majority is necessary to nomination in a Democratic convention. There followed a series of maneuvers in the best Tammany manner to overcome this obstacle. The most important was the announcement from the Roosevelt-Farley forces just a week before the convention met that they would use their pledged delegates to end the two-thirds rule. Each convention makes its own rules, which are adopted by an ordinary-majority vote, and the Roosevelt people had that vote. At least, so they believed. Governor Roosevelt, waiting in Albany, took the position that the two-thirds rule was undemocratic and that it was high time some one had the courage to discard it. (He conveniently overlooked the fact that he was vigorously opposed to such action at the 1924 convention, when abrogation of the rule would have meant victory for William Gibbs McAdoo, who at the start was the chief contender against his own candidate, Alfred E. Smith.) Other leading Democrats, Senator Glass, Al Smith, James R. Cox and John W. Davis among them, vehemently denounced the Roosevelt-Farley maneuver as grossly unfair, as an attempt "to change the rules in the middle of the game." Farley was unruffled. He declared that Governor Roosevelt had instructed him to carry the fight to a finish. In Albany the Governor told the press he had "no comment" to make.

The following Monday, however, the Roosevelt camp was alarmed by an unlooked-for development. Even many of the ardent Roosevelt delegates found this trickery more than their hardened professional stomachs could hold. They began to desert to the opposition by the dozen, at least some of them abandoning the Roosevelt cause altogether. The desertions "over the movement to abrogate the two-thirds rule," said the dispatches from Chicago, " were showing signs of running into a stampede when from Albany came the order today to ' cease firing.' " On the verge of defeat as the result of this shabby maneuver, Franklin Roosevelt suddenly discovered that he believed and had always believed in fair play. "This is no time for petty strife and momentary advantage," he telegraphed Farley. "It is true that the issue was not raised until after the delegates to the convention had been selected, and I decline to permit either myself or my friends to be open to the accusation of poor sportsmanship or of the use of methods which could be called, even falsely, those of a steam-roller." [27]

With peace restored, the convention returned to its original division. Governor Roosevelt had the largest single block of votes, but not enough to win the nomination. The remainder were scattered among eight or ten minority candidates, most of them "favorite sons." Of these, only former Governor Smith appeared to be a serious contender. If they had been held together, the opposing delegations could have prevented the nomination of Franklin Roosevelt. But this was not to prove possible. The Smith-Shouse forces could not make a dent in the Farley machine. Moreover, the " favorite son " delegations could not be held in line. Each of the "favorite sons " was doubtless secretly hoping that the lightning would strike him if Governor Roosevelt could really be stopped, but each of them also knew that to protect his political position in his own State he had to be on the winning side in the national convention. When it became apparent that Jim Farley had built his machine both wisely and well, the " favorite son " delegations were ready to jump to the Roosevelt band-wagon as opportunity or advantage offered. The California group was the first to go — upon what terms has never been disclosed. The rest promptly followed.

Franklin Roosevelt's nomination (as distinct from his subsequent election) was the product, not of popular unrest, but of traditional political maneuvering. Had the Democratic nomination for the Governorship of New York not been thrust upon him in 1928, he would in all likelihood not have been in the running for the Presidency four years later.* Had not Jim Farley helped him in 1930, his plurality that year would probably not have been nearly so large.† And had Farley failed to sell him to a majority of the party workers in 1931–32 — an arduous task, for despite his family name and his victories in 1928 and 1930, there was no popular demand for him west of New York, a drawback his unimpressive record at Albany had done nothing to overcome — it is more

* According to many of his friends and all of his biographers, this honor was forced upon him. He was still a sick man and wanted to avoid the strain of public life. His friends hold that Al Smith, fearing for his own chances in New York, virtually tricked him into running as the gubernatorial candidate on the Smith-Robinson ticket. One biographer quotes him as having told Smith at the time that "you're hitting below the belt." Another declares there is "ample evidence that if ever a man was drafted for office it was Roosevelt." If this version be true, then certainly a large part of the credit for putting him into the White House should go to Al Smith. However, the Smith people were later to contend that Franklin Roosevelt (and especially his wife) wanted merely to be coaxed into accepting the nomination and never had any real thought of refusing.

† Here again friends have given him credit that probably should go to another. It is worth noting that in 1934 Governor Lehman, a relatively drab and uninspiring figure, with none of the Roosevelt pretensions to political omniscience, personal charm or crusading fervor, rolled up an even larger plurality for reelection than had Franklin Roosevelt in 1930. No less interesting is the fact that Farley directed the campaigns of both men. This might seem to indicate that it was not the Rooseveltian personality or shrewdness, but instead, perhaps, Farley's political skill that was responsible for the impressive vote-getting ability Franklin Roosevelt displayed in 1930.

than possible that the Presidential nomination in 1932 would have gone elsewhere. In other words, had he relied upon some-one less capable and energetic than Jim Farley, without ques-tion the shrewdest political specialist the country has known for years, he might never have reached the White House.

9

RELENTLESS DEFLATION

∽

In the case of the election, however, the normal political forces were to be swamped by new currents that had arisen from the economic crisis. In the fall of 1932 deflation was still grinding away the security and property of millions of petit-bourgeois voters. This class had been blinded, no less than the upper bourgeoisie, by the deceptively dazzling prosperity of the 1920's. There was little apparent unrest. The voice of reform was weaker than it had been at any time since the 1870's. But after three years of depression reform was again lifting its head. The miners marching in West Virginia, the farmers striking in Iowa, the school teachers going hungry in Chicago, the small manufacturers, shopkeepers, white-collar workers and factory mechanics who everywhere were being crushed under the weight of the crisis were demanding change, were demanding that a capitalism rampant, but no longer triumphant, be brought under control. These people were to turn to the Democratic nominee, not because his name happened to be Roosevelt, not because they had any more faith in the Democratic Party than in the Republican Party, but because they were seeking deliverance from most of the things Herbert Hoover seemed to stand for. In brief, they were to turn to Franklin Roosevelt (as they doubtless would have turned under the circumstances to any Democrat, even to a Roman Catholic such as Alfred E. Smith) because the deflation was still pressing them down and the Hoover Administration was apparently helpless to stop it.

It was not that President Hoover was not equally desirous of halting the relentless deflation. No public man in the country was at that time more worried, frightened, than he. Within the scope of his economic and social prejudices, which greatly limited his action, he did perhaps as much as a disillusioned representative of the capitalist class could have done. It is certain that he would have wiped out the war debts had he had the courage to face the hostile nationalist opinion of the country. As it was, he threw himself with surprising eagerness at the opportunity offered by Germany's plight in June, 1931, to suspend service on this huge indebtedness for a year (for which he was loudly applauded by both capitalist parties and by all sections of the bourgeois press). Only the intransigence of France robbed the Hoover moratorium of the effect it would otherwise surely have had.

But in the meantime, frustrated abroad, President Hoover was to seek in his own way to stem the deflation at home. He had tried prayers. He had believed that if confidence were maintained, if employers would refrain from laying off their help and would not cut wages, if consumers would go on buying and spending as usual, the crisis would not materialize. But prayers availed him nothing. It was not want of confidence that had set off the depression, started prices tumbling, and compelled industry to curtail its activity and consumers to check their spending. It was instead the other way about.

He next decided that it would be best to let the depression die a natural death. In time prices would fall so low that consumption would again be stimulated and the economic machine started on another upward spiral. In the words of George Soule:

[The Hoover Administration] turned a deaf ear to the growing clamor for enforcement of the anti-wage reduction agreement, for some form of public unemployment relief, for a different kind of help to the farmers, for a large public-works program based on borrowing. . . .

97

This was the period which gave rise most of all to the legend that the depression President was a spineless mass of jelly, that he was incapable of action. Yet he was still pursuing a definite policy, a policy endorsed in theory both by the financially powerful and by the conservative economists . . . the way to remedy the disease was to let it run its course without interference. The economic order was a self-compensating one, and if left alone would get into balance. If wages were allowed to sink, that would reduce costs, profits would therefore reappear and furnish a bait for production, output would increase and employment would turn up. Existing goods would wear out, inventories would reach a minimum, and finally simple necessity would require enlarged production. Disparities in prices would be corrected by the force of competition. Prices that were too high would be driven down. Inflated capital values would perforce be written off. The disappearance of weaker banks would strengthen the others. Eventually the banks would adjust their assets to lower values and begin to lend again. All that was necessary was for the politicians to keep hands off. . . .[28]

The capitalist-entrepreneur class welcomed this policy. They could and did live upon their accumulated fat — for a while. The lower middle class was in no such fortunate position. They had no reserves to fall back upon, or else their reserves were soon exhausted. But the Hoover policy had one notable flaw. It was all very well to wait for inflated values to be written off, but what would happen if not only their inflated value, but the capital claims themselves were to be written off in any considerable number? What would happen if the earnings of railroads, industrial corporations, business houses, property owners, farmers and other debtors should fall so low that they would be forced into wholesale repudiation of their obligations?

And this did begin to happen in the last half of 1931. President Hoover quickly pitched his *laissez faire* policy overboard. When capital assets began to crumble, he set himself to the task of shoring them up through the Railroad Credit Corporation and later the Reconstruction Finance Corporation. Loans were poured out to railroads and banks and other corporations in order to protect their outstanding debts and save capitalism from the menace of wholesale defaults. The President was no longer content to let the deflation run its natural course, but sought to halt it when it started to undermine the towering structure of capital claims, though this was the one thing that needed deflation. He was, paradoxically, endeavoring to save capitalism from the ravages of the crisis by keeping the crisis alive. More than that, he sought to do this by lending money, that is, by heaping up still more capital claims.

There was no general objection to this expansion of the public debt to preserve the private indebtedness of the capitalist class. Even the petit bourgeoisie did not object to it as being unsound economic practice which was likely to prolong the depression, but complained principally on the ground that they were not sharing in the supposed benefits. But the lesser bourgeoisie did object, and very loudly, to cancelation of the war debts, though that also would have served to protect private debts and would have had the added merit of helping to scale down the gigantic capital-claims structure which was impeding recovery. Wall Street saw this clearly. Its spokesmen — Albert Wiggin, Thomas W. Lamont, Benjamin M. Anderson and others — thrust forward at every conceivable opportunity the suggestion that cancelation of the war debts would give economic recovery a decided fillip, though they doubtless also kept in mind the fact that their own financial stake in Europe would thereby be strengthened.

Their propaganda, the report of the Basle Committee (which Wall Street largely dominated), the actual impoverishment of Germany, and the forces Herbert Hoover had set afoot with his moratorium — all contributed to the decision that was finally reached at Lausanne on July 8, 1932. While President Hoover lacked the hardihood to say flatly that he favored cancelation, he did as much as anyone to bring about the repudiation that eventually followed. It was widely believed, especially in France, that Germany would not resume payments after the Hoover holiday, at least not on the scale called for in the Young Plan. Fearing this, Premier Laval of France visited Washington in October, 1931, with a view to determining whether the United States would forego part or all of its war-debt claims in the event German reparations were further reduced or abolished. The President naturally could not commit Congress, without whose authority there could be no change in the existing debt agreements. But he plainly intimated that a new debt agreement might be needed after the expiration of the moratorium and that " the initiative in this matter should be taken at an early date by the European powers principally concerned." [29] Here, unquestionably, was an invitation to Europe to scale down its intergovernmental debts, with an implied promise that the United States would reduce its debt claims when Europe had acted. It was so interpreted by Pierre Laval upon his return to Paris and this interpretation was given additional support when on December 10 the President sent a special message to Congress asking that a new funding commission be created to reconsider the war debts.

No one seems at that time to have thought of complete cancelation of the intergovernmental debts. In British circles, for example, the most that was talked about was a 25 per cent reduction all around. But two days before Christmas came the Basle Report, which indicated quite pointedly that Germany was no longer in a position to pay and that it would be to the advantage of the world if the whole slate were wiped clean. On January 9 Chancellor Brüning of Germany stated very simply, on the basis of the Basle Report, that his country would under no circumstances resume payment and that it was idle, therefore, to talk of anything less than complete cancelation. The international debt conference, which had first been scheduled to be held at The Hague in December and then postponed to January, was again postponed. Five months of wrangling and maneuvering failed to shake either Chancellor Brüning or the hard facts of the world's economic impasse. Eventually the conference was convened in the little Swiss town of Lausanne and on July 8 the Allied statesmen, bowing to the inevitable, declared German reparations forever ended.

For reasons of political prestige, as well as financial stability, they felt that their governments could not afford to continue paying the United States now that payments from Germany were to cease. And so they entered into their "gentlemen's agreement," which provided that the Lausanne convention regarding reparations would not be ratified until "a satisfactory settlement" had been arranged between the creditors of Germany "and their own creditors." The Allied statesmen appeared to be taking away with one hand what they had given with the other, for it seemed certain that the United States, their chief creditor, would never consent to any reduction in its claims. But since it was even more certain that Germany would never resume payment, the "gentlemen's agreement" was actually an understanding looking toward repudiation of the war debts. Whatever explanations and apologies London and Paris were subsequently to offer, the fact remains that European repudiation was based upon and dates from Lausanne.

Compared with the total of the world's capital claims, the sum of the intergovernmental war debts was not very big. It amounted in all to approximately thirty billion dollars. Yet the cancelation of this capital indebtedness served to relieve the international capital structure of a particularly onerous load. This was not only because the intergovernmental debts had created a delicate transfer problem that acted as a damper upon world trade, but also because it meant that productive capital, which was carrying an immense burden of its own, would no longer have to carry in addition the obligation of meeting the charges upon a vast amount of non-existent capital. That the lifting of the war-debt load was to prove sufficient to stem the deflation, at least for a time, soon became evident.

10

THE LOWER DEPTHS

✺

THIS seems to have been true of the situation in the United States, although the momentum of some of the deflationary forces, as well as certain special conditions, was still to precipitate a bank panic in the early part of 1933. The country's largest capital market, the New York Stock Exchange, reached its lowest point, significantly enough, on the very day the Lausanne agreement was signed. The most important capital goods industry — steel — touched bottom in the same week, when it was operating at 12 per cent of capacity, and then followed the securities market into higher ground. Foreign trade dropped to $186,200,000 in value in July, the lowest it had been since August, 1904, and from then on showed multiplying signs of recovery.[30] The employment index likewise established its low in July, when it stood at 55.2, and then climbed upward (though it fell back temporarily to 55.1 in the panic month of March, 1933). The payroll index followed a similar course.[31]

Even commodity prices, but particularly those having to do with such capital goods as building materials, metal products and machinery, revived somewhat immediately after July 8 — but the revival, alas, was followed by another sharp slump in the general price level. For this there were several reasons, some economic, others apparently political or psychological. Although the pressure on the capital-claims structure had been relieved to a considerable extent, the prices of some commodities were still too high in relation to consuming power. Agriculture, moreover, presented a special problem. The continued fall in farm prices tended to depress all other prices.

It is possible, nevertheless, that had the banking system been stronger the panic of 1933 might have been averted. But not only were many of the banks loaded down with worthless South American and European paper and with urban and farm mortgages of increasingly dubious value. Not only were their funds tied up in deflated domestic securities that could only be marketed at a loss. The banks were also victims of their own mismanagement and of lax government inspection. During the boom years the official examiners had been lenient because they did not want to do anything that might impede the upward course of prosperity. During the depression they had been lenient because they feared the effect on public opinion of a wholesale closing of banks. Nor was this an accidental development. It was a policy conceived and executed by the authorities in Washington. For example, in issuing a call for reports on the condition of the banks as of the close of business on June 30, 1932, the Comptroller of the Currency ruled that in evaluating their security holdings they could disregard the prevailing market quotations and list these assets at their " intrinsic value." In short, the banks were encouraged to pad their assets in order to show that they were solvent, when in fact many of them were not. Even when some houses were proved beyond any doubt to be hopelessly insolvent, they were permitted to remain open. In the case of the Harriman National Bank in New York City, for instance, the Comptroller of the Currency subsequently declared that to have closed this house (which continued to accept deposits for nine months after examiners had found it insolvent and had found evidence of criminal mismanagement) "would have created such excitement that it might have been heard throughout the United States. The banking situation was critical. We were endeavoring to keep the banks open and some of the bankers themselves had to be encouraged to go on." [32]

The Harriman Bank was not in a class by itself. F. G. Awalt, acting Comptroller of the Currency, testified before a Senate committee that "between five hundred and six hundred defalcations" by bank officers "are annually uncovered by the Comptroller's staff and sent to the Department of Justice." Assistant Attorney-General Nugent Dodds said that he did not know " of a national bank in the country that hasn't had false entries in its statements to the public." [33] Moreover, some of the larger banks had got themselves entangled in a network of security and realty affiliates and holding companies, by means of which they gambled with their depositors' money to enrich their own officers and directors. This was the case, it will be recalled, with the Bank of the United States.

Toward the end of 1932 the strain upon this rotten system became more than it could bear. It was bound to break and finally did break in those areas where the economic crisis had gone deepest and where the banking system was the weakest. There was a preliminary rumble from the Mountain States in the first week of November when a twelve-day suspension was decreed for all of the banks in Nevada. This was followed by a proclamation by the mayor of Gibson City, Illinois, in the heart of the corn belt, closing the one remaining bank in his city for a period of thirty days in the interest of " the public welfare." Panic promptly seized this farming region. Within a fortnight sixteen banks were closed in St. Louis; bank " holidays " were declared in Rock Island, Moline, and East Moline, Illinois, and in Muscatine, Iowa; other banks shut their doors throughout Illinois, Iowa, Missouri and Kansas. Although the banks in this area had been well shaken down as the result of twelve years of chronic depression, the larger economic crisis was now undermining the surviving strong banks.

Then in the middle of February came the Michigan moratorium, which really precipitated the financial panic. The national panic would doubtless have developed in any case, but the fact that it started in Detroit had peculiar significance, for it was there that the crisis had brought the contradictions of capitalism into sharper relief than anywhere else in the country, the Chicago metropolitan area alone excepted. It was there that petit-bourgeois unrest had been more in evidence than in any other city, and it was there that the class struggle, with its tremendous pressure upon manufacturers and bankers as well as upon small merchants and other lower-middle-class elements, had been brought more boldly into the open.[34]

The Michigan banking system fell apart at the first blow. In the words of John T. Flynn:

These Michigan magicians had invented something brand new in the way of banking. It was not so completely new, of course, as they supposed, for group banking has broken out in this country at intervals, and almost always with disastrous results. But this was group banking with more virulent tumescence and higher temperature and some new complications. It was a combination of unit banking and branch banking, security manufacture, real estate exploitation, and numerous other lines, including running a garage, and all brought together under the control of a holding company like a utility web or department store chain. There were, of course, holding companies running wild among banks in other places. But in Michigan two groups — two holding companies — set out to capture the entire banking resources of a whole State. . . .

In other cities one bank might fail and the others, somewhat strained, might continue. But in Detroit failure of one meant the failure of all. And they did fail. Not just two banks, but 178 banks closed their doors. A great industrial city and a rich industrial and agricultural State were left for months almost without money. It was the most comprehensive bank failure in our history, and it marked the crash of the kind of banking which these magicians gave Michigan.[35]

Panic spread into neighboring States, its tempo rapidly increasing. It suddenly broke out simultaneously in widely separated areas. Maryland's " holiday " began on February 25. Then State and municipal executives everywhere seemed to be trying to outdo one another in restricting banking operations or in declaring "holidays." On March 3, despite Governor Lehman's protestation of a few hours before that New York was " safe " and he was not worrying, the panic hit the leading financial center of the country. And within forty-eight hours a new President of the United States was to close the few remaining banks with his proclamation of a nation-wide " holiday." It seemed to many that the lowest depths had been reached, that the whole country was going to smash.

Panic does not arise without cause. In this instance the principal cause was readily apparent. There was, however, a contributing factor which cannot be ignored. The people had been gradually losing faith during three years of depression not only in their leaders, but in all of their institutions except one. This one exception was the state. They believed that with a strong man, a forceful leader, in control of the destinies of the state the relentless deflation could be brought to a halt. The nomination of Franklin Roosevelt had given the people reason to hope. He seemed to promise positive, energetic action. His dramatic flight to the Chicago convention after his nomination was a symbol of action. His campaign was based on the use of the same symbolism. He traveled far and wide; he apparently possessed boundless energy as well as courage. He talked directly to thousands of people, nay, to millions, for his radio audience could hear his voice and so sense his " charm," his air of carefree gallantry in the face of infinitely difficult problems, his great confidence in himself. He was a man to inspire hope when hope was most needed. It is possible that the panic might have come sooner had not Franklin Roosevelt kept up the spirits of the lower classes until after the election.

As it was, the panic began almost immediately thereafter. Once elected, Franklin Roosevelt retired into silence. There was noticeable a prompt and sharp letdown in the hopes of the people. They had wanted a man of action and now they saw that they would have to wait four months before he could take office. The man who remained in the White House could do nothing to reassure them. He was thoroughly beaten, discredited. American democracy had stated in no uncertain terms that he no longer enjoyed popular confidence. Congress ignored him. The bankers and industrialists could not afford to deal with him, for he was soon to leave office. Foreign governments were in the same position, for any arrangement they might make with him could and probably would be overturned by his successor. Thus, for four months the Federal Government had at its head a man who was helpless to act. Coupled with the growing pressure of the economic crisis, this was enough to sap what life there remained in public confidence.

No less ominous was the silence and inaction of Franklin Roosevelt. He observed with painful precision all of the proprieties of his position. Herbert Hoover was still the President; he himself could not assume that office until March 4. Hence it would be out of place for him to act in any way, for any action or suggestion on his part might, as he suggested, embarrass or be resented by " those now vested with executive and legislative authority." [36] Not that he had no opportunity to act at this time. He had such an opportunity thrust upon him by Herbert Hoover. A week after the election the latter had asked his successful rival to confer with him with regard to war debts, armaments and the scheduled international economic conference. He pointed out that none of these matters could be disposed of during his remaining few months in office. He went so far as to confess his own helplessness by declaring that Congress was now looking to his successor and not to him for leadership. " If there is to be any change in the attitude of the Congress," he said in his telegram to the President-elect, " it will be greatly affected by the views of those members who recognize you as their leader and who will properly desire your counsel and advice." [37]

Franklin Roosevelt replied that he would be " glad to cooperate in every appropriate way." A few weeks later he did meet with Herbert Hoover in the White House. But it all came to naught. He would not assume responsibility without power. In subsequent correspondence with the President he declared: " I think you will recognize that it will be unwise for me to accept an apparent joint responsibility with you when, as a matter of constitutional fact, I would be wholly lacking in any attendant authority." [38] But this, of course, was nonsense. He had before him a number of alternatives, any one of which he could have followed without offending his delicate sense of authority. Indeed, he had definite responsibility as the leader of the largest political party, not only in Congress, but in the country. He might well have exercised this responsibility in such a way as to have made possible a real measure of cooperation between Congress and himself on the one hand and the White House on the other regarding war debts and like questions. In his capacity as party leader he could have issued a statement, or a series of statements, outlining what he believed should be done and what he intended to do. Herbert Hoover had already suggested that he would have been only too happy to receive such guidance. This method, moreover, would not in any way have transgressed " constitutional fact," and it would have reassured the lower middle class.

His refusal to take any action whatever had the opposite effect. The people could not be expected to understand the narrow distinctions he drew with respect to personal responsibility. They were not yet aware of his strange reluctance to share authority with anyone. They knew only that they had a President who could not act and now they saw that they also had a President-elect who apparently would not act. The hope the latter had aroused with his symbolic flight to Chicago and had kept alive through his campaign began to dwindle. The man on the street was ready to believe the stories he had heard of the new President's indecision and mental confusion. Popular confidence, none too robust in any case, gave way to suspicion and suspicion to despair. It was no difficult matter for fear and panic to take charge thereafter.

PART THREE

BALLYHOO

❧

THE AMERICAN bankers and industrialists had no intention of surrendering because popular panic had closed the banks. They knew they could no longer deal with Herbert Hoover. Nevertheless, had the panic come somewhat earlier in his term, the finance and industrial capitalists would not have hesitated to work through him and he would have been compelled to take action of one sort or another. He might have blundered. He might have called out the troops or in some other way have stupidly aggravated the situation. But in all human probability he would in the end have done precisely what his successor was to do. He would have listened to the bankers, accepted most of their suggestions, and then with their help salvaged the banking system, the good houses along with many bad ones, in such a way as to disturb as little as possible the foundations of that system.

But since Herbert Hoover's hands were tied, this task was left to Franklin Roosevelt. For many long hours immediately before his inauguration on March 4 he discussed with bankers and others the question of devising some means of checking the panic. No agreement was reached, mainly because some of the President's advisers, notably A. A. Berle, wanted to overhaul the entire system before reopening the banks. This was opposed by others, including Raymond Moley, and especially by the bankers themselves. In consequence the President found it necessary to proclaim a national " bank holiday " pending agreement upon a definite plan. The conferences continued for three days before a plan was drawn up that met with the approval of the bankers. Emergency legislation was prepared and sent to Congress, which had been convened in extraordinary session, and that body hastily enacted the legislation without even stopping to read it. Within a few days the new President announced that the "sound" banks would resume business at once. In a radio address from the White House on March 12 he declared:

. . . we start tomorrow, Monday, with the opening of banks in the twelve Federal Reserve Bank cities — *those banks which on first examination by the Treasury have already been found to be all right.* This will be followed on Tuesday by resumption of all their functions *by banks already found to be sound* in cities where there are recognized clearing houses. That means about 250 cities of the United States. On Wednesday and succeeding days, banks in smaller places all through the country will resume business, subject, of course, to the Government's physical ability to complete its survey. . . . Let me make it clear to you that if your bank does not open the first day, you are by no means justified in believing that it will not open. *A bank that opens on one of the subsequent days is in exactly the same status as the bank that opens tomorrow.* (Italics mine.)

In brief, within a week the new President had weeded out the bad banks and was allowing only the good ones to reopen — or that at least was the impression he conveyed to the country. In point of fact, it was a physical impossibility for the Treasury, the new President, or any other human agency to have determined within the space of a week just which banks were sound and which were not. It would have required months — and an army of examiners — to have gone over the books of a single one of the larger New York houses. The talk, then, of "examination by the Treasury" was decidedly misleading.

Yet many banks were known to be insolvent without such

careful examination. It might have been that the Administration's hurried survey was intended only to segregate these and bar them from reopening. But what actually took place? According to Ralph Robey, a conservative financial writer of recognized authority, it became apparent almost at once that bad banks were being allowed to reopen along with the good. The first intimation that the program, to quote Mr. Robey,

was not to be carried out with circumspection came with the opening of the banks in the twelve Federal Reserve cities on Monday. Some of the banks licensed to resume operation without restrictions were known to be insolvent unless new capital had been poured into them during the holiday. It was possible that it had been. It was not probable. One could only hope that if new capital had not been added such liberality in the granting of licenses would not be carried beyond the large cities.

On Tuesday, with the opening of banks in some 250 other cities, almost the last basis for hoping that licenses would be granted only to solvent institutions was wrecked. It would have been impossible to raise enough capital to bolster up so many weak institutions. With the reports of openings throughout the rest of the country on Wednesday, the last shred of hope for a genuine clean-up of the banking system disappeared. It was obvious we again had resorted to pulling a white rabbit out of the hat. It was a better white rabbit than the National Credit Corporation or the Reconstruction Finance Corporation, but it would not meet the problem. Thousands of banks were open that were unsound. We still did not have a solvent banking system.[1]

Franklin Roosevelt could easily enough have chosen to nationalize the banks. There is no doubt that at this particular moment the country would have supported him in anything he did. He was again confronted with the sort of incontrovertible fact which has always seemed to him necessary to daring action on his part. It is ridiculous to suppose, however, as many liberals and social reformers have done, that he would have nationalized the banks in such a way as to have pointed the country toward socialism. Nationalization would simply have meant control of the banking system by a state which in its turn was controlled by the capitalist class. In any case, it was not necessary to take such a drastic step; the needs of capitalism could still be fairly well met with the banks remaining in private hands. Secondly, the people were obviously satisfied with his grandiose action in closing and reopening the banks. He was content to let well enough alone.

For it was not what he did, but his manner of doing it, that aroused the nation. His national "bank holiday" proclamation had been merely a device to gain time. To return to Ralph Robey, it could be interpreted "only as evidence of a lack of any real leadership — of a lack of ability to appraise a situation with promptness and act accordingly." Yet to the public it spelled ACTION. This is what the lower middle class had been praying for. Popular confidence was revived as though by magic. Nothing fundamental in the economic system had been changed. The sharp reversal in public sentiment had been brought about by a melodramatic accident and by ballyhoo from the White House (aided, it is true, by a "charming" radio voice which was a distinct relief from the dreary Hooverian tone).

From then on came one imperial gesture after another. Government by ballyhoo had become the order of the day. The President took frequently to the radio, talked directly to the people themselves, and in the meantime kept up a steady bombardment of Congress with his spectacular plans. The whole movement was so rapid and dramatic that few persons could stop long enough to assess the worth of this scheme or that. The currency was swept off the gold standard with an almost joyous unconcern for its consequences. Beer was made lawful and prohibition ostentatiously repealed — grand and symbolic gestures with which to help liberty-loving Americans take their minds off other matters. The Tennessee Valley project was announced — the man dared even venture into *socialism!*

Experiment followed experiment with breath-taking speed. Billions were appropriated for public works, additional huge sums for direct unemployment relief. Cut-throat competition would be abolished and employers compelled to be fair in dealing with one another and with their employees. More than that, they would be forced to pay their help the " wages of decent living." The workers themselves were to be free to organize, nay, they were even to have the support of the law in this. The farmers were to get relief, *real* relief at long last; they would be paid for plowing under their crops; they would show the world how to grow rich by producing less wealth. Home-owners burdened with mortgages would be helped. The wicked speculators of Wall Street would be made to wear the yoke of a Securities Act. No class, group or geographical section was ignored in this vast outpouring of plans from the White House.

Even after Congress adjourned in June the show went on. Europe had just welshed again on its war debts; President Roosevelt gave Europe a figurative " punch on the nose," to the delight of the nationalists, with his cablegram of July 3 to the London Economic Conference. In July the AAA began recruiting farmers for its " destroy-and-prosper " campaign. In the same month the NRA got busy. And organized labor opened its campaign for 25,000,000 members — " The President Wants You to Join the United Mine Workers." In August came the Blue Eagle drive with its threat of boycott and its ballyhoo unparalleled in time of peace; and the " cracking down " on Henry Ford, not justified by any law, but because Ford refused to follow the formula of noise and pageantry which the Rooseveltians had prescribed for an ailing business community. There followed the CWA, for the jobless had to be put to work to save their souls from the terrible dole; the Treasury's gold-buying scheme, the invention of a farm expert who believed that the law of supply and demand could be overcome by daily manipulation of the price of gold; the gesture of recognizing the Soviet Union, which Franklin Roosevelt and his advisers felt, as they later tacitly confessed, would provide the long-sought foreign market needed to absorb the American goods surplus. And then Congress again.

That there was some merit in this multitude of proclamations and plans and experiments is obvious. But the method employed in publishing the various programs and panaceas can hardly be said to have been conducive to sound or clear democratic thinking. The people were given no time to ponder or debate any single plan. Public opinion was given no chance to crystallize at any one point. Everything had perforce to be swallowed whole. When trouble arose in any quarter, when criticism of this or that fallacy or mistake began to be heard, the President plunged quickly and with a resounding crash of publicity into some other startling experiment; and the applause that was always sure to follow such audacity just as quickly drowned out criticism and complaint.

The first year of the Roosevelt Administration was not all ballyhoo by any means. Indeed, the publicity methods used seem to have been devised primarily to keep popular enthusiasm whipped up while the President was setting forth on his course of "bold, persistent experimentation." For this he needed authority, sweeping authority, and plenty of expert help. He was already in possession of an office the immense possibilities of which were beyond measuring. Sir Willmott Harsant Lewis, the Washington correspondent of the London *Times*, a few years before had written that " in the political life of America the Presidency is everything, all power and all glory have been drawn up into the White House." [2] Another eminent student of American politics, William Bennett Munro, had declared that the powers of the office had " now expanded far beyond what the framers of the Constitution intended. Today this Presidential hegemony, this overpowering authority, seems to be the outstanding fact in American government." [3]

In addition, the capitalist-entrepreneur class had for a year or longer done everything it could to enhance still further the prestige and power of the office, not because it loved Herbert Hoover more, but because it loved Congress less. Indeed, it was afraid of Congress, it was afraid of any institution through which American democracy, being slowly and ruthlessly ground down by the forces of deflation, might express its discontent and its desire for change in concrete form. Hence the upper bourgeoisie resorted to various means of discrediting Congress. Politicians, business men, bankers, clergymen, newspapers both liberal and reactionary — all took a hand in the game. Many prominent capitalists and newspapers even went beyond impersonal criticism of Congressional democracy. They heaped personal abuse on individuals and groups in the national legislature. Senators and Representatives were ridiculed directly and by name. Nor was it mere coincidence that the principal targets of this defamation were members of the Progressive bloc, for the Progressives alone had until then represented by faith and earnest works the political needs of the lower middle class.

Before long the pressure of this " public " opinion had become so strong that not only were the voters convinced of the incorrigibility of Congress, as was evidenced by comments one heard on every hand, but Congress was rapidly losing confidence in itself. Many of the leaders on Capitol Hill openly admitted that they were ready to abdicate. Toward the end of the 1932–33 session Speaker Garner brought out his plan to confer powers of a dictatorial nature upon the incoming President.[4] That these were powers which the Constitution had explicitly invested in the legislative branch of the government not only did not disturb Mr. Garner, but seemed to him to make it even more desirable that they should be transferred to the executive branch. On the other side of the capitol Senators Byrnes and Bratton advanced a similar though somewhat more modest proposal.

The suggestion that Congress surrender a large part of its authority to the President was acclaimed throughout the country, especially by the press. For example, Walter Lippmann, who in September, 1931, had asked whether it was "conceivable that Congress and the voters would abdicate their power in favor of the President and a committee, or that men could be found who were wise enough to do the job and rash enough to try it," [5] had by February, 1933, come to the conclusion that "if ever the circumstances were such as to justify a resort to extraordinary powers under popular government, those circumstances now exist." [6]

Franklin Roosevelt himself, it will be remembered, had in March, 1930, denounced "government by oligarchy masquerading as democracy." He had said that "the doctrine of regulation and legislation by 'master minds,' in whose judgment and will all the people may gladly acquiesce, has been too glaringly apparent in Washington during these last ten years. Were it possible to find 'master minds' so unselfish, so willing to decide unhesitatingly against their own personal interests or private prejudices, men almost god-like in their ability to hold the scales of justice with an even hand — such a government might be to the interests of the country, but there are none such on our political horizon, and we cannot expect a complete reversal of the teachings of history." These were strong words, to which it would be hard to find a satisfactory answer. But what was his position three years later?

He started off with the necessary concessions to democracy and the Constitution. In his inaugural address he said: "I am prepared under my constitutional duty to recommend the measures that a stricken nation in the midst of a stricken world may require. These measures, or such other measures as the Congress may build out of its experience and wisdom, I shall seek, within my constitutional authority, to bring to speedy adoption. . . . Our Constitution is so simple and practical that it is possible always to meet extraordinary needs by changes in

emphasis and arrangement without loss of essential form. . . .
It is to be hoped that the normal balance of executive and legislative activity may be wholly adequate to meet the unprecedented task before us. . . . We do not distrust the future of
essential democracy. The people of the United States have not
failed." He also warned, however, that the crisis might neces-
sitate " temporary departure from that normal balance of public procedure," in which case he would " ask the Congress for
the one remaining instrument to meet the crisis — broad executive power to wage a war against the emergency, as great as the
power that would be given to me if we were in fact invaded by
a foreign foe."

Subsequent developments and the Supreme Court were to
reveal that this genuflection before the Constitution and reference to the wisdom and experience of Congress were gratuitous. The President placed his own interpretation upon the
basic law and proceeded promptly to dictate his own program
to Congress. Indeed, at the close of the extra session of 1933 it
was found that only one bill of any consequence enacted in
those three months, the Glass-Steagall banking law, had origi-
nated in Congress. All the rest had been handed down to Congress by the President, and they were all approved, in some
cases by unanimous vote.

Moreover, though the President had never asked at any one
time for "broad executive power to wage a war against the
emergency," many of the measures enacted at his command
greatly extended his already vast power. Among other things,
he was given authority to regulate transactions in credit, currency, gold and silver, and foreign exchange; to regulate the
currency in various ways, for example, by reducing the gold
value of the dollar in any proportion up to 50 per cent of its
existing gold content; to regulate business competition, curtail
overproduction, improve wages and shorten hours of labor by
a system of " codes of fair competition," and to license industries and trades for the purpose of enforcing such codes; to

regulate the banks to a greater extent than theretofore, and to acquire stock in State and national banks; and to allocate production of certain crops and lease land for the purpose of withdrawing it from production. Some measures merely stated general objectives in broad and generous terms, leaving it to the President to define policies, that is, actually to draw up his own legislation. Other measures, while ostensibly defining policies, gave him virtually unlimited power to lay down his own rules and regulations, or to change them at his pleasure, that is, again to write his own laws.

The President needed, of course, expert assistance and guidance in exercising this sweeping authority. He had a "brain trust" in being. Such a council of advisers was not unusual, though Franklin Roosevelt perhaps drew more heavily upon the universities for advisers than had any of his predecessors. Its real significance lay in its connection with the extensive authority granted to the President. He delegated much of this power to the score or more of recovery agencies, emergency commissions, and research bureaus. In his name they issued orders and decrees, laid down rules and regulations, made laws of their own which could be enforced under penalty of fine or imprisonment.

In short, here were "master minds" regulating and legislating. Here were Franklin Roosevelt's "almost god-like men" presumably seeking "to hold the scales of justice with an even hand." And it was all being done in the name of democracy. The reformers and intellectuals in the Administration – the President himself, Madame Perkins, Messrs. Ickes, Tugwell, Hull, Richberg – literally swamped the newspapers, magazines, radio and dinner tables in trying to explain and defend what they were doing. They admitted they were holding and exercising extraordinary power, but contended, in the words of Professor Tugwell, that their whole program was no more than an effort "to strengthen the democratic process," [7] or, to quote Dr. Richberg, that it was " an essentially democratic and individualistic endeavor." [8] Besides, were not all the people gladly acquiescing in the judgment and will of these " master minds " — thanks to the unceasing ballyhoo from the White House?

☼ 2 ☼

MONEY IS OUR GOD

ᔋ

FRANKLIN ROOSEVELT's immediate and primary task was to halt the deflation. He might concurrently try out his various notions regarding reform and reconstruction, but events would not permit him to forget that the forces of depression were still active.

Yet at the very outset of his term he took two major steps that were deflationary in potential effect, if not wholly in purpose. The national "bank holiday" had left in the hands of conservators, i.e., receivers, a number of small banks considered too weak to meet even the vague and generous requirements of the new Administration. Their failure to reopen tied up almost $5,000,000,000 in bank deposits and, of course, reduced the liquid purchasing power of the country to that extent. Soon thereafter Congress enacted the economy program the President had promised, and this would have resulted in a budgetary saving of something like $1,100,000,000 had it been carried through, and thus was also deflationary in that it would have cut heavily into buying power. Obviously the President could not go much further along that road.

The trick, as he and his advisers seem to have understood the problem, was to raise prices. On March 16 he sent to Congress his farm-relief bill. In its original form it made no provision for monetary changes of any sort. Instead it sought merely to raise farm prices by restricting production. This could not be done in a day or a month, but would take perhaps a year, if not longer. The farmers would not wait. New signs of revolt spread over the grain belt. The farmers, fed for generations upon the propaganda of the free-silver advocates and other currency tinkers, insisted upon currency reform as the one quick way of boosting prices. Political pressure from that quarter drove the Administration into experimenting with the currency.

Doubtless the President meant to take a hand in this game in any case. In his speech of May 23, 1932, at Oglethorpe University he had said that " whether it be an original cause or an effect, the drastic change in the value of our monetary unit in terms of commodities is a problem which we must meet straightforwardly. It is self-evident that we must either restore commodities to a level approximating their dollar value of several years ago, or else that we must continue the destructive process of reducing through defaults or through deliberate writing down of obligations assumed at a higher price level." So some kind of manipulation of the dollar was clearly in the President's mind.

Nevertheless, when the test came, he had no policy, no program, no definite ideas as to how to go about adjusting the dollar to what he considered the realities of the economic situation. Even after two years of currency tinkering Lionel D. Edie, a distinguished economist and a not unfriendly critic of the Roosevelt program, reported that the Roosevelt monetary policy was " still in the experimental stage." According to Professor Edie, the policy was based upon "a hastily conceived philosophy. It did not exist before the inauguration. It was brought into existence under duress of economic and political circumstances. Expediency and compromise figure largely in its final definitions. . . . But one idea rises above all questions of method, and that is the determination that prices must be raised sufficiently to enable the American people to shoulder the debt burden." [9]

President Roosevelt's initial move was to take the country

off the gold standard in April. This was really his first major experiment. It was neither deliberate nor carefully planned, but was done piecemeal, requiring at least three Executive Orders and one Joint Resolution of Congress before he was in any sense satisfied. Even then it was some time before the public really understood that the gold base had been abolished. Its confusion may partly be attributed to the fact that during the campaign Franklin Roosevelt and his party had given the country excellent reason to suppose that the gold standard would be zealously guarded. The Democratic platform had advocated " a sound currency to be preserved at all hazards." In his own campaign speeches the Democratic nominee had emphatically declared for " a sound currency " and had repeatedly announced his " unqualified acceptance " of the party platform.

It can be argued, of course, that a " sound " currency need not necessarily be one based on gold. But this quite ignores the fact that a vast majority of the American people had come to regard only that currency as sound which is founded upon the gold standard. This is the one moral that may be drawn from the conclusive defeat of the free-silver party in 1896. Moreover, neither the Democratic nominee nor his party made any effort to disabuse the voters of their belief that the party platform was speaking of a gold currency. Not once was it said that the contemplated " sound " currency would be built upon some other basis. On the contrary, there is available evidence suggesting that Franklin Roosevelt was himself thinking in terms of a gold currency. In his Brooklyn campaign speech, for example, he declared:

The business men of the country, battling hard to maintain their financial solvency and integrity, were told in blunt language in Des Moines, Iowa, how close an escape the country had some months ago from going off the gold standard. This, as has been clearly shown since, was a libel on the credit of the United States. No adequate answer has been made to the magnificent philippic of Senator Glass the other night, in which he showed how unsound was this assertion.

Herbert Hoover may have been in a state of panic when he spoke in Des Moines, but that would hardly excuse his political rival from making such a sweeping gesture of allegiance to gold if he had at that time any notion of pulling the currency down from its gold base. And it cannot be forgotten that Franklin Roosevelt later offered Carter Glass the portfolio of Secretary of the Treasury, although Senator Glass was known to be one of the most ardent champions of the gold standard.

The President subsequently sought to justify his action in abandoning gold on the ground that the metal was being hoarded or sent out of the country by selfish interests and individuals. In talking over the radio on May 7, 1933, he said that conditions had arisen

which very readily might have meant, first, a drain on our gold by foreign countries, and secondly, as a result of that, a flight of American capital, in the form of gold, out of our country. It is not exaggerating the possibility to tell you that such an occurrence might well have taken from us the major part of our gold reserve and resulted in such a further weakening of our government and private credit as to bring on actual panic conditions and the complete stoppage of the wheels of industry.

This statement was based on that philosophy of fear which Franklin Roosevelt had himself denounced only two months before. Grover Cleveland had refused to succumb to panic when faced with exactly the same problem. At that time, in the words of Benjamin M. Anderson,

the gold reserve was never large enough to be comfortable. There were heavy foreign withdrawals. There was heavy domestic hoarding. The government had a heavy deficit. There were powerful political influences opposed to the gold standard, and in 1896 a major political party made its campaign against the gold standard, with the result for a long time uncertain. The gold reserve had to be replenished again and again by emergency measures. In February of 1895 it got down to $42,000,000, which was only 11 per cent of the paper money outstanding against it. . . . When the gold reserve went down to $42,000,000, President Cleveland notified the bankers in New York that he must have more gold, and they got it for him. This represented the low point of President Cleveland's reserve. He kept on paying as a matter of course. That was what the gold was for.[10]

Franklin Roosevelt did not have to contend with such a persistent and extensive drain upon the gold reserve. On the contrary, though a small amount of gold was beginning to move out of the country, there still remained far more than enough to have given the currency all of the protection it could have required. To quote the New York *Times*, on the day " the United States officially abandoned the gold standard, the gold holdings of the Federal Reserve System reached the highest total since September 16, 1931, when the record high of $3,-485,739,000 was established. Except for a short period preceding the abandonment of the gold standard by England, the gold reserves of the Federal Reserve System have never before exceeded the current total [as of April 19, 1933] of $3,365,-595,000." The reserve ratio in that week stood at 61.5 for the country as a whole. It takes a very lively imagination to picture the American dollar being in any danger at the time Franklin Roosevelt forced it off its gold base.

It is true that to a very modest extent gold was being hoarded or sent out of the country, but the movement was unnatural and illogical. People were hoarding because they were afraid. Gold was in flight because of panic and for no other reason. The movement could quickly have been halted by the restoration of confidence in financial institutions and the currency. For under normal circumstances gold simply cannot be made to flow out of a country with high tariff walls and a favorable balance of trade.

The dollar remained strong in the foreign exchange market

for months after the Roosevelt Administration's first assault upon the gold standard in March. It went to a discount only under the persistent hammering of the Administration through adoption of the Thomas currency amendment to the farm bill, the Joint Resolution of June 5 repudiating the gold-payment clause in private and government bonds, the President's flouting of stabilization at the London Economic Conference, his gratuitous denunciation of the gold standard as "a fetish of the international bankers." After each such attack the dollar underwent a sinking spell, but each time recovered and began to work its way back to parity — until the White House launched another offensive.

Finally, in the last week of October, the President brought out his gold-purchase plan. Under this scheme it was intended, in the words of the President, " to control the gold value of our own dollar at home." Gold would be purchased by the United States Government in the world market; this would force the price of the metal up; the dollar would go down in the same proportion, and commodity prices would rise. It was an ingenious scheme and might have worked had there been that intimate relationship between gold and commodity prices which Professor Warren and his associates had claimed. While gold went up and the dollar down, commodity prices did not respond as per schedule. The plan was thereupon abandoned, although President Roosevelt had said in his radio speech of October 22 that this device for manipulating the gold value of the dollar from day to day was being adopted as " a policy and not an expedient." He had looked upon it as a positive and permanent means of moving " toward a managed currency."

It is true that earlier, immediately after the gold base was abandoned in April, prices had climbed rapidly. But the rise was due mainly to the belief that the dropping of the gold standard would soon lead to outright inflation. A speculative boom developed on the stock and commodity exchanges. Manufacturers hastened to turn out more goods than the market would ordinarily consume. They wanted to increase their inventories before the anticipated inflation sent costs out of sight. Even the consumer, fearing the effect of an abnormal price rise upon his buying power, hurried to lay in a supply of staple goods. In short, it was the fear of higher prices that was primarily responsible for the rise. That the currency experiment was a minor factor in so far as its direct economic effect was concerned was seen in July when the price boom suddenly collapsed. The Roosevelt policy had proved too weak to support it. As was to have been expected, the prices of commodities directly affected by world market conditions continued to respond to changes in the value of the dollar. The general price level, however, lagged behind. Indeed, though the dollar had depreciated approximately 37 per cent by the end of 1933, the wholesale price index had in the same period risen only 18 per cent.[11] It was evident that the price level was not being restored by this sort of experimentation with the country's money.

Toward the end of December, before settling down to more or less permanent stabilization of a devalued dollar, the President had one more fling at currency rigging. Under political pressure from the silver States he directed the Treasury to announce that it would buy all newly mined domestic silver at 64½ cents an ounce. The market price was in the neighborhood of 43 cents. For months nothing happened. Then slowly the market price crept up to the Treasury price. When this occurred, the Treasury twice within a month boosted its quotation, finally leaving it pegged at approximately 77 cents. It was contended the rise in silver would give a fillip to commodity prices in general and would strengthen the currency. This did not follow. The only appreciable effect at home was to enrich silver-mine owners and speculators. Commodity prices did not respond in any way, while the influx of gold was more than enough to meet the requirements of a strong currency. Among the silver-standard countries, however, the

Roosevelt policy worked havoc, notably in China, and from the British financial press came the stern warning that if this policy were to disrupt the Indian rupee something more than a polite and formal protest would be forthcoming from the British Government.

Meanwhile the confusion engendered by the Roosevelt Administration's various monetary maneuvers was retarding business recovery, or so business men complained. Their protests gave the President the excuse he needed to abandon the Warren gold-buying fiasco, which was daily becoming more ridiculous even in the eyes of the inflationists. In the following month, January, 1934, he asked Congress to make more specific the power to regulate the currency that had been bestowed upon him in the Thomas amendment to the Agricultural Adjustment Act. At his demand he was authorized to devalue the dollar by not less than 40 and not more than 50 cents. The next day he reduced the gold content of the dollar to 59.06 per cent of its former weight. Though this action by no means closed the door to further manipulation of the currency, to all practical purposes it amounted to more or less permanent stabilization of the dollar, for it was not likely that the President would soon again try any rash experiments in this field.

None of the theories had worked exactly, or even approximately, as his advisers had predicted. Some gains were recorded, but these were largely offset by the disturbing effect this experimentation had upon business. Though the President had declared only three months before that it was impossible for anyone to say at what point the dollar could be safely stabilized and that the Government would not in any case move to fix its value at any given point until "we have restored the price level," [12] he now considered it advisable to disregard this statement, but, of course, without the slightest assurance that the new dollar would "not change its purchasing and debt-paying power during the succeeding generation."

It should be added that prices did continue to rise, though not materially, after the President had devalued the dollar. The rise, however, must be attributed to other influences than the currency policy. Some of it resulted from the enormous expenditure of public funds; some from the drought of 1934; some from the deliberate destruction of wealth under the direction of the AAA; some from the monopolistic practices encouraged by the NRA; and some from the simple fact that in certain fields the deflation had run its course.

The juggling of the currency was bound to lead to repudiation. It also led to the repudiation of Franklin Roosevelt by himself. In that part of his Brooklyn campaign speech in which he denounced Herbert Hoover for having intimated that the country was once in danger of going off the gold standard, he had said that this threat was "a libel on the credit of the United States." He continued:

I might add that Senator Glass made a devastating challenge that no responsible government would have sold to the country securities payable in gold if it knew that the promise, yes, the covenant, embodied in these securities, was as dubious as the President of the United States claims it was. . . . The President is seeing visions of rubber dollars. This is only part of his campaign of fear.

Yet within a few weeks of his assumption to power he was himself to repudiate this sacred covenant. By the resolution of June 5, 1933, which Congress adopted at his dictation, the gold-payment clause in both private and Government bonds was outlawed. The resolution declared that provisions requiring "payment in gold or a particular kind of coin or currency" were "against public policy," and provided that "every obligation, heretofore or hereafter incurred, whether or not any such provision is contained therein," shall be discharged "upon payment, dollar for dollar, in any coin or currency which at the time of payment is legal tender for public and private debts."

When the resolution of June 5 was challenged in the courts, the President sent his legal representatives to the Supreme Court to argue that no Congress could by its action bind any succeeding Congress. The court replied that the Administration was claiming for the Government the right to ignore its pledge and alter the terms of its obligations whenever it found their fulfillment inconvenient. The Administration's argument, the court went on, assumed " that the Constitution contemplates a vain promise, a pledge having no other sanction than the pleasure and convenience of the pledgor." Under the Rooseveltian interpretation of the Government's sacred covenants, the court ruled, the credit of the United States would be " an illusory pledge."

The Roosevelt Administration itself had sold gold bonds at the start, and not only to the upper stratum of the *rentier* class, the usual market for such obligations, but to members of the lower middle class. To quote a speech made in Congress on January 25, 1935, by Representative Daniel A. Reed, of New York:

In April, 1933, $500,000,000 of notes or baby bonds were offered to the public in denominations of $100 each, so that the little man, the laboring man, the school teacher, the doctor, could buy these bonds. To encourage their purchase a statement was issued by the Secretary of the Treasury that the bonds would all be paid, principal and interest, in gold of the then standard. Within three months the Government that had made that promise repudiated it.

The President sought further to justify his action in his radio speech of May 7 by declaring:

If the holders of these promises to pay started in to demand gold, the first-comers would get gold for a few days, and they would amount to about one twenty-fifth of the holders of the securities and currency. The other twenty-four people out of twenty-five, who did not happen to be at the top of the line, would be told politely that there was no more gold left. We have decided to treat all twenty-five in the same way, in the interest of justice and the exercise of the constitutional powers of this government. We have placed everyone on the same basis in order that the general good may be preserved.

This was mostly nonsense. Not all the obligations he mentioned fell due simultaneously or within the compass of a few days. Hence not all of these people could possibly have demanded payment in gold at once. What is more important is the fact that the demand for gold was based upon fear of the President's vague and haphazard currency policies. To overcome this fear it was not necessary to lock up gold and threaten hoarders with imprisonment.* All that was needed was to create public confidence in the currency.

There was no social justification for the gold policy. No social reform or betterment could have been or can be derived from manipulation of the currency. Money is merely a form of accountancy, an index or reflection of property relationships. It cannot create wealth nor control its distribution. It may be juggled in such a way as to disrupt social relationships for a time, but it cannot permanently alter the basic relationships between the major economic-interest groups or classes. For the differences between these classes are based not upon differences in money income, but upon the property relationships which are the source of income.

* At this writing, more than two years later, gold was still locked up, which was as though Franklin Roosevelt were saying he still could not trust the people to have confidence in his currency policy.

WORLD-SAVING INTERLUDE

∽

WHILE the President's academic advisers were grinding out
legislative measures for Congress to adopt in the spring of
1933, and while Congress was mechanically pondering and
passing these bills, he himself found time for a brief moment
to appear in the world-saving role of Woodrow Wilson. To
judge by the enthusiasm with which his policies were being
received at home, the United States liked his " bold, persistent
experimentation." Might not the world also profit by a bold
experiment or two?

He began by inviting the leading statesmen of forty-two
nations to confer with him in Washington. One or two little
incidents served to mar the great occasion. While Ramsay
MacDonald and his associates representing Great Britain were
on the high seas bound for Washington, the President announced the action that formally took the dollar off the gold
standard. This seems to have hurt the feelings of Prime Minister
MacDonald and his colleagues, who believed, perhaps ungen-
erously, that President Roosevelt had deliberately chosen that
particular moment to abandon gold because he knew that this
action would strengthen the bargaining position of the United
States and that the British spokesmen, being aboard a ship in
the middle of the Atlantic, would hardly be able to take the
necessary defensive measures respecting their own currency.
A similar view was entertained by many Washington correspondents and most of the financial writers in New York City,

but from what we know of the haphazard manner in which the President was then managing his currency policy it is rather hard to believe that upon this occasion he was moved by any Machiavellian purpose.

At any rate Ramsay MacDonald and the rest of the European company appear to have lost their resentment the moment they were brought face to face with the President's boundless personal " charm." He met these delegates singly or in national groups. To all appearances the spokesmen of one nation had no idea what he was saying to the representatives of any of the other nations. Nor has the exact nature of any of these conversations ever been divulged, even to the American people. Nevertheless, after each conference an official communique was issued from the White House to inform the public as to the general conclusions reached. These explanations were all more or less alike. They all stressed the immediate necessity for international action looking toward stabilization of currencies and liberalization of commercial policies. They all emphasized the need for reviving world trade through international cooperative effort. For example, the statement published jointly by President Roosevelt and Guido Jung, the Italian Minister of Finance, said in part:

The world faces a crisis of the first magnitude. If normal life is to be resumed, the World Economic Conference must be made a success. It must not only meet soon, but come to its conclusions quickly. The task is so complex and difficult that unless it is approached by all nations with the fullest and sincerest desire to arrive at a result, the conference cannot succeed. . . .

A truce in the field of tariffs and other obstacles to international trade is essential if the conference is to undertake its labors with any hope of success. We are in agreement that a fixed measure of exchange values must be reestablished in the world and we believe that this measure must be gold. . . .

Along with the measures which must be taken to restore normal conditions in the financial and monetary field, and stability in international exchanges, must go hand in hand measures for removing the obstacles to the flow of international commerce. . . . We are both determined to approach the problems of the World Economic Conference with the firmest resolve to bring its labors to success.[13]

Franklin Roosevelt's second appearance in his world-saving role came a few weeks later. Before the World Economic Conference could meet in London the Hitler crisis shook Europe. The Nazi dictator was to address the Reichstag on the subject of Germany's military condition, and it was generally anticipated that he would deliver a speech setting the world at defiance. Partly to forestall Hitler, and partly no doubt for other reasons, the President selected this moment to send a stirring plea for peace, both military and economic, to the heads of fifty-four governments. That section of his message discussing international politics and the disarmament question and proposing still another " pact of non-aggression " may have persuaded the Nazi leader to be more temperate, but essentially it was of a piece with the meaningless Kellogg Pact, the unenforceable Stimson Doctrine, and the Wilsonian thesis that war can be used to end war — it was benevolent in intention, but devoid of reality. However, the message also contained the following paragraph:

The World Economic Conference will meet soon and must come to its conclusions quickly. The world cannot await deliberations long drawn out. The conference must establish order in place of the present chaos by a stabilization of currencies, by freeing the flow of world trade, and by international action to raise price levels. It must, in short, supplement individual domestic programs for economic recovery by wise and considered international action.[14]

Within a few weeks the President announced the personnel of the delegation he was sending to London. With one or two exceptions, alas, the men selected were third-rate. Most of them were without experience in delicate negotiations of this sort and were ignorant of international economics and European politics. The delegation arrived in London with no clear instructions, no program of action, and no explicit or defined authority. It was beset from the start with internal wrangling and made no effort to conceal this dissension. Indeed, the delegates continued to quarrel publicly among themselves while the London press stood frankly aghast at such conduct. Once the American representatives were on the verge of reaching a minor agreement, but were promptly told, in effect, that such decisions must be left to the White House and not be undertaken by the men who had presumably been sent over to make them.

Naturally this brought the London conference to an impasse. The other delegates could not deal with the Americans and the President was too far away to take a direct hand in this task which he had described as " so complex and difficult." Then it was announced that Raymond Moley, dean of his staff of academic advisers, would go to London. He rushed off by seaplane to Nantucket Island. There he was picked up by the destroyer Bernadou, which carried him to the Amberjack II, the yacht aboard which the President was spending his vacation. Hurried consultations followed, final instructions were given to Assistant Secretary Moley, and then he sped to New York, again by airplane. From New York he sailed for England, announcing en route that he would fly from Cobh in Ireland in order to get to London in time to save the conference, which was about to collapse. The Moley episode was very much in the dramatic Rooseveltian manner. It spelled ACTION. It thrilled the American people and encouraged the delegates at London to believe that at last Franklin Roosevelt was sending someone who could really speak for him, that at last the President of the United States would redeem the pledges he had publicly given in April and May.

Unhappily, the air of expectancy and hope was soon dissipated. Raymond Moley did not fly from Cobh to London; he proceeded to England by steamer. He did not electrify the conference upon his arrival; instead he further depressed it by making it known that he had no new instructions, no real authority to speak for the President. The theatrical action attending his departure from Washington had quite obviously been nothing more than a part of that government-by-ballyhoo to which the Roosevelt Administration was addicted. The conference could not be saved by such deception.

Yet Moley and his fellow delegates did attempt to work out some sort of an agreement. Under his direction the effort succeeded where the previous efforts of the American delegation had failed. His proposal met with the general approval of the other delegations. It was not the sort of agreement the Roosevelt statements of April and May might have led the country to expect. It fell far short of the original goal of the conference itself. But it was a step in the direction of currency stabilization, however modest, and it signalized the first meeting of minds on the general question of trade revival since the depression began.

President Roosevelt would have none of this tentative agreement. He rejected the proposal out of hand. Nor was he content to stop there. He followed his rejection with his astounding cablegram of July 3. In this message he declared that he would

regard it as a catastrophe amounting to a world tragedy if the great conference of nations, called to bring about a more real and permanent financial stability and a greater prosperity to the masses of all nations, should, in advance of any serious effort to consider these broader problems, allow itself to be diverted by the proposal of a purely artificial and temporary experiment affecting the monetary exchange of a few nations only. Such action, such diversion, shows a singular lack of proportion and a failure to remember the larger purposes for which the economic conference was originally called together. . . .

Our broad purpose is permanent stabilization of every nation's currency. Gold or gold and silver can well continue to be a metallic reserve behind currencies, but this is not the time to dissipate gold reserves. When the world works out concerted policies in the majority of nations to produce balanced budgets and living within their means, then we can properly discuss a better distribution of the world's gold and silver supply to act as a reserve base of national currencies. . . .

This document, belligerent in tone and showing such deep contempt for the conference he had helped to bring into being, was actually another repudiation of Franklin Roosevelt by himself. Here he was damning the efforts of the conference, lame though they may have been, to reach the very goal which he himself had emphasized was so necessary to the salvation of the world. Here he was declaring that the necessary basic reforms could not be achieved in London after all, could not be achieved by "wise and considered international action," but would first have to be attained by the action of individual nations in balancing their budgets and living within their means. Would the United States, it might have been asked at that time, balance its own budget and live within its means? Amusing, too, was Franklin Roosevelt's opposition to the tentative London proposal on the ground that it was " a purely artificial and temporary experiment " — this from the man who had become the world's chief exponent of experimentation in political economy.

But the time for saving the world had passed. The role no longer became Franklin Roosevelt. While his delegates were floundering about in the fog of the London conference, he and his expert advisers were at work on a domestic program based upon the assumption that the United States could solve its own problems quite without regard to world economic conditions. This was not only true of the Roosevelt currency experiment, but also of the agricultural program and the industrial recovery plan. Having set forth upon this nationalist road, it was no longer practicable for the President even to pretend that salvation might be had through international effort.

☼ 4 ☼

DESTROY AND PROSPER*

_ഗ_

IT was inevitable that Franklin Roosevelt should want first
of all to do something for the farmer. He had never been a
working farmer, it is true, but he had lived among working
farmers and knew something of their difficulties and attitudes.
Throughout his public career he had always put the farmers'
interests first. In his own words: "I lived on a farm in the
State of New York for fifty years; I ran a farm in the State
of Georgia for eight years; ever since I have been in public
life I have made it a point to travel over the country and in so
doing I have maintained a practical interest in the farm problems of the various parts of the country at first hand; finally,
as Governor of the State of New York, the farm products of
which now rank fifth or sixth among the States, I have in four
years devoted myself to building a farm program." † [15]

* With apologies to _The Nation_, in whose columns this phrase was
first used to describe the mad lengths to which capitalism _in extremis_ is
prepared to go in the hope of saving its profit margin.

† This did not mean, of course, nor did Franklin Roosevelt apparently
intend to imply, that the farm program he worked out as Governor of New
York had in any real or enduring sense solved the economic problem for
the farmers of that State. The farmers there were just as poorly off, relatively speaking, as the farmers elsewhere in the country when he left
Albany. This was especially true of the dairy farmers, among whom unrest
took a violent form only a few months after Franklin Roosevelt had assumed the Presidency. Even a year later it could be asserted, as the Erie
County Dairymens' Association did assert, that 90 per cent of the farmers
of Western New York were "virtually destitute." (New York _Times_,
August 9, 1934.)

There were other reasons why the farmers had to receive immediate attention. For one thing, they constituted the largest single group in the lower middle class. They could bring more political pressure to bear upon the authorities in Washington than any other petit-bourgeois group. Lastly, and more importantly, the farm crisis was of a special nature. While the business depression might prove to be only another cyclical affair, the farm crisis, which had already run twelve years, appeared to be permanent.

Franklin Roosevelt had inferentially promised to do something for the farmers in his Atlanta speech of May, 1932. During the campaign he presented a farm program in a speech at Topeka, Kansas, on September 14, 1932. He asserted that the Hoover Administration and its two predecessors had "failed utterly to understand the farm problem as a national whole, or to plan for its relief." He said that "they destroyed the foreign markets for our exportable farm surplus beginning with the Fordney-McCumber tariff and ending with the Grundy tariff, thus violating the simplest principle of international trade, and forcing the inevitable retaliation of foreign countries." The Republican tariff he called "a ghastly fraud."

He criticized the Hoover Farm Board. "When the futility of maintaining prices of wheat and cotton through so-called stabilization became apparent," he said, "the President's Farm Board, of which his Secretary of Agriculture was a member, invented the cruel joke of advising farmers to allow 20 per cent of their wheat lands to lie idle, to plow up every third row of cotton, and to shoot every tenth dairy cow. Surely they knew that this advice would not — indeed could not — be taken. It was probably offered as the foundation of an alibi." For the rest, he declared, the Republicans had simply insisted that nothing could be done for the farmers until general business conditions improved.

In place of the "ghastly tariff fraud" Franklin Roosevelt

offered a Democratic tariff policy looking toward the negotiation of " agreements with individual countries permitting them to sell goods to us, in return for which they will let us sell to them goods and crops which we produce." The first result, he said, would be to " assist substantially the American farmer in disposing of his surplus." This sounded pleasant, but it ignored economic history. It ignored the fact that the farm crisis was not peculiar to America, but world-wide in scope. To quote Louis M. Hacker:

The United States had become a creditor nation; instead of being compelled to export raw materials to pay interest on foreign borrowings, it had to be prepared to receive these on the account of American portfolio and direct investments abroad. The savings of American rentiers and the undistributed profits of American corporations were now invested in those newer lands — Canada, Mexico, South America, Africa, Australasia, the Far East — which could balance their international payments only by selling in the world market those foodstuffs and fibers which we ourselves kept pouring into Europe up to the World War. Ironically enough, not only did the United States have to prepare to be displaced in foreign markets but it faced the probable necessity of making room in its home market for imported agricultural goods to compete with those domestically produced. . . .

Again, many of our former customers had been completely lost to us or were definitely turning away. England was trying to favor the agricultural wares of its oversea dominions and such good customers for its manufactured products as Argentina; Italy and Germany, the lessons of the war ever fresh in their minds, were striving to attain national self-sufficiency; other nations of Europe favored the agricultural products of the Danubian countries, Poland, and Denmark in order to obtain trade advantages for their own finished-goods surpluses; Japan, trying to hold its bitterly won lead in the India cotton-goods market, was promising to purchase Indian raw cotton in return. Everywhere in the world new areas were being opened to cultivation — for agricultural wares are the cheapest and quickest goods peoples harassed by debts can produce.[16]

In brief, the world market had shrunk, while the capital structure had expanded prodigiously. Goods, ever more goods, had to be produced and sold to satisfy these capital claims. Everywhere nations, "harassed by debts," i.e., by capital claims, were pouring out goods and hunting markets in which to sell them. These nations, the United States along with the rest, sought at the same time to protect their home markets. Their tariff and trade walls were not the cause, however, but the effect of the shrinkage of the world market. Reciprocal trade agreements would merely shift the relative weight of this effect without doing anything to disturb the cause.

If Franklin Roosevelt knew this, he gave no sign of it. Yet he did acknowledge that at best his tariff policy would be slow in stimulating foreign trade. Hence other means would also have to be devised to help the farmer. Since he apparently saw that tariffs interfered with the flow of commerce, one might have supposed that he would look in some other direction for his panacea.* Instead he promised " to provide for the farmer a benefit which will give him, in the shortest possible time, the equivalent of what the protected manufacturer gets from the tariff." He would " make the tariff effective."

But how could the principle of the tariff be applied to an agricultural economy so largely dependent upon the world market? This was not made clear in his Topeka speech. As it could not be done by imposing a tax upon products which the country exports on net balance, it would appear that he

---

* It may be doubted that Franklin Roosevelt ever actually recognized the fallacy of the tariff system. In a speech at Sioux City, Iowa, a fortnight later, for example, he declared that the " excessive, outrageously excessive rates " of the Grundy tariff " must come down." But he said this would be done in such a way as to " injure no legitimate interest " and that rates would be put " as low as the preservation of the prosperity of American industry will permit." The desire to protect " legitimate " interests and " the prosperity of American industry " has always been the first consideration of the protectionists. It is the very keystone of their philosophy. Nor was President Roosevelt to bring down the excessive Grundy rates. Instead, by devaluing the dollar, he actually increased them by 69 per cent!

was advocating payment to the farmers of an equalization fee or other subsidy to give them the benefit of a fictitious domestic price level arbitrarily established at a point above the world level. That is exactly how the tariff works, although in the case of the protected manufacturers the tribute is collected directly from the consumers rather than through the state.

He said that his " plan must finance itself." The farmers, he held, would never think of seeking " access to the public treasury." If this was a promise that the subsidy would in no sense constitute a levy upon the general income of the nation, it was mere quibbling. No subsidy can be anything else. In this particular case the income of the farmers was to be increased, not by increasing farm wealth, i.e., real farm income, but by means of a processing tax. While this would, perhaps, enable the farmers to buy more of the goods of other industries to the exact amount of the subsidy or tax, those from out of whose income this tax would have to be paid would find their real income — and their purchasing power — reduced by the same amount. At best, it would represent a transfer of real income from one group of consumers to another. At worst, and especially if the production of farm wealth were actually to be curtailed, it would represent not only a transfer of income, but an absolute reduction in total national income. Far from financing itself, the Roosevelt plan could be financed only at the expense of general income.

And curtailment of farm production was also in his mind. He said that his plan would have to be so applied " that the increase in farm income, purchasing and debt-paying power will not stimulate further production." In short, production was to be controlled or limited by agreement or law. Elsewhere the same experiment had been tried in one way or another. The British had sought to save their native rubber industry with the Stevenson Plan. Brazil had limited production by burning millions of sacks of coffee. Other methods had been followed with regard to copper, tin, steel, sugar, wheat, fruit. But all of the control plans had failed. When the Hoover Farm Board urged that the American cotton crop be limited by plowing under the growing surplus, the fallacy of its proposal was quickly exposed. Democratic leaders denounced it as "economic blasphemy," while Franklin Roosevelt ridiculed it in campaign speeches and said it would not and could not work.

Such attempts to cure economic ills by creating artificial scarcity through what is euphemistically called "planned production" are not hard to explain. The productive forces of capitalism have reached the point where they seem to promise an era of abundance. But abundance, alas, has a depressing effect on prices. Low prices, in their turn, depress profits. And a falling rate of profit threatens, not only individual industries, but the very foundation of capitalism. Therefore, in the words of Lewis Corey, "capitalist production reacts against abundance and resorts to 'planned limitation' of output. . . . Thus, capitalism, the historic creator of abundance, becomes the enemy of abundance." [17]

It was upon this reasoning that President Roosevelt based the farm program he handed to Congress on March 16, 1933. The bill provided for the expected subsidy, but payment of the subsidy was made conditional upon the individual farmer's acceptance of such limitations upon his output as the Agricultural Adjustment Administration might consider necessary. The subsidy was to be financed by a processing tax, ostensibly to be levied against processors, but which would inevitably be collected from consumers in the form of higher prices. Later other subsidies, notably direct loans on cotton and corn in storage, were added.

The general objective of the program was to restore farm prices to the statistical "parity" with other prices that obtained in 1909–14. This, it was held, would again make the farm dollar equal to the city dollar in buying power. It would enable the farmer to buy more of the products of the factory, which would help the urban worker by adding to factory employment. And with more people on factory pay rolls there would be more money with which to buy farm products. It would seem, in a word, that here was *the* solution of the economic problem.

Some doubt might have been felt on this score, however, since not only the contemplated subsidy, but also the " parity " scheme, was, in effect, an attempt to revive the domestic market at the expense of the buying power of the domestic market. If the hypothetical " parity " were attained, it would mean that farm prices had been increased in relation to the general level of prices. This would compel consumers either to use a larger proportion of their income in buying farm goods, or else to buy fewer farm products. In the first case the manufacturing and other non-agricultural industries would suffer, production and employment would be retarded, and urban buying power would be decreased. In the second case the farmers would be deprived more immediately of the supposed benefits of the price rise, for while they would be getting more money per unit of their product, they would be selling less. In other words, the attainment of " parity " would not by itself bring the promised and necessary increase in domestic demand.

Nor would higher wages meet this difficulty, for higher wages mean higher production costs and such costs must either come out of profits or be passed on to the consumer in the form of higher prices. The former would serve to prolong the stagnation in industry, which was depressed because the rate of profit was already too low. And if there were an increase in industrial prices, the desired " parity " would obviously not be attained. Nothing but a genuine and broad expansion in business activity, which would increase pay rolls without increasing real wages or the general price level, would suffice to restore the farmer's home market on anything like the basis that existed in 1909–14.

Franklin Roosevelt himself was not altogether sure that his farm experiment would succeed. Yet he insisted that it be tried. In a message accompanying the bill he sent to Congress on March 16 he said: " I tell you frankly that it is a new and untrod path, but I tell you with equal frankness that an unprecedented condition calls for new means to rescue agriculture. If a fair administrative trial is made and it does not produce the hoped for results, I shall be the first to acknowledge it and advise you." To a public living on little more than eager but nebulous hope this was accepted as splendid, inspiring candor. In fact, it was something considerably less than that. As a politician the President must have known that he could never afford to acknowledge failure. He had committed himself to a course of action from which he would find it difficult to depart without suffering loss of prestige and political strength. Moreover, simple analysis would have shown the inherent weakness of his plan without going to the trouble of actually experimenting with the food supply and income of the nation. Perhaps the President had not bothered to study the plan and so was not aware of its defects, or else he was saying, in effect, that the desperate illness of agriculture was such as to justify any cure, even a demonstrably false cure.

In any case, the campaign of limitation and destruction, with all the usual Rooseveltian ballyhoo, was started in July, 1933. County agents everywhere arranged " pep " meetings at which the Roosevelt plan was sold to the farmers. Wheat farmers were induced to cut their acreage by some 15 per cent. Cotton growers were persuaded not only to reduce their acreage for the coming crop year, but actually to plow under about a third of the cotton then growing. Other basic crops were dealt with in similar fashion. Pigs were slaughtered and thrown away. In the language of the Milwaukee *Journal:*

The government plan was to convert these pigs into meat, to be given to local agencies for relief purposes. Funds for their purchase had already been provided through the process tax on pork, so there was no worry about that. Besides the meat, from which no returns were expected, there would be the lard and some fertilizer by-products that would be the property of the government.

But very soon it was found that the pieces of meat from most of these pigs could not be handled successfully by the packing machinery. Baby hams and baby shoulders from pigs were just too small to be put through the process. So the government decided it would salvage what grease it could — not the clean, white lard we know, but just grease to be used as a base for soaps — and make all the rest of the pig into fertilizer.

Quickly the fertilizer processes were clogged to the stopping point with the abundance of pig meat. A way had to be found to discard it. The packers thought of the Mississippi, flowing not far from their doors. They actually did throw some of this material into the river. But that could not go on. So they bought themselves a farm, and today, in great pits dug for the purpose, they are burying the sweet, tender meat of these pigs, drawn from the farms that were once the pride of America.[18]

It was Franklin Roosevelt who at Topeka only a short year before had denounced the Hoover Farm Board for having, as he said, "invented the cruel joke of advising farmers to allow 20 per cent of their wheat lands to lie idle, to plow up every third row of cotton, and to shoot every tenth dairy cow." This advice, he declared, "would not — indeed could not — be taken." Yet now, in 1933, this very program was being put into force, and under the direction of the same Franklin Roosevelt.

THE FARMERS COLLECT

∾

WHILE it was not until July that the farmers were asked to sign crop-limitation contracts and not until August that the Southern planters took to plowing under the 6,000,000 acres or so of growing cotton that was finally destroyed, the farmers began collecting almost at once after March 4, 1933. Farm prices shot upward as soon as the grain and cotton exchanges were reopened following the bank holiday. Wheat, selling in the neighborhood of 50 to 55 cents just before the holiday, rose to $1.25 by the third week of July. December cotton, quoted at 6.72 cents at the time of the panic, went to 12.20 cents. Corn, which had been around 30 cents, touched 77 cents before the reaction came in July.

Practically the whole of this rise occurred before the farm program itself became effective. What had set off the boom was in part the temporary revival of confidence that attended the President's gesture in closing and reopening the banks, but in far greater part it was due to his action in forcing the dollar off gold. From the middle of April, when the gold standard was formally abandoned, until the middle of July the country witnessed a spirited flight from the dollar. Many were convinced that monetary inflation was imminent and lost no time in turning their currency holdings into commodities and equities. The July reaction put an end to the speculation. Farm prices were shaken down. But they remained 50 to 70 per cent higher than they had been prior to March 4.

Even after the crop-curtailment program had been launched the change in the value of the dollar was to remain the dominant factor with regard to wheat and cotton. When the currency was stabilized in January, 1934, wheat settled down to around 90 cents, where it stayed for at least the next eighteen months. At that level wheat, as compared with its price before the gold base was abandoned, had risen no more than was necessary to offset the depreciation of the dollar. Neither the Roosevelt destroy-and-prosper program nor yet the even more destructive drought of 1933–34 was able to lift it above this point. Cotton, at 10 cents a pound, likewise had no more than risen in a proportion almost exactly equivalent to the cut in the gold content of the dollar. Subsequently cotton was — for a time — to go up to 12 cents again, not because of the " planned " production, but solely because the Roosevelt Administration sought to peg the price by lending the planters 12 cents a pound on cotton they had in storage. It was presumed that since the farmers were thereby assured a 12-cent return in any case they would keep their cotton off the market whenever the quoted price fell below this figure and that the check upon the market supply would in its turn tend to keep the price at the pegged level.

" Planned " limitation failed as a price-control device in the case of wheat and cotton because both of these crops are on a net export basis. So long as this condition obtains the price of both is and must be fixed in the world market. No such piddling regulation as President Roosevelt undertook would suffice to remove this obstacle. Only by drastically scaling down domestic production — at least 25 per cent in the case of wheat and as much as 55 per cent in the case of cotton — until it is just sufficient to satisfy domestic demand can national price-control through crop limitation be made effective. Short of this, short of virtually ruining the Southern States and dealing a body blow to hundreds of communities in the Wheat Belt, cotton and wheat must remain subject to world market conditions. The single alternative is international control of the world supply. But where is the body to enforce such control? The Roosevelt Administration tried this approach with respect to wheat. But the London Wheat Agreement broke down when Argentina insisted on exceeding its export quota and there was no one to prevent it from doing so.

Corn, livestock and a few other farm commodities were later to rise in price to an extent greater than the proportionate reduction in the gold content of the dollar. No doubt production control was of some benefit, but its contribution to the rise was not of measurable consequence. Government loans on corn in storage were probably more effective. It may be noted, however, that the major part of the rise did not take place until after the drought of 1934 had virtually depleted the surpluses of these products and had greatly reduced current supplies. For example, approximately 55 per cent of the beef cattle in the country was lost or had to be prematurely slaughtered because of the drought. There can be little question that the dry weather was here the most important factor.

In 1932 the farmers had been marching in protest against their economic plight. In the following years they were content to stay at home, collect their gains and applaud their benefactor. The price rise gave them a cash income from the sale of their products amounting to $5,534,000,000 in 1934,* compared with $4,889,000,000 in 1933, and with $4,328,000,000

* Not all of this gain in cash income was due to the increase in demand for farm products. A considerable part — the AAA reports do not reveal how much — came from the forced sale of livestock during the 1934 drought. As a result of the drought many farmers lost their entire herds and had to begin building up again from the bottom. The tremendous loss of beef cattle also was to result in much higher prices for beef in the retail market, thus throwing an extra burden on the consumers. The AAA could have used its resources in buying feed for livestock in the drought areas. Thereby it could have helped to reduce the surplus of grain and at the same time have helped to maintain a balanced retail-price structure, which supposedly was one of its objectives. Instead the AAA fostered the destruction of livestock as a matter of deliberate policy, using approximately $100,000,000 of its processing-tax money for this purpose. The real cost, of course, ultimately came out of the pockets of the livestock raisers and the urban consumers.

in 1932. To this were added the "benefit payments," i.e., the subsidies they were paid for curtailing their production, and these amounted to $557,000,000 in 1934 and to $162,000,000 the year before. In 1934, then, they received a total amount of $6,091,000,000, which was about 25 per cent more than their cash income of 1932, though still some six billion dollars less than their income of 1929.[19] They collected in other ways as well. The corn and cotton loans helped them. And approximately $1,500,000,000 of farm indebtedness was refinanced on "easy terms" by the Farm Credit Administration, though by far the greater benefit from this refinancing went to the money lenders and not to the farmers.

No one need imagine that this was all done without cost to the country or the farmers themselves. The consumers lost through depletion of their buying power. In the early part of 1935, with the desired "parity" between urban and farm prices still some points off, signs of what the Department of Agriculture was pleased to call "consumer resistance" began to appear.[20] Market reports spoke with growing frequency of "the disinclination of the consuming public to pay the higher prices demanded" and predicted that unless consumption increased "prices are likely to go far lower."[21] The Bureau of Agricultural Economics deemed it expedient to refer, rather enigmatically, to "weakening demand." The Secretary of Agriculture told a House committee that if meat prices went much higher, there would be "a great outcry on the part of the population in the cities," and such an outcry seemed to be developing in June and July, 1935, with the beginning of organized buyers' strikes in New York, Detroit and other cities. In brief, Franklin Roosevelt's farm-relief scheme was not financing itself, but was being financed out of the income of the consumers and they were increasingly disposed to spend less of their money on farm products.

In his Topeka speech Franklin Roosevelt accused the Republicans of having "destroyed the foreign markets for our exportable farm surplus" with their tariff. After more than two years in office he himself had done nothing to restore these markets. On the contrary, farm exports continued to dwindle. On March 9, 1935, the Department of Agriculture reported:

The smallest January volume of farm products in more than twenty years was shipped out of the United States this year, according to the Bureau of Agricultural Economics. The bureau's index is 57 compared with 62 in December, and with 93 in January a year ago.

The January index of cotton exports is 68 compared with 109 in January last year. Exports this January were 486,000 bales against 782,000 bales a year ago. Total exports for seven months ended January 31 were 3,325,000 bales compared with 5,929,000 bales during the corresponding period of 1933–34. Volume of cotton exports has declined 44 per cent, and value has declined 27 per cent.

January exports of wheat and flour, including flour milled from Canadian wheat, were 1,310,000 bushels, one of the smallest monthly exports on record. Total exports of wheat and flour from July 1 to January 31 were 14,830,000 bushels compared with 18,-607,000 bushels during the corresponding period of 1933–34. The bureau says that during this period imports exceeded exports by 16,000 bushels.

All products except fruits were exported in less than pre-war volume in January. The index figures are: grain and products, 17; animal products, 33; dairy products and eggs, 69; wheat, including flour, 14; tobacco, 97; hams and bacon, 18; lard, 45. All figures compare with a pre-war base of 100.

The answer is to be found both in the world agricultural crisis and in the Roosevelt policies. The world can produce more than enough foodstuffs to feed itself, more than enough cotton to clothe itself, more than enough, indeed, to meet its debts, if only there were buyers enough. But because of this very abundance countries everywhere have been seeking to protect their own farmers and peasants by this or that artificial means. Thus, while the pressure has increased, markets have become smaller. Countries that might otherwise buy a large part of their foodstuffs and raw materials abroad have been fostering production at home, partly because they, too, want to make themselves as self-sufficient as possible, and partly because the tendency to self-sufficiency on the part of other countries has reduced or cut off markets for their manufactured and other wares, thus leaving them without enough exchange to buy foodstuffs and cotton abroad. President Roosevelt has contributed to this development. He was bitter in his denunciation of the Grundy tariff, but he was himself to devalue the dollar, which had precisely the same effect upon American foreign markets. His efforts to help the farmers by manipulation of domestic farm prices were to have an even more drastic effect. This was notably true in the case of cotton, which has not only been the largest single export crop grown in the United States, but the largest single export item in American foreign trade, the next three, in the order of their value, being machinery, automobiles and petroleum.

For years the European powers, seeking to make themselves independent of the American cotton supply, have been encouraging production in their colonies, mainly in Africa, with a view both to increasing the yield and improving the quality, especially the latter, for it is the superiority of the American staple that has given it such a wide advantage in the world market. They have spent enormous sums on research, educational campaigns, port improvements, highways and irrigation projects. By the end of the 1920's they were beginning to meet with modest though appreciable success. Since then, moreover, the Soviet Union has taken to promoting cotton production on a broad scale. While the Roosevelt Administration has been paying bonuses to Southern farmers for not planting cotton, the Soviet Government has been paying bonuses to its state and collective farms producing yields above the average in quantity and quality. By 1935 the Soviet Union was in a position to export between one and two million bales. This was equal to the reduction in the American carry-over which Secretary of Agriculture Wallace hoped to achieve in the same year. Brazil has offered an even greater threat. The State of São Paulo increased its production from approximately 250,000 bales in 1933 to between 900,000 and 1,000,000 bales in 1935. According to W. L. Clayton, a leading cotton factor of Houston, Texas:

Cotton is raised in all of the thirteen states of Brazil, but Mr. Benjamin Adler, an authority on cotton in that country, calls attention to the fact that the two states of São Paulo and Minas Geraes alone comprise in excess of 200,000,000 acres of potential cotton land served by railroads and dirt roads already constructed; that the cost of producing cotton there is extremely low, the yield on virgin land is high and the quality is good.[22]

In the crop year 1934–35, it may be noted, a total of only 73,400,000 acres was planted to cotton in all of the producing countries of the world. Hence the threat from Brazil is not without importance.

But so long as the price mechanism was not interfered with the American staple remained supreme in the world market. According to figures prepared by A. H. Garside, economist for the New York Cotton Exchange, world production of all kinds of cotton during the five crop seasons from 1924–25 to 1928–29 averaged 25,494,000 bales, of which the United States produced an average of 15,172,000 bales, or about 60 per cent. In 1931–32 American output increased to 16,877,000 bales, while foreign production dropped to 9,658,000 bales. But for the season 1934–35, that is, for the first full season to which the Roosevelt restrictions and price-fixing applied, American output was only 9,700,000 bales, while foreign production had jumped to 12,750,000 bales, or about 57 per cent. In that season the American price was pegged at 12 cents. The world price, on the other hand, remained two to three cents lower. Foreign mills, which ordinarily prefer American cotton because of its superior quality and are willing to pay a modest premium to get it, simply turned to other countries for their supplies when the Roosevelt price-pegging policy increased the premium to 20 per cent or more. The extra quality was insufficient to overcome the advantage which lower prices gave competitors who were using non-American cotton.

To meet this situation the American Government must either withdraw its support, thereby forcing the planters down to an economic status lower than that which existed before 1933, since the enlargement of the world production areas and the increase in competition will keep the world price down, or else it must continue to fix prices and pay subsidies. It was warned by events in the cotton market early in 1935 that it can follow no other course. In February the pound sterling fell rather sharply. This enabled those producing countries whose currencies are linked with sterling to offer their cotton at lower prices. The effect was to weaken the world market and widen the gulf between American and world prices. About the same time it became known that Russia had finally put its cotton on an export basis. Lastly, the Agricultural Adjustment Administration had delayed announcing whether it would make storage loans on the 1935 crop, and this led to reports that the price peg would be pulled out. On March 11 cotton prices dropped precipitately, the May delivery falling as much as $10 a bale at one time. Not until assurances came from Washington that the price-fixing policy would be retained did the market recover, and even then the price did not return to the 12-cent level.

The crop-loan plan had another disadvantage. With conditions in the world market tending to pull the domestic price down, cotton would and did continue to pile up in the warehouses. By the spring of 1935 the Government held 5,500,000 bales in storage, which was more than half of the existing surplus. It was hoped, of course, that by keeping this surplus off the market, prices would stay up, but the mere existence of such a reserve tended actually to keep prices depressed. Traders had always to consider that the supply in storage might at any time be released, so that the effect upon trading was almost the same as though the surplus in storage were really in the market. In other words, the Roosevelt Administration was resorting to the very sort of " stabilization " the Hoover Farm Board had tried and which Franklin Roosevelt himself had in his Topeka speech denounced as " futile."

But as foreign markets dwindle and the domestic surplus continues to increase relative to effective demand, the Government must pay out an ever larger subsidy in the form of crop loans. The only alternative is further curtailment of the domestic crop. The latter course would eventually reduce domestic production to a basis where it would be just enough to meet domestic demand. Then, and then only, would price control through limitation become effective; but then American cotton exports, which in the good years of the previous decade made up in value as much as one-fourth of the total exports of the country, would be virtually wiped out, and the economy of the Southern States would be dealt a disastrous blow. Only slightly less disastrous to the profit economy of the country as a whole, however, would be the continued payment of an ever larger subsidy to the cotton planters.*

* In August, 1935, after considerable political maneuvering and bickering, the cotton loan was finally reduced from 12 to 10 cents. This meant that the price-fixing policy was being definitely scrapped as a failure. The domestic market was again almost completely under the influence of world market conditions. The domestic price was then fluctuating between 10 and 10½ cents, which was only slightly above the world price, the difference representing the premium that foreign mill-owners are usually willing to pay for the superior American staple. Since the grower now had nothing to gain by borrowing on his cotton and putting it into storage, it was believed that all of the current crop would be disposed of in the market in the normal manner. Thus the steady accumulation of cotton in Government warehouses, which was hanging like a deadweight over the market, would be halted, although the surplus already accumulated by the Government would remain a depressing factor. At the same time it was supposed that the restoration of a normal domestic price would help the American growers to recapture their lost foreign markets. This remained to be proved, of course,

Not only has the Roosevelt policy been destroying foreign markets and impairing domestic buying power, but it has also been undermining the efficiency of American agriculture as a whole. The President's destroy-and-prosper theory called for reduced output and not necessarily for reduced acreage. With acreage alone cut and the farmers left free to adopt more efficient methods, which they could afford to do with the financial help they have been getting from Washington, production would not be substantially lessened and in many cases might even be increased. The vast potentialities of improved agricultural efficiency have been discussed by many authorities, including O. W. Willcox, formerly Assistant Professor of Soils at Iowa State College. Dr. Willcox may, of course, be going to the extreme when he holds that with intensive scientific cultivation a farmer ought to be able to feed " at least 15,000 people on a subsistence level " from " one square mile of well managed land," so that to " feed the 125,000,000 people of the United States on a similar level would require only 8,333 square miles (5,353,120 acres), which is hardly more than a sixth of the plow land now being cultivated in the State of Illinois." [23] Yet he has fairly well established that through intensive cultivation yields of the major crops can be enormously increased — corn by 800 per cent more than the present average yield, wheat 1100 per cent, cotton 1200 per cent — although, of course, only at the cost of a greater capital outlay.[24]

The Willcox study has been challenged by other students,

---

for the first two years of the Roosevelt cotton experiment had greatly stimulated cheaper and more efficient production elsewhere and it was possible that the markets that had been lost to these other producing countries could not be regained. In any case, it seemed evident that this new competition would tend to keep the world price depressed. The reduction of the cotton loan naturally did not mean that cotton growers were no longer to be subsidized, for, as suggested above, the Administration would not dare risk reducing the income and living standards of the farmers to the extent that such a course would involve. In consequence, the cotton farmers were promised a bounty that would assure them a 12-cent return on their cotton whatever the price their crop might fetch in the market.

but even if we dismiss it and look to our own recent history, we can see what efficiency will do for agriculture. In the words of Louis Hacker, " between 1919 and 1929, on a stationary cultivated acreage, the output of American farmers increased more than 20 per cent! " [25] In his 1933 report the Secretary of Agriculture indicated that this progress could and doubtless would continue. He suggested, for example, that with only a relatively minor improvement in methods we could retire 30 per cent of our 100,000,000 corn acres and still produce a normal crop.

Obviously, the Roosevelt Administration could not be content merely to limit acreage. It would also have to check efficiency. Though the Roosevelts and Tugwells might talk loftily about retiring submarginal lands, it is almost imperative that such lands be retained, for to take them out of production and leave only the better soil and the more alert farmers at work would be to invite an increase in average yield that would tend to defeat the purpose of the destroy-and-prosper formula. The crop-reduction scheme in fact has been applied to poor and good soil alike. No distinction has been drawn between the efficient, low-cost farmers and the high-cost, submarginal farmers. The Roosevelt Administration has sought to underwrite them all.

Even so the experiment was to run afoul of the efficiency problem in the first year. More than 15 per cent of the growing cotton crop was destroyed in 1933 at the behest of the Administration. It was supposed that this would result in a 15 per cent cut in that year's total output. But at the end of the year it was found that the total yield harvested was actually larger than it had been the year before. What happened was that many of the planters spent their benefit payments on extra fertilizer and the like with an eye to increasing the yield per acre in anticipation of the promised higher prices. That could not go on if production were to be effectively limited. The Bankhead Cotton Control Act was rushed through Congress. This law not only limits acreage, but authorizes the establishment of maximum production quotas for individual planters. No matter how efficient he is, the individual farmer may raise only so much cotton for the market. If he raises more, he is subject to penalty. In short, under the Bankhead Act efficiency has been made unlawful.

Why the same thing has not yet occurred in connection with other basic crops may be largely ascribed to the 1933–34 drought.* The dry weather destroyed far more of the corn, wheat and livestock than the Roosevelt program called for. At this writing it was still too early to determine whether the 1935 season would bring any change in the situation, though it appeared morally certain that if improved methods, coupled with normal weather, were to result in greater output to the detriment of domestic prices, there would inevitably arise a demand that grain farmers and livestock producers also be licensed, a demand that the more efficient be penalized to protect the less efficient.

* Tobacco and potatoes have since been made subject to a control similar to that exercised in the case of cotton under the Bankhead Act.

☼ 6 ☼

ABUNDANCE IS IMMORAL

⌒

WOULD President Roosevelt take any other attitude with regard to business enterprise? If he had to choose between the
profit mechanism and the larger needs of society, would he
compromise the one the better to serve the other? Or would
he again, as in the case of farming, have recourse to the devices
of monopolism to save business and industry from the consequences of abundance. As Governor of New York, it is true,
he had sharply criticized the " ever-growing aggregations of
capital " and had asked whether monopolism was not carrying the country toward "a new feudal system." And he had
advocated the doctrine of " complete separation of business
and government."

But he had already indicated that the doctrines he had
espoused so enthusiastically in Albany were not necessarily
those he would follow in Washington. He had already shown,
too, that he considered the crisis to be the product of business
and political immorality rather than the result of the interplay
of contradictory forces inherent in capitalism. He was to deal
with the abundance that had broken down the capitalist machinery mainly as a problem in morals. And it clearly seemed
to him that this immorality could only be dealt with by the
state, or in any case only by business enterprise with the advice and assistance of the state. Only thus could the depression
be halted and business prosperity restored, as he indicated in
what was perhaps his most significant campaign address, that

delivered in San Francisco on September 23, 1932, in which
he declared:

Recently a careful study was made of the concentration of business in the United States. It showed that our economic life was
dominated by some 600-odd corporations who controlled two-
thirds of American industry. Ten million small business men divided the other third. More striking still, it appeared that if the
process of concentration goes on at the same rate, at the end of
another century we shall have all American industry controlled
by a dozen corporations and run perhaps by 100 men. Put plainly,
we are steering a steady course toward economic oligarchy, if we
are not there already.

Clearly, this calls for a reappraisal of values. . . . Our task now
is not discovery or exploitation of natural resources or necessarily
producing more goods. It is the soberer, less dramatic business of
administering resources and plants already in hand, of seeking to
reestablish foreign markets for our surplus production, of meeting
the problem of underconsumption, of adjusting production to
consumption, of distributing wealth and products more equitably,
of adapting existing economic organizations to the service of the
people. . . .

Nor today should we abandon the principle of strong economic
units called corporations, merely because their power is suscepti-
ble of easy abuse. In other times we dealt with the problem of an
unduly ambitious central government by modifying it gradually
into a constitutional democratic government. So today we are
modifying and controlling our economic units.

But he went on to say:

As I see it, the task of government in its relation to business is to
assist the development of an economic declaration of rights, an
economic constitutional order. This is the common task of states-
man and business man. It is the minimum requirement of a more
permanently safe order of things.

Happily the times indicate that to create such an order not only
is the proper policy of government, but it is the only line of safety

for our economic structures as well. We know now that these economic units cannot exist unless prosperity is uniform, that is, unless purchasing power is well distributed throughout every group in the nation. . . .

That is why some enlightened industries themselves endeavor to limit the freedom of action of each man and business group within the industry in the common interest of all; why business men everywhere are asking a form of organization which will bring the scheme of things into balance, even though it may in some measure qualify the freedom of action of individual units within the business.

And further:

. . . the individuals who claim and hold control of the great industrial and financial combinations which dominate so large a part of our industrial life . . . have undertaken to be, not business men, but princes — princes of property.

I am not prepared to say that the system which produces them is wrong. I am very clear that they must fearlessly and competently assume the responsibility which goes with power. So many enlightened business men know this that the statement would be little more than a platitude, were it not for an added implication.

This implication is, briefly, that the responsible heads of finance and industry, instead of acting each for himself, must work together to achieve the common end.

They must, where necessary, sacrifice this or that private advantage; in reciprocal self-denial must seek a general advantage. It is here that formal government — political government, if you choose — comes in. Whenever in the pursuit of this objective the lone wolf, the unethical competitor, the reckless promoter, the Ishmael or Insull whose hand is against every man's, declines to join in achieving an end recognized as being for the public welfare, and threatens to drag the industry back to a state of anarchy, the government may properly be asked to apply restraint. Likewise, should the group ever use its collective power contrary to the public welfare, the government must be swift to enter and protect the public interest.

At first glance it would appear that he really meant to have the state control the " strong economic units " in the public interest, that is, with a view to liberating the forces of abundance from the strangle-hold of private monopoly. Some passages of the speech would seem to support this interpretation; for instance, his reference to the task of " meeting the problem of underconsumption." Yet he also said that this task was not necessarily one of " producing more goods." Rather did he consider it " the soberer, less dramatic business of administering resources and plants already in hand," of seeking " foreign markets for our surplus production," and of " adjusting production to consumption." * In other words, the emphasis was to be on control or limitation of production, and that, of course, is of the very essence of monopolism.

Nor did he have in mind anything like actual state control of the " strong economic units," as he clearly showed by his declaration that " the task of government in its relation to business is to assist the development of an economic declaration of rights, an economic constitutional order." He declared that the " responsible heads of finance and industry, instead of acting each for himself, must work together to achieve the common end." He pictured the common end in terms of business morality. He was persuaded that pauper wages and sweatshop conditions and the insufficiency of purchasing power could be corrected only by awakening in the leaders of the com-

---

* He was even more explicit on this point in a campaign talk delivered over the radio from Albany, New York, on October 6, 1932. In this speech he said that the reforms he was planning " will make possible the approach to a national economic policy at home which will have *as its central feature* the fitting of production programs to the actual probabilities of consumption. At least the issue will no longer be confused by the impossible hopes of selling in foreign markets which cannot now pay for our products. There will no longer be that excuse for the overbuilding of American industries. And they can begin the process of accommodation to markets on which they can count which has been too long delayed." This is economic nationalism stated baldly and simply. It plainly reveals that it was Franklin Roosevelt's purpose to adopt a policy of curtailing and limiting production, which would obviously mean a decrease in purchasing power and in living standards.

munity a sense of moral responsibility toward the less fortunate members of the community. The " lone wolf " and the
" unethical competitor " would have to go, while " the princes
of property " would have to behave themselves, if prosperity
were to be brought back. The state would have to guide and
assist them, but not disturb their leadership, i.e., their control.

What he did not see was that the immorality of modern
capitalism arises not from the immorality of the capitalist
" leaders," but from the contradictions inherent in capitalism
itself. He apparently did not see that purchasing power was
being held back not because of business immorality, but because of fundamental economic limitations. Moreover, the
" princes of property " themselves considered the lone wolves
immoral, not because they were dishonest in any pedestrian
sense, not because they sweated their labor, but because their
independent operations, their price cutting, their " unfair "
trade practices — which represent nothing more than price
cutting by indirect rather than direct methods — run counter
to the *mores* of modern capitalism. For how can the market
be controlled, production adjusted to consumption, the profit
margin protected and prosperity restored, if business men of
this stripe are allowed to produce as they please and to sell
their goods in the market at any price they might fetch?
Clearly, the monopolists, the real princes of property, would
have no difficulty in standing with Franklin Roosevelt on this
high moral ground.

It is no less certain that they would welcome any " economic
constitutional order " that permitted them to " work to-
together," not only in driving out the wolves, but in reviving
the rate of profit. Such cooperation would seek to substitute
market and price control for " anarchic " competition. It
would obviously and inevitably result in strengthening monopoly, particularly since the effective economic power would
be left safely in the hands of the finance and industrial monopolists. Indeed, Franklin Roosevelt promised that under his

plan the state would even assist in this cooperative effort by applying restraint to any reckless or unethical business man who might threaten "to drag the industry back to a state of anarchy."

Other passages point in the same direction. For example, he did not hesitate to speak with approval of the "enlightened" industries which "themselves endeavor to limit the freedom of action of each man and business group within the industry in the common interest of all," but he did not say that his "enlightened" industries are the great monopoly industries or that the freedom of action they limit is the freedom of the market. He gave direct encouragement to those who were "asking a form of organization which will bring the scheme of things into balance," but he did not say that this "form of organization" is the trade association, the modern vehicle of monopoly and a device by which business had in recent years gotten around the anti-trust laws. He added, to be sure, that if "the group" should "ever use its collective power contrary to the public welfare, the government must be swift to enter and protect the public interest." But this promise was gratuitous and could not be redeemed, for monopoly cannot possibly use its collective power except in a manner contrary to the public interest.

Throughout the depression business had carried on ceaseless propaganda to break down the anti-trust laws. The Chamber of Commerce of the United States was one of the most active agencies in this drive. Numerous individual financiers, industrialists and other spokesmen for the capitalist-entrepreneur class added the weight of their own opinions upon every suitable occasion. To quote an Associated Press dispatch published in 1932, "the picture of industries producing more than they can sell and selling what they do without profits, has brought from such widely divergent persons as Chairman J. Raskob, of the Democratic National Committee, Gerard Swope, president of General Electric, and Nicholas

Murray Butler, of Columbia University, proposals for changing the laws governing big business. President Hoover has favored some change designed to meet conditions. . . . Leaders in both parties feel that because of the depression, a revision of the anti-trust laws has at least some chance of adoption." [26]

While Herbert Hoover "favored some change," it was Franklin Roosevelt who finally brought it about. He gave the country the National Industrial Recovery Act. This law expressed in concrete terms the objectives of his San Francisco speech. It also met in every important particular the specifications the monopolists themselves had laid down, as John T. Flynn has shown in a study of the circumstances attending the conception of the Recovery Act. Mr. Flynn traced the development of the NRA idea through the various economic "plans" brought forward by the capitalist-entrepreneur class from 1925 to 1932. Summing them up, he wrote:

Thus, then, the matter stood at the end of 1932 as Hoover prepared to move out of the White House. The Chamber of Commerce and what is called Big Business had a program which included (1) modification of the Sherman anti-trust law; (2) self-rule by trade associations under codes of practice to regulate production, prices, and trade practices; (3) authority to shorten hours and establish minimum wages; (4) a long-term plan for setting up unemployment, disability, and old-age insurance.[27]

The first three points were covered in the Recovery Act; the fourth President Roosevelt was not to propose until two years later.

Nor was the resultant system of "codes of fair competition" a new departure in government or political experimentation. Actually all of the basic principles of this system, excepting only those dealing directly with labor,* had entered into a

---

* Even the labor provisions can be traced to earlier laws, notably to the war-time laws of the Wilson Administration and the Railway Labor Act, while the collective-bargaining section is hardly more than a rewriting of a similar provision of the Norris-LaGuardia Anti-Injunction Act of 1932.

similar scheme recognized and supported by the Federal Trade Commission and the Department of Justice under Presidents Coolidge and Hoover. In his book, "Trade Associations and Industrial Control," Dr. Simon N. Whitney declares:

Not only were trade associations, after 1925, released from pressure by the Department of Justice, but they were also receiving active aid from two branches of the Federal Government. The Department of Commerce was extremely energetic in rendering them assistance and counsel of various sorts. For a time it seemed that the Federal Trade Commission would be even more helpful. In 1919 the Commission, in pursuance of its basic purpose of preventing unfair competition, began to hold what were later called "trade practice conferences." It would invite the members of an industry to a meeting, under the chairmanship of one of the Commissioners, at which rules to govern selling practices would be adopted. The whole Commission, after considering these rules, would announce either approval (and therefore purpose to enforce), simple "acceptance," or definite disapproval of each specific regulation.

About 1924 the character of these conferences changed. The regulations which were being adopted ceased to be mere prohibitions of practices, like commercial bribery and misbranding, which were already illegal. Practices which had never been recognized as unlawful began to find their way into the codes. Naturally the interest of the business community increased. Conferences came to be called less often at the request of the Commission and more often at that of the trade associations. Moreover, they became more frequent. At first only two or three had been held each year, but in the late 1920's the number grew rapidly, reaching fifty-seven in the fiscal year 1929–30.[28]

Then, however, the Federal Trade Commission began to be troubled by the tendency of the trade associations to exceed the authority given them in these "codes of practice." The Commission had approved a rule against "selling below cost for the purpose of injuring a competitor" — which, in-

cidentally, was the guiding principle in all of the price agreements under the NRA code system — but the trade associations were interpreting the rule in such a way as to bar all
price cutting. " As a result of its growing doubts," Dr. Whitney continues, " the Commission decided in 1931 to reconsider the whole program. It proceeded to revise the great
majority of the codes, the reported purpose being 'to tighten
up on the associations, which, it has been said, were leaning
too heavily toward price fixing, more or less indirectly, and
in the direction of a lessening of competition.'" But so vigorously did business protest " that the Commission shortly afterward reversed itself again, at least partially." [29]

The change in policy disturbed the trade associations and
some of them lost heart. They were upset also by the fact that
Herbert Hoover, upon whom they had counted for generous
assistance, was more inclined than his predecessor to give heed
to the anti-trust laws. During his term of office the Department
of Justice brought dissolution suits against eight leading trade
associations. In five of these cases dissolution was ordered by
the courts, while the remaining three had not yet been decided
when Herbert Hoover retired in favor of Franklin Roosevelt
and his NRA. Moreover, the depression had worked great
havoc among these groups. To quote Dr. Whitney again:
" In the early part of 1933 many trade organizations, unable
to cope with the increasing severity of the depression, had become dormant or had even disbanded, and the whole trade
association movement was practically in a state of collapse."
But then " the Recovery Act galvanized it into life again and
simultaneously into a prominence never known before." [30]

The monopolists saw at once that the law was cut to their
order and said as much. Gerard Swope, of General Electric,
declared it would give industry its " opportunity to demonstrate how effective and constructive its leadership can be."
J. S. Tritle, of Westinghouse, hailed Franklin Roosevelt as
" the great sponsor of a united front on the part of industry

and government." [31] Henry I. Harriman, president of the United States Chamber of Commerce, said: " Today's passage of the National Industrial Recovery Act constitutes a most important step in our progress towards business rehabilitation. . . . The act will permit legitimate business enterprise to lift itself above the destructive competition which has prevented recovery and which has been threatening to bring about complete economic demoralization." [32] John D. Rockefeller, Jr., looked upon it as a " great and promising adventure in reconstruction." [33] Charles M. Schwab, Eugene G. Grace, Tom M. Girdler and other steel industrialists were lavish in their praise, especially after the first year of price-fixing and market control under the steel code. [34] Other monopolists were no less enthusiastic.

Yet business as a whole hesitated. It had its doubts about the man Roosevelt. He had been playing to the petit-bourgeois gallery, in words if not in deeds. He had been talking of the needs and rights of the workers. He had brought men and women of reputed collectivist tendencies into his Administration. He might be a radical himself. His tampering with the currency — always the hallmark of radicalism in the eyes of the financial and industrial East — suggested that he was. So, too, did his insistence that he be empowered to license individual businesses or entire industries as a means of enforcing the Recovery Act. The licensing power was considered a distinct threat to free enterprise. Equally alarming to the monopolists was the inclusion of the collective bargaining provisions in the law.

Moreover, the price boom that followed abandonment of the gold standard made it possible for numerous business men, large and small, to pile up earnings for the first time in three years. Wages were still at depression levels, costs were low, rising prices meant higher profit margins. Business was naturally reluctant to sacrifice this advantage by subscribing to the minimum-wage provisions of the Recovery Act. Actually no sacrifice was involved, but that was not known at the beginning.

The unanticipated stubbornness of the business community was met with another outpouring of that ballyhoo to which the Roosevelt Administration had accustomed the country and to which the country still thrilled. Washington officials, from the President down, beat the tom-toms of alternate fear and hope. General Hugh S. Johnson, an obscure protégé of Bernard Baruch, the banker, directed the ballyhoo in the role of Recovery Administrator. He warned that " we may have a new collapse " unless business men hastened to come under the benevolent wing of the NRA. Donald Richberg, a lawyer for the reactionary Railway Brotherhoods, who had been chosen to act as chief counsel for the NRA, asserted in a speech in New York that communism was the only alternative to this great Rooseveltian experiment. President Roosevelt himself, taking his case to the people over the radio, spoke darkly of the "economic hell of the last four years," from which we would not emerge if business men refused to take the necessary " courageous action." In that case, he said, " the great opportunity . . . will pass us by and we will go into another desperate winter."

There followed a period of red fire, speeches, parades, the like of which the country had never seen in time of peace. The New York *Herald Tribune* of September 14, 1933, reported that more than 2,000,000 persons had turned out the day before "to see New York's greatest demonstration — the attempt of 250,000 men, women and children to parade up Fifth Avenue in honor of the national recovery program." The demonstration was described as " a civic pageant of enthusiasm and unanimity such as New York has never seen before . . . a frolic which will be long remembered by those who saw it." To the red fire was added the blue eagle — a truly magnificent symbol of coercion and boycott. Only those business enterprises which had in one way or another agreed to abide by the Recovery Act were permitted to attach the sign of the blue eagle to their products. Consumers were urged in countless ways — by public statements, radio speeches, mass meetings, newspaper advertisements, house-to-house canvasses — to buy nothing that did not bear the blue eagle. This was boycott pure and simple, although, in keeping with the moral tone of the great adventure, General Johnson and other officials roundly denounced those who dared to call it by its right name. The drive went on in other directions. Employers who paid low wages, whether sweatshop operators or merely victims of the fall in the rate of profit, were held up to public scorn, called traitors, " chiselers." To cap the campaign — and to show that the Roosevelt Administration was no more afraid of big industrialists than it was of sweatshop owners — the President and General Johnson threatened to " crack down " on Henry Ford.

There was nothing in the Recovery Act requiring Henry Ford, or anybody else, to state publicly that he would comply with the President's reemployment agreement or the automobile code. Nor could General Johnson show, as he admitted, that the Ford Company was not complying. This did not disturb him. He would show that the Government was boss. President Roosevelt gave him all the support he could, closing the Government market to Ford products and imperiously forbidding companies and individuals who had borrowed Government money to use any of it in buying such products. The Detroit manufacturer did not make the open confession of faith demanded of him. He would not even talk about the matter. In the end the NRA ballyhoo broke asunder upon his intransigence. The moral was obvious. The NRA was not big enough to bring a powerful industrialist to heel as Johnson had implied it could and would do. No other factor contributed as much to the subsequent deflation of General Johnson and his organization as this silly attempt to coerce a hard-boiled capitalist by pompous but empty bluff.

The business community in general, however, was beginning to perceive that the NRA really had its interests at heart. The impetus of anticipated inflation had spent itself and business men again stood in fear of ruthless competition. The Roosevelt Administration gave the various trade and industrial groups what practically amounted to blanket authority to write their own terms. There was hardly a pretense of protecting labor or the consumers — except in those industries where labor was already strongly organized. Johnson had only one thought in mind, and that was to produce results. Within a few months he had placed 90 per cent of American business under codes. The code structure erected was undeniably impressive. President Roosevelt did not blush in taking credit for this accomplishment, though afterward he had no hesitancy in attributing the subsequent failure of the code system to the fact that business had been allowed to write its own terms.

For recovery did not follow. The entire idea was based upon a fallacy, upon the notion that by limiting or destroying wealth we can recover wealth. The avowed objective of the NRA was to adjust production to visible consumption, to rig the law of supply and demand in favor of profits. Every code restricted production in one way or another. Most of them also restricted consumption through manipulation of prices. Some even went so far as to impose limitations upon the introduction or use of new machinery. This was the Rooseveltian solution of the capitalist crisis.

True, the President believed that " temporary " limitation of production was no serious matter since " the pent-up demand of this people is very great " and had only to be tapped to release a flood of buying power. The tapping could be done by raising wages while holding prices down pending recovery. In his statement of June 16, 1933, he declared:

I am fully aware that wage increases will eventually raise costs, but I ask that managements give first consideration to the improvement of operating figures by greatly increased sales to be expected from the rising purchasing power of the public. That is good economics and good business. The aim of this whole effort is to restore our rich domestic market by raising its vast consuming capacity. If we now inflate prices as fast and as far as we increase wages, the whole project will be set at naught. We cannot hope for the full effect of this plan unless, in these first critical months, and, even at the expense of full initial profits, we defer price increases as long as possible.

This was, alas, not good but thoroughly bad economics. Certainly a depression cannot be overcome by adding to costs, but only by cutting costs — meaning wages primarily, for most other costs are fixed. Yet here was the President telling business that it ought to take a directly contrary course. He was proposing, in effect, not only that this depressed condition be prolonged, but that it be deliberately intensified. Business, looking to its profits, naturally did not heed his advice and could not have heeded it without bringing on another sharp drop in business activity. The pent-up demand of the people was not to be tapped in this way.

But, of course, the NRA was not entirely a failure. As was to be expected, it greatly facilitated the advance of monopolism. It was necessary in this connection to make certain concessions to the lag in public opinion. The country had not yet come to understand that trade has to be more or less restrained, that production has to be limited, if the profit system is to be preserved. The lesser bourgeoisie and workers still felt — and correctly — that monopolism was not to their interest. Hence the Roosevelt Administration had perforce to persuade them that black was white. Upon signing the recovery bill, President Roosevelt solemnly announced that " the anti-trust laws still stand firmly against monopolies that restrain trade and price fixing which allows inordinate profits or unfairly high prices." The law itself laid down the rule that the codes to be adopted must not be " designed to promote monopolies or to eliminate or oppress small enterprises." And for the next two years NRA officials continued to insist that the code system was not promoting monopoly. For example, General Johnson vehemently asserted that statements to the contrary were "stark, unqualified, unjustified misstatements of fact . . . something more than modern sedition, a little less than modern treason." [35]

It is hardly necessary to repeat here that the NRA had for its one objective restraint of trade under the guise of planned limitation or adjustment of output. Not only was this true in theory, but in its various reports the Darrow Board presented a great deal of factual evidence, though only a small part of all the evidence available, to show that it was also true in practice. It is surely not without significance that in attempting to defend the NRA, Messrs. Johnson and Richberg should have presented no clearly reasoned and factually substantiated arguments, as men confident of the soundness of their position would have done, but sought instead to damn the Darrow Board with vituperation and invective. But even if we set aside the Darrow reports out of deference to the apologists for the NRA, we may still turn to the no less conclusive evidence to be found in the reports of the Federal Trade Commission, which the President had gone out of his way to pack with friendly appointees,* and of the Consumers Advisory Board of the NRA itself.

Ironically enough, the Industrial Appeals Board, created by Johnson to take the place of the Darrow Board, was in its first report to offer still more factual evidence of the monopolistic character of the NRA code system. In the summer of 1934 the code authority of the cotton-textile industry had, with the permission of the NRA, ordered a 25 per cent curtailment of production for three months on the ground that this was necessary to keep prices from bogging down. Upon in-

---

* For which he was later criticized by the Supreme Court who denounced his summary removal of one member of the Commission as unlawful.

quiring into the situation the new board came to the conclusion that in all probability the net effect of the order was "merely to transfer some amount of production from the small plants accustomed to operate a few machines intensively to the larger plants which have not been utilizing the full machine capacity allowed to them under the code and order." [36] In other words, the smaller enterprises were being penalized to provide the larger companies with more business. With this damaging report General Johnson's hand-picked Industrial Appeals Board appears to have vanished from the public prints.

NRA officials set up "the little man" as the sole standard of judgment whenever the monopoly cry was raised. They implied that if it could be demonstrated that "the little man" was being hurt, they would concede the validity of the criticism. Actually there is no record of their ever having conceded this despite the abundance of valid proof lying ready at hand. There can be no question that the strongest units in each industry or trade group dictated the terms of their respective codes. No one could imagine, for example, the steel trust not laying down the rules that were to govern the steel industry, or the telephone monopoly allowing itself to be bound by regulations drawn up by the few surviving independents in that field. One has only to read the records of the NRA hearings on the major codes to understand who wrote them. I have before me a stenographic transcript of the hearing on the electrical equipment code. This shows one small manufacturer after another arising to testify that not only did he not have a hand in writing the code, but that the General Electric-Westinghouse group did not even bother to consult him. Yet the code was approved virtually as originally written.

Furthermore, in most of these industries the NRA simply handed over control to the already dominant corporations and factions. These groups had been ruling their industries through trade associations in various disguises, whose boards of directors they controlled. In almost every case the NRA invested the boards of directors with power to act as code authorities for the industries in question. Thus, the monopoly control which theretofore had been exercised more or less clandestinely by the dominant groups was given the sanction of law. The power of the state was employed to reenforce one of the principal devices by which the monopolists had for years been crushing their smaller rivals and extending their power.

Nevertheless, the monopolistic tendencies of the NRA could not be measured by the fate of " the little man " alone. For modern monopoly does not consist in large ownership — witness the wide distribution of industrial shares — but manifests itself mainly through control of production and through manipulation of markets and prices. If a trade association made up entirely of small enterprises, of " little men," all of equal strength, resorts to similar control and manipulation, the effect upon the national economy is precisely the same as though these enterprises were under a single ownership.

Under the NRA legislative power was delegated to the President by Congress, while he in his turn delegated this power to the trade associations, for the codes they wrote and he approved had the force of law. The Fascist corporations in Italy are founded upon the same principle, although the Italian corporations give the workers and consumers a somewhat larger voice and more equal representation than American workers and consumers were given in the NRA trade associations.[37] President Roosevelt saw no harm in this delegation of legislative authority to private enterprise. So convinced was he of the moral soundness of his course that he could conceive of no possible objections to it, constitutional or otherwise. Indeed, he regarded the Constitution as a miraculously flexible document that could always be stretched to meet the needs of any unusual situation, or at least to enable a sincere and responsible leader to show the community the way out of a critical situation.

No man was more astounded than he, therefore, when in

179

May, 1935, the Supreme Court declared the Recovery Act unconstitutional. For the first time since he had entered the White House he was left literally speechless. Although theretofore he had never hesitated to speak out on a moment's notice, it was several days before he could bring himself to comment publicly on the problem created by the Supreme Court's ruling. And then he was to talk dourly, bitterly. He preached that " gospel of fear " which, in his campaign speech in Brooklyn, New York, he had justly accused the Republicans of spreading in a last desperate effort to stave off defeat. He said that the court's action had turned the country back to the " horse and buggy " era and warned that if the court's philosophy were to be generally followed it would mean 36-cent wheat and 5-cent cotton for the farmers and would bring other dire consequences down upon the rest of the nation.

His first thought, according to the Washington correspondents, was to propose an amendment to the Constitution which would have the effect of erasing State lines and of increasing the authority of the executive branch of the Federal Government to deal with business matters. On July 4, 1929, he had said that he wanted " to preach a new doctrine: a complete separation of business and government." On March 2, 1930, he had asserted that the preservation of States' rights " is not a cry of jealous commonwealths seeking their own aggrandizement at the expense of sister States. It is a fundamental necessity if we are to remain a united country." But in a White House press conference on May 31, 1935, he asked if the country really considered it wise to strip the Federal Government of power to intervene in business. He declared, said an official transcript of his talk to the press, that " this country cannot go back to the era of the thirteen States and have its national decisions based on forty-eight sovereignties. . . . It cannot relegate to the States the adjustment of agriculture or the determination of national or social or economic problems."

His second thought was to go along with the Supreme Court,

and this he did. It was not that he had abandoned his idea of seeking an amendment to the Constitution, for there was no evidence that he had. But he would not fight for this idea. He was, after all, a righteous conformist, not a real rebel. Yet he clung to the philosophy expressed in his San Francisco speech. He still believed that " the responsible heads of finance and industry, instead of acting each for himself, must work together to achieve the common end." At his behest Congress extended the life of the NRA until April, 1936, and while it was to be continued only as a skeletonized agency without any real power, the President soon made it clear that the real purpose of keeping the NRA alive was to assemble data for use in formulating a new and comprehensive industrial-control program to be submitted to Congress during its 1936 session. Moreover, the monopolistic NRA trade associations, which the Recovery Act had exempted from prosecution under the anti-trust laws, but which had now been deprived of that exemption by the Schechter decision, were left undisturbed. The Department of Justice made no move to bring them into court under either the Sherman or the Clayton Act. On the contrary, the Administration adopted the policy of encouraging these associations to turn to the Federal Trade Commission for approval of "voluntary" codes, much as had been done from 1925 to 1931.

7

WAGES OF DECENT LIVING

☙

PRESIDENT ROOSEVELT had addressed the promises of his Recovery Act to the workers as well as to business. In his statement of June 16, 1933, he said:

The law I have just signed was passed *to put people back to work* — to let them buy more of the products of farms and factories and start our business at a living rate again. . . .

In my inaugural I laid down the simple proposition that nobody is going to starve in this country. It seems to me to be equally plain that no business which depends for existence on paying less than living wages to its workers has any right to continue in this country. By " business " I mean the whole of commerce as well as the whole of industry; by workers I mean all workers — the white-collar class as well as the men in overalls; and by *living* wages I mean more than a bare subsistence level — I mean the wages of *decent* living. (Italics as in original.)

At no time in history have the bulk of the workers received anything resembling " wages of decent living." [38] At the height of our prosperity in the 1920's there were lumber workers earning no more than $10.48 a week, machine-shop helpers earning $11.78, bituminous miners getting $10.34 — to say nothing of the countless sweatshop employees, mill hands and others whose earnings averaged much less. Late in 1928 the Labor Bureau, Inc., prepared a " Minimum Health and Decency Budget " based on the cost of goods and services required by an American worker's family consisting of father, mother and three children. It was declared that this budget set " the bottom level of health and decency below which a family cannot go without danger of physical or moral deterioration." It followed the pattern established by the federal Department of Labor, which frankly admitted that its budget " does not include many comforts which should be included in a proper ' American standard of living.' " For a family in New York it was estimated that an income of $41.74 a week would be needed; for Chicago the figure was placed at $46.98. Yet in September, 1928, the New York State Department of Labor reported that $29.72 was the average weekly earnings of factory employees in that State, and Illinois reported average factory earnings of $29.11.

Even the highest-paid factory employees did not earn enough to attain to the minimum regarded by the Labor Bureau, Inc., as the bottom level of safety. In New York, for example, only newspaper typographers and book and job printers were in or near the " Minimum Health and Decency " class, drawing average earnings respectively of $44.81 and $39.50. All the rest were below that line, the majority far below. And in Illinois only the newspaper printers, whose average earnings were $45.84, and the construction workers, with $43.80 per week, approached the minimum of $46.98 set for the city of Chicago. The National Industrial Conference Board, an employers' research organization, estimated that the average minimum cost of maintaining " a fair American standard of living for the family of an industrial worker " in New York City was $31.92 a week. So the average New York worker was in 1928 earning $2.20 a week less than he needed to maintain what even in the judgment of the employers was a " fair " standard of living.

Nor were New York and Chicago exceptional. During this period 18.5 per cent of the American people as a whole — according to a study prepared not for some radical organization, but for the International Chamber of Commerce — had incomes so low that they could properly be classified as paupers. At least, these 22,000,000 Americans were regarded as living at or below the "bare subsistence" level, while many of them had, indeed, to be supported in part or in whole by society. Another 16.8 per cent were included in the "Minimum for Health and Efficiency" class, while still another 25.2 per cent were earning only enough to assure them of an existence at what the orthodox economists called the "Minimum Comfort" level. These three groups together made up "the poorest class" in Professor Wilford King's income studies, which Professors Paul Nystrom, Irving Fisher and other conservative economists have used as the bases of their own studies. Franklin Roosevelt might have been willing to place the workers in the higher ranges of this group in his "decent living" category, but Professor Fisher has indicated that they hardly belong there. Discussing the problem in 1928, he wrote:

. . . The poorest class alone, comprising 76,000,000 people, received about 38.6 per cent of the national income, or $34,740,000,-000, less than $460 per person. This class includes not only manual and office workers, but the small business men, many managers, and most engineers as well. . . . [Their income is] little more than enough to buy the minimum requirements of an average family of five among the industrial or office workers in New York City, as estimated during 1926 by the National Industrial Conference Board. The Conference Board's budgets allow nothing for emergencies — "for a vacation, for unemployment, for old age, for savings of any kind."

To be earning barely enough to get along on, with nothing left over for unemployment or old age or a vacation or an emergency of any kind, can certainly not be regarded as decent living.

Naturally, when the Wall Street debacle put an end to the dream of perpetual prosperity for the upper reaches of American society, the earnings of the workers also came down. Some thirteen to seventeen million were stripped of their earnings altogether and forced to live upon the dole or upon the charity of relatives and friends. The manufacturing pay roll index fell from its high point of 112.9 in September, 1929, to its low point of 37.1 in March, 1933. The employment index dropped from 109 in September, 1929, to 58.8 in March, 1933. Of course, prices fell, too, though this was of apparent benefit only to those who managed to hang on to some kind of work and in their case the benefit was more than offset by the decline in earnings. The Bureau of Labor Statistics of the Federal Department of Labor has estimated that the average weekly earnings of all factory workers was $25.26 in 1929, but only $17.44 in 1932, a decrease of 31 per cent.* [39] According to the same agency's index of " the cost of goods purchased by wage earners and low-salaried workers," living costs had gone down only 23 per cent in this period.[40] In brief, three years of depression had measurably widened the already broad gulf between wage income and a decent standard of living. Franklin Roosevelt promised, in effect, not only that he would reverse this trend, but that he would eliminate the disparity. The American workers might have remembered that his predecessor likewise had promised to abolish poverty.

After the first half year of the recovery experiment launched so confidently on June 16 the American Federation of Labor reported, on the basis of official statistics, that the gulf was growing wider:

In wages, there have been definite gains under codes for the lowest-wage groups; but workers of average or higher wages have been forced to a lower living standard. Hourly wage rates average higher by 5½ cents per hour, but in many cases this is not enough to compensate for shorter hours; and in no case is it enough to compensate for higher prices.

Workers' income in our sixteen chief producing and distribut-

* These figures are arrived at by dividing the weekly wages in all manufacturing industries by the total number of wage earners employed in each of the two years, as reported to the Bureau of Labor Statistics.

ing industries averaged $20.53 a week in November, 1932, and $20.56 in November, 1933. Meanwhile, food prices are up 7 per cent and prices of clothing and furnishings are higher by 21 per cent, so that workers' real buying power is considerably lower.[41]

A few months later the Federation asserted that "the individual worker made no gain whatever in ' real ' wages from March, 1933, to March, 1934. His average weekly wage increased 9.7 per cent, but this was completely offset by a 9.3 per cent increase in the cost of living." [42] In August, 1934, the Federation's reports were fully substantiated by the first official survey to be undertaken by the Roosevelt Administration. This survey, prepared by Donald R. Richberg, then Executive Secretary of the Executive Council, began by asserting that the workers' buying power had been greatly improved. Richberg said:

It is estimated that total wages in manufacturing industries increased from $96,000,000 a week in June, 1933, to $132,000,000 a week in June, 1934, or 37.5 per cent. When this increase of 37.5 per cent is compared with an increased living cost of 9.6 per cent, there remains despite increased cost of living a net increase of 25 per cent in the total purchasing power of manufacturing wage earners.

But Richberg seems quickly to have realized that it is individual and not total purchasing power that matters to the individual worker. In his next paragraph, he said:

The individual wage earners did not obtain a similar increase — the average per capita weekly earnings in manufacturing rising only 8.5 per cent. Therefore, the average manufacturing worker's purchasing power remained practically unchanged; although by shortening hours he "shared his work" with new employees, without an individual loss in " real wages." [43]

Donald Richberg felt that a 1 per cent decline in real wages was no loss at all. He would have to concede, however, that the

186

trend was not toward but away from " wages of decent living." At most, according to his own statement, the gulf between low wages and decent living " remained practically unchanged."

But even as he was publishing the results of this survey, the cost of living was rapidly rising. His report was dated August 26. Three days before the press had reported that " another rise in the general level of wholesale commodity prices, ascribed chiefly to advances in the farm prices, foods and fuel, and lighting material groups, was announced today by the Bureau of Labor Statistics." On the same day it was being predicted that " meat prices next winter will be the highest since the world war." On August 28 dispatches from Washington told of an increase of 1.2 per cent in retail food prices during the preceding fortnight. The price rise from August to September alone, according to the National Industrial Conference Board, " depressed real weekly earnings of wage-earners 2.1 per cent."

Toward the end of 1934 evidence was increasing that a large part of the cost of such business recovery as had developed was coming out of the pockets of the workers. In October the National Industrial Conference Board declared that " real weekly earnings were 16.2 per cent below those of five years ago." [44] Leo Wolman, labor economist and a prominent member of the Roosevelt Administration, agreed that real wages had fallen, but thought the proportion was not quite so great. He placed the decrease in this period at 12.8 per cent for employees in manufacturing, though he held that there had been an actual increase for workers in other lines of activity. He declared, however, that in the 18 months from June, 1933, to the last quarter of 1934 real wages had declined for all workers employed in manufacturing, the extractive industries (except bituminous and metalliferous miners), the public utilities, wholesale and retail trade, and on the railroads. The decline in real weekly earnings ranged from 2.2 per cent in manufacturing and among telephone and telegraph workers to 11.1 per cent in anthracite mining.[45]

So that during the first year and a half of Franklin Roosevelt's experimentation with the law of supply and demand the movement was decidedly away from "wages of decent living." Not that business did not benefit, for while the bonanza spirit of 1929 had by no means been recaptured, industrial earnings showed a marked gain. The net profits (less deficits) of 1,935 companies increased 32 per cent from 1933 to 1934, according to the National City Bank.[46] The Standard Statistics Corporation reported that 418 companies earned profits totaling $911,000,000 in 1934, as compared with $605,000,000 in 1933, and only $49,000,000 in 1932.* After all, the NRA system was devised in the interest of profits, not of wages. It is the profit system that the capitalist "planners" seek to save, not the consumers or wage earners.

The expansion in business activity did help a small number of wage earners by giving them new jobs. How many were "put back to work" can only be guessed at.† At the start

* The gain in profits by the corporations included in the National City Bank's survey, said the bank in its monthly letter for April, 1935, "does not necessarily mean that the composite statement for all corporations in the United States, numbering over 500,000, will make a similar showing for 1934, when the official figures compiled by the Treasury Department from income-tax returns become available several months hence. Whereas a tabulation of published reports for the year 1933 showed a profit of $1,314,000,000, the Treasury figures for all corporations showed in 1933 a net deficit of $2,359,000,000." Since the net worth of the 1,935 companies included in the National City Bank's survey was estimated at $48,572,000,000, it is seen that the average net worth of these companies was in excess of $25,000,000. Thus, they were among the very largest in the country. It follows that the bulk of the smaller corporations lost money in 1933. There is nothing in the business or industrial indexes for 1934 to suggest that this disparity between the giant corporations and the smaller companies was overcome in that year. In other words, it would appear that the Roosevelt experimentation has been of help neither to the worker nor the small business man, while it has helped to pile up earnings for the big business houses and monopoly interests.

† In "Seeds of Revolt," pp. 33–4, I wrote: "It has long been possible to obtain data concerning profits and prosperity. We keep a close check on the rise and fall of prices, on the expansion and contraction of corporate

President Roosevelt put his own guess at what might seem to be a reassuringly high figure, but as the months wore on he found no opportunity, in face of the known facts, to increase his first estimate. In a radio speech on October 22, 1933, he said: ". . . there were about 10,000,000 of our citizens who earnestly, and in many cases hungrily, were seeking work and could not get it. Of these, in the short space of a few months, I am convinced that at least 4,000,000 have been given employment — or, saying it another way, 40 per cent of those seeking work have found it." In his annual message to Congress on January 3, 1934, he declared that " several millions of our unemployed " have been " restored to work." In a second broadcast on June 28, 1934, he asserted that " I could cite statistics

---

earnings. . . . These statistics and many like them we record with utmost fidelity. For they tell how rich we are. We want to know nothing else. Above all, we do not want to know how poor we are, or how many paupers there are among us. Hence, as a matter of national policy, we do not record the number of the jobless or probe too deeply into their requirements."

This criticism was directed, of course, at the Hoover Administration. But it can be said to apply just as well to the Roosevelt Administration. The Bureau of Labor Statistics has improved its methods to a minor degree. The Federal Emergency Relief Administration has compiled records of the number of families on relief. But it is still true that " we do not record the number of the jobless or probe too deeply into their requirements." The Estate Counsel *News Letter* summed up the situation in able fashion when, in its issue of December 3, 1934, it said:

> The Bureau of Labor Statistics issues no employment figures, but compiles an index number only. This index covers manufacturing industries only; is therefore not broadly conclusive. Secretary Perkins sometimes issues a statement on unemployment, but break-downs of her figures are seldom available for months afterward. Strangely enough, the Administration policy is to *include those on relief rolls as EMPLOYED. . . .* Variation between American Federation of Labor figures and those of the Bureau of Labor Statistics is partially accounted for by the fact that the A.F.L. includes all relief roll workers as UNemployed.

> In the service industries, which includes all sorts of non-manufacturing groups such as barbers, waiters, filling station attendants, professional people and those working on their own account — employment figures are almost totally lacking. Those in the management group are taken to have stable employment which they do not have. Taken as a whole, the study shows that our major recovery problem — unemployment — is the problem on which we have available the least reliable statistics.

to you . . . to show hundreds of thousands reemployed in private industries and other hundreds of thousands given new employment through the expansion of direct and indirect government assistance of many kinds." In still another fireside talk over the radio, delivered on September 30, 1934, more than a year after the NRA was initiated, he went back to his original guess. "The emergency purpose of the NRA was to put men to work," he said, "and since its creation more than four million persons have been reemployed." In his 1935 message to Congress, however, he gave no reemployment figures at all, but instead mentioned the desirability of providing jobs for the " 3,500,000 employable people now on relief, pending their absorption in a rising tide of private employment " — a neat understatement from which the unwary might be led into supposing that as of that date there were only 3,500,000 men and women in want of work.

Soon after taking office the President had declared: "I am going to be honest at all times with the people of the country." [47] But he was something less than candid in discussing unemployment. For instance, he asserted that there were only 10,000,000 persons looking for work when he entered the White House. The actual figure was much nearer 17,000,000. The American Federation of Labor estimated the total in March, 1933, to be 13,689,000.* But this estimate failed to include various groups, farm hands and others, while it also presumed that the ratio of unemployment among the unorganized was the same as among the organized workers, whereas the ratio has always been higher among the former. Both Lewis Corey and the Alexander Hamilton Institute, giving proper consideration to the neglected groups and other factors usually ignored, but working from independent material, came to

* The National Industrial Conference Board placed the total at 13,-300,000, while *Business Week* had earlier estimated that 15,250,000 were jobless in November, 1932.

the conclusion that the correct total was in excess of 17,000,000. Mr. Corey placed it at 17,252,000.

The President's contention that by October his recovery program had put 4,000,000 persons back to work could not have been based upon reliable and comprehensive official statistics, for no such statistics existed. Nor could it have been based upon private estimates, for they were all lower. The best the National Industrial Conference Board could do was to estimate that the number of jobless had been reduced by 2,110,000 from June to October, that is, from the time the recovery program was launched to the date of the President's radio speech; [48] while the American Federation of Labor declared that 2,082,000 workers had been rehired in this period.[49] From then on, moreover, employment remained fairly stationary, fluctuating within a range of a few hundred thousands. The National Industrial Conference Board showed an additional gain of about 672,000 jobs in the next nine months, but this had been more than wiped out by the spring of 1935.[50] On the other hand, the American Federation of Labor refused to acknowledge any such gain. It admitted that from October, 1933, to June, 1934, a hundred thousand jobs had been added, but held that this was more than canceled by the fact that "the increase in those seeking gainful work was about 300,-000." [51]

The stagnation in the reemployment movement after October, 1933, doubtless disturbed the President, though he gave no outward sign of his concern. It also disturbed a certain section of the business community — the United States Chamber of Commerce, for example. This body met the situation with the usual exorcism. It challenged the validity of the unemployment estimates of the American Federation of Labor and announced (in the summer of 1934) that the number of jobless was below 7,000,000, though it offered neither data nor statistics in support of its contention. According to the Chamber's statement: "If all the reliable data to be had are gathered, and if there is care to err upward rather than downward — in order that there may be no chance of intelligent criticism of the result as too small — there is reached for July an estimate under 7,000,000 for persons in unemployment for all reasons." Even this was only "a gross figure," which could be further "refined" by weeding out various categories. This done, "the estimate of those who in July were out of employment by reason of business conditions cannot exceed 5,000,000." Among the groups to be weeded out would be the "several million persons" who are "normally" unemployed, as well as "many persons that are unemployable." [52]

This reference to the existence of an "unemployable" class was to provide the Roosevelt Administration with a new method of reducing unemployment. All that was necessary was to point out that many of the jobless were simply "unemployable" and so were not a part of the problem with which the Administration was dealing. Later in the year the President's Relief Administrator announced that the "unemployables" on the relief rolls were being turned back to the States and municipalities to be cared for. And in his 1935 message President Roosevelt himself took up the refrain. He talked not of the jobless, but of "these 3,500,000 employable people now on relief."

Omitting the fantastic conclusions of the Chamber of Commerce, whose statistical legerdemain convinced no one, the other and more dependable agencies are found in general agreed that at most three million workers were reabsorbed by industry and commerce after two years of Rooseveltian experimentation. These three million undoubtedly benefited in being transferred from the pauper wages of public charity to the more substantial but still far from adequate wages of normal employment. However, this still left a vast group dependent upon the dole. And surely no one will say that these millions, making up approximately one-fourth of the working class, were not also entitled to a "proper American standard of living."

Without doubt there was a marked improvement in the technical methods of distributing relief under Franklin Roosevelt as compared with the situation that existed under Herbert Hoover. The former's acknowledgment of the Federal Government's responsibility in the matter was a distinct contribution toward sound social relationships. In some cases, too, the jobless were even better paid after March, 1933, than they had been before. Yet the improvement in method was of little concrete importance to the bellies that had to be fed and the backs that had to be clothed. It mattered little to them if their pitifully small dole came from Washington or from their county poor supervisor. Moreover, though Franklin Roosevelt appeared at the start to be willing to make relatively generous concessions to the jobless, the profit system could not afford such luxuries; and so the higher relief wages some of them received in the beginning did not last very long.*

The Federal Emergency Relief Administration began operations in the latter part of May, 1933. Its first task, in which it was on the whole eminently successful, was to bring order

* First in point of time in the development of the relief program came the small but far from insignificant Civilian Conservation Corps. This semi-military body had a standing enrollment of about 350,000 men, though more than a million men passed through the corps in its first two years. They were paid $30 a month, but the Administration prevailed upon them to remit most of their wages for the keep of their dependents. In the first seventeen months about $136,000,000 was paid to the CCC workers, of which approximately $113,000,000 was sent home. Actually, therefore, their wages averaged $5.10 a month, or about $1.18 per week. In addition, of course, they received their own keep. But it was not the purpose of the President to provide these youths who voluntarily accepted servitude with anything like adequate wages. He promised them nothing more than moral and physical rehabilitation. Through the CCC, he said, "we can take a vast army of these unemployed out into healthful surroundings. We can eliminate to some extent at least the threat that enforced idleness brings to spiritual and moral stability." In the meantime, too, the Civilian Conservation Corps enabled the Government to get a lot of useful work done at wages far lower than it would have had to pay had it sought to hire men for these tasks at the then prevailing rates.

out of the chaotic relief situation in the country. Another early objective was to substitute work relief for direct relief where-ever possible and to standardize work-relief policies and wage scales. It established, or sought to establish, a work-week of 35 hours, with a minimum wage of 30 cents an hour to be paid in cash. This would have provided a minimum weekly wage of $10.50, below which the Relief Administration hoped that none of the State or local organizations would go. Apparently to make sure of this, it issued instructions to the effect that relief wage rates should be kept high enough to meet the mini-mum pay rates President Roosevelt considered necessary to the success of his reemployment program for private industry.

In September of the following year it was found that the weekly earnings of workers on relief averaged $18.42 in Penn-sylvania and $16.78 in New York. Earnings in other States were less, the lowest being Kentucky, with a weekly average of only $3.70.[53] Since the Bureau of Labor Statistics reported average weekly earnings in the manufacturing industries to be $18.59 in the same month,[54] it would appear that the work-relief beneficiaries in New York and Pennsylvania were prac-tically as well off as the workers who held regular factory jobs. It must not be forgotten, however, that the relief-wage averages in those two States were increased somewhat by the higher rates paid to the white-collar workers on relief. (The State organizations had been advised that the white-collar workers should be employed on projects that would pay them enough to "provide for health, decency and comfort com-mensurate with the previous standard of living of the family." No such requirement was laid down for the mechanics or semi-skilled and unskilled laborers on relief. They were kept on a minimum-need rather than a standard-of-living budget.)

In the meantime the Civil Works program had been launched with the customary ballyhoo. The NRA had failed to produce the anticipated recovery. There were still at least ten to fourteen million workers without regular employment. On November 8, 1933, therefore, the President announced that " four million men now out of employment will be put to work " under a plan to be administered by the CWA, which he was creating for the purpose. They were not to be " put back to work " in the sense in which he had used this phrase in signing the recovery bill, though that was obviously the impression he sought to convey to the public. He spoke of these workers becoming " self-sustaining employees on Federal, State and local projects " and declared that they would " be taken completely off the relief rolls." Actually they were merely to be transferred from one type of relief project to another.

In the same announcement the President said that approximately two million of these workers had been " earning relief in the form of wages for part-time employment on made-work projects. The total amount earned by the members of any one family is less than $20 a month in most of the localities." It was to be presumed, therefore, that under the CWA their relief earnings would be increased. Earnings were increased — until the CWA blew up a few months later. By the middle of January, 1934, more than four million jobless workers had been enrolled by the CWA. At that time their total weekly earnings were $62,024,854, and their average weekly wage $14.72.[55] But also at that time the original funds set aside for this work were being rapidly exhausted. The CWA program was sharply curtailed. Hours of employment were cut from thirty a week to twenty-four in some communities and to fifteen in the smaller towns and rural areas; and earnings were reduced, of course, in like measure. By the end of March the whole program was dropped.

When the CWA collapsed, the Roosevelt Administration charged that the failure was largely due to the " grafting " and " chiseling " of local business men and politicians. One CWA official implied that the Administration had really not wanted to spend so much money on these "made" jobs, which consisted mostly in raking leaves, trimming trees and digging ditches, but had been forced to do so by pressure from Congressmen and from small merchants.[56] There can be little question that petty graft existed, that Congressmen were anxious to see their constituents provided for, and that the small merchants profited when the CWA workers spent their wages. But the real reasons for the failure of this experiment are to be found elsewhere. With his usual disregard for economic realities, Franklin Roosevelt had once again gambled on an early return of prosperity. He was no doubt sincere in wanting to see the unemployed paid more than $20 a month, and he apparently believed that if recovery were to turn up by the spring of 1934, the Government could be more generous and pay them, say, $60 a month. But the expected recovery did not put in its appearance. The President had to choose between the jobless and the profit system, for it was clear that the latter could not afford to keep its unemployed at the cost of $14.72 a week for very long.

Also to be considered was the question of competition with private enterprise. Employers complained that they could not keep their workers when the Government relief agencies were offering more pay for less work. The facts in many cases seem to have supported this complaint. Yet the protest was a reflection, not only upon the low wages being paid by private enterprise, but also upon the Roosevelt minimum-wage policy. For if a $14.72 weekly wage scale for CWA workers could be regarded as offering serious competition to private employers, it must follow that the general average of wages for workers in the lower ranges was below this meager level. The complaints of the employers undoubtedly helped the President to arrive at his decision to drop the CWA. The Relief Administration attempted, however, to continue to hold up relief wages on other projects by insisting on retention of the minimum rate established in the beginning. This appears to have been done in a few of the larger industrial States, as may be seen from the figures given above for Pennsylvania and New York, but it met with growing opposition from public officials and employers everywhere. Finally, the Relief Administration was also compelled to surrender. In November, 1934, it rescinded its original order calling for a minimum rate of 30 cents an hour. Thereafter the rate was to be set by the local agencies, which for the most part were dominated by the employers.

Meantime the number of applicants for relief continued to grow. By February, 1935, more than 22,000,000 persons — one-sixth of the total population of the country — had been reduced to accepting public charity. The problem was frightening the capitalist-entrepreneur class. This class could no longer oppose Federal relief for the jobless, but it insisted that relief be distributed as economically as possible. It went so far as to favor the cash dole, which not long before it had bitterly denounced as destructive of the morale of the working class. The National Industrial Conference Board published figures to show that work relief cost two to three times as much as direct relief. A prominent spokesman for the capitalist class, Winthrop W. Aldrich, chairman of the board of the Chase National Bank, argued in support of direct relief that England " has refused to go further into debt, has balanced its budget, and is taking care of the unemployment relief by *a cash dole*, similar to our home relief, derived from taxation." In the United States, he said, " there are very powerful forces at work to bring about heavy public borrowing to make work." [57] Borrowing would make heavier taxes and heavier taxes would press further upon the rate of profit. The capitalist-entrepreneur class felt that it would rather have the hated cash dole. It would rather risk demoralization of the working class than put up with this growing threat to profits.

Franklin Roosevelt, however, still believed it essential that the morale of the workers be maintained by keeping them at work. In his 1935 message to Congress he said:

A large proportion of these unemployed and their dependents have been forced on the relief rolls. The burden on the Federal Government has grown with great rapidity. We have here a human as well as an economic problem. When humane considerations are concerned, Americans give them precedence. The lessons of history, confirmed by the evidence immediately before me, show conclusively that continued dependence upon relief induces a spiritual and moral disintegration fundamentally destructive to the national fiber. To dole out relief in this way is to administer a narcotic, a subtle destroyer of the human spirit. It is inimical to the dictates of sound policy. It is in violation of the traditions of America. Work must be found for able-bodied but destitute workers.

This was the old tory argument, the old fear that the workers might lose the habit of work, to the detriment of the existing economy. It was also in keeping with the traditions of Hyde Park. Yet the President was learning at the same time that he could not be too moral in his views without inviting increasingly stern opposition from the beneficiaries of the existing economy. Therefore, in announcing a new work-relief program in 1935, he proposed that "compensation on emergency public projects should be in the form of security payments which should be larger than the amount now received as a relief dole" — that was to reassure the unemployed — "but at the same time not so large as to encourage the rejection of opportunities for private employment or the leaving of private employment to engage in government work" — and that was to reassure the employers. He also declared that "preference should be given to those projects which will be self-liquidating in the sense that there is a reasonable expectation that the Government will get its money back at some future time" — which was to persuade the capitalist class that the

heavy new expenditures his program involved would not necessarily lead to new and heavier taxation, but would somehow
be recovered by the Government.

On June 16, 1933, the President had said that "no business
which depends for existence on paying less than living wages
to its workers has any right to continue in this country." Under his 1935 relief program, which was to provide "useful"
jobs for 3,500,000 "employables," the Government would be
far and away the largest business and the largest employer of
labor in the country. The wages to be paid would not be
equivalent to the wages paid in private industry, low as they
are, for the President's lieutenants in Congress had succeeded
at his behest in defeating an amendment to the relief bill that
would have compelled him to pay this labor at the prevailing
wage rates. Nor could the relief wages be as high as the meager
rates paid under the original CWA, for employers had complained that these had encouraged the rejection of opportunities for private employment. The average, therefore, would
have to be less than $14.72 a week. Although the relief bill
was signed by the President in April, five months later (September, 1935) the new plan had not yet been put into operation so it was not possible to determine precisely what the
average earnings under this scheme would be. However, the
President had announced a scale of wages ranging from $94
a month for professional and technical work in the largest
industrial centers of the North down to $19 a month for un-
skilled work in the smaller communities of the South. It was
presumed, on the basis of relief operations in the past, that this
scale would mean an average wage for the country as a whole
of $35 to $40 a month, or less than $10 a week. This would
be slightly higher than the average monthly earnings of $33.32
reported to the Relief Administration in April, 1935, but still
far below a decent living wage. In other words, though he
considered it highly immoral in 1933 for any private business
to pay its help less than "living wages," in 1935 the President

had no hesitancy in having the Government hire 3,500,000 " emergency " workers — more than one-tenth of the working population of the country — and pay them pauper wages.*

This policy would inevitably have disastrous effects upon wage rates elsewhere. There would develop a tendency to displace regularly employed municipal, State and Federal workers with the far cheaper " emergency " employees. That has been the constant history of all work-relief schemes throughout the depression, as the studies of the National Research League and other agencies have shown. No State or municipality has succeeded in putting this temptation behind it, while even the Federal Government has, through the CCC and FERA, used pauper labor on relief to get necessary work done that would otherwise have been done by higher-paid regular employees. Much more important would be the effect upon wage rates in private industry. The American Federation of Labor held, with complete justice, that " a relief wage established on a lower basis than the prevailing rates of pay will tear down our wage standards and, either directly or indirectly, cause reductions in the wages of the American working people." Private industry, indeed, would be foolish to continue paying higher rates while the biggest employer in the country was getting useful work done at less pay.

* It is interesting to note that in its *Monthly Labor Review* for May, 1935, the Department of Labor published a " Budget for Dependent Families, Based on Prices as of November, 1934." For a family of five, including an unemployed man, his wife and three children, it was estimated that a minimum monthly income of $90.77 would be needed. So that under the President's 1935 relief plan not only would the workers draw considerably less than living wages, but the great bulk of them would be paid at a rate far below that which this Government agency held essential to their minimum requirements.

8

LABOR'S MAGNA CARTA

∽

HAD the workers been organized they could readily have defended themselves against attacks upon the wage structure. Franklin Roosevelt appeared to be willing to help them get themselves organized. The appearance was misleading. His support of the collective-bargaining provisions of the Recovery Act was to prove no more than another gracious but empty gesture. It could not have been otherwise. Were labor organized to such an extent that it could effectively resist any real deflation of wages — the variable costs of capitalist industry — the depression would be prolonged and perhaps intensified. The only other costs that could then be deflated to meet the fallen price level and restore the profit margin would be the capital claims, the fixed costs of industry, but the President was endeavoring before all else to check the deflation of the capital-claims structure. This was the keystone of his recovery program. He could not consistently, therefore, support any movement that would give the workers power to hold up the wage structure. He might attempt to set up minimum wages in trying out various means of preventing the deflation from bringing on actual starvation, but control even of these minimum wages he would keep in the hands of the capitalist class.

Nor would class-interest permit him, for other reasons, to lend any real support to organized labor. The essential goal of working-class organization, though its conservative leaders may never recognize it, is the transfer of economic power from the bourgeoisie to the workers. The complete organization of labor would be revolutionary in itself, for if this were achieved, the capitalist class could not move without the consent of labor and then only upon such terms as labor might be ready to lay down. In short, by helping to strengthen organized labor President Roosevelt would be aligning himself with the workers in their revolutionary struggle against his own class. To be sure, revolution in this sense is a distant and probably unattainable goal. Nevertheless, every increase in the strength of organized labor is a step in that direction, for the stronger the workers become the more control or economic power they obtain for themselves. In his study of the problem E. E. Cummins saw this clearly, when he asserted:

The real conflict between employer and employee centers around matters of control. The laborer aims to improve his economic condition — to increase his wages, shorten his hours, better his working conditions — but if he is a member of a trade union, he aims to do this largely by obtaining greater control over industry through his organization. The radical labor organizations are thus seen to be less fundamentally different from the more conservative organizations than might appear at first glance. The radical union seeks to overthrow the present economic system in so far as that is necessary to place the control of industry in the hands of the workers. The conservative union asks for " more and more now " and believes fundamentally in the system of collective bargaining, but after all collective bargaining is " a step in the process of control." The conservative laborers not only want higher wages, they want some share in the determining of those wages. They not only want shorter hours and better working conditions, they also want a voice in the control of those conditions. They are continually wanting more and more control, just as they are ever demanding more and more wages, and shorter and shorter hours, and better and better working conditions.[58]

For this reason employers have always fought the conservative as well as the radical unions and have opposed every attempt to extend the principle of independent collective bargaining. For every time they yield on the question of hours or wages or working conditions they thereby yield a certain part of the control over their own business. A few might be willing to raise wages and shorten hours voluntarily, but even they want to have the final and complete say in the matter. The only collective bargaining employers ever really tolerate is that which is collective bargaining in name only, in brief, the wholly spurious bargaining of company unions which they control.

Once the bank crisis was out of the way President Roosevelt's advisers set themselves to the task of drawing up a plan for business recovery and industrial rehabilitation more or less in accordance with the position he had taken in his San Francisco speech. While they were deliberating Congress was acting in response to the pressure of organized labor. On April 8 the Senate, by a vote of 53 to 30, passed the Black bill providing for the establishment of a 30-hour week for the employees of all industries operating in interstate commerce. Later the same bill was repassed, and by another large vote, under a motion to reconsider. At the same time a similar measure, more extensive in scope, was reported favorably in the House, though Secretary of Labor Perkins had warned that the President would never approve it. An impressive majority was in sight in the lower chamber for this bill. It appeared that labor would get what it wanted. Here was an example of the political power of labor being translated into economic power. If the organized workers could extend their control over working conditions to this extent, they might obviously in the future extend it further by the same means.

John T. Flynn has said:

The question of protecting labor from starvation wages and long hours was now no longer a doubtful issue. . . . What was wanted now was a substitute that would protect employers from these statutory limitations on work periods and wages. The next move was to save the employers. When, therefore, the NRA act was brought forward, it was to defeat the Black and Connery bills, to turn the subject over to employers and to give them, besides, something they had wanted for years but dared not now insist on — the modification of the anti-trust laws and the privilege of self-rule in industry.[59]

And this was, in truth, accomplished by the Recovery Act. That measure not only left organized labor with no semblance of control over minimum wages or working hours, but also took this power out of the hands of Congress and gave it over to the NRA trade associations, which, of course, were to be controlled by the employers. Labor was given no more than an " advisory " voice in the exercise of this control.

Nor did the Administration's original draft of the recovery bill, as prepared by General Johnson, make any provision whatever for collective bargaining. Indeed, the draft was so phrased that even the existing trade unions would have found it difficult, if not impossible, to continue to bargain collectively as they had done in the past. It was only upon the insistence of certain officials of the Department of Labor that Section 7a was ultimately written into the bill. And these officials had to fight long and hard against the opposition of colleagues in the Administration to get this collective-bargaining " guaranty " into the law.

Once it was included President Roosevelt lost no time in trying to turn it to political advantage. Upon signing the bill he declared that the workers " are here given a new charter of rights long sought and hitherto denied." For this he was quite willing to take the credit, which the workers, who earnestly wanted to believe that they had his support, were just as willing to extend to him.

But Section 7a was not a " new charter of rights." There was a time, it is true, when trade unions were outlaw organizations, which the state and the courts, as well as the employers, sought to suppress. But as a result of the long struggle of pioneers in the labor movement, trade unions came in time to be recognized as having lawful status. And this implied legal recognition of the principle of collective bargaining. Many Federal and State laws — for instance, the Clayton Act of 1915 — took cognizance of its legal standing. The regulations of the National War Labor Board declared that "the right of the workers to organize in trade unions and to bargain collectively, through chosen representatives, is recognized and affirmed." The railway labor laws of 1920 and 1926 made it "the duty" of the workers and the railroads to enter into agreements, arrived at through independent collective bargaining, "concerning rates of pay, rules, and working conditions." The Norris-LaGuardia Act of 1932 provided:

Sec. 2 . . . the public policy of the United States is hereby declared as follows:

Whereas . . . though he [the worker] should be free to decline to associate with his fellows, it is necessary that he have full freedom of association, self-organization, and designation of representatives of his own choosing, to negotiate the terms and conditions of his employment, and that he shall be free from the interference, restraint or coercion of employers of labor, or their agents, in the designation of such representatives or in self-organization or in other concerted activities for the purpose of collective bargaining or other mutual aid or protection.

Section 7a of the Recovery Act lifted both the purpose and most of the language of this earlier law. Thus, while it could be held that employers were still seeking to deny this right, it was hardly accurate to suggest that Section 7a represented a "new charter of rights."

Franklin Roosevelt was at no time to seek honestly to enforce this supposed guaranty to labor. Even before the bill was enacted his spokesmen sought to sabotage it. Donald Richberg once tried to rewrite it in such a way as to distort its meaning and, in effect, guarantee the open shop.[60] At another time an amendment was offered in the Senate declaring that:

"Nothing in this title shall be construed to compel a change in the existing satisfactory relations between employees and employers. . . ." This was so obviously an attempt to protect company unions that Senators Norris, Wheeler, Wagner and other "friends of labor" promptly arose to expose it. When its true nature was revealed, Senator Clark of Missouri, its sponsor, could only say in its defense, that both General Johnson and Donald Richberg favored it. He declared that "Mr. Richberg, one of the authors of the bill, well known as one of the leading labor lawyers and a leading representative of labor unions, was present and not only accepted the amendment, but said he thought it was very beneficial to the bill." [61] Yet it was to these two men, Johnson and Richberg, that Franklin Roosevelt was to delegate his broad power to administer the Recovery Act, including Section 7a.

The steel industry, bell-wether of American big business, announced through Robert P. Lamont, then president of the American Iron and Steel Institute, that it would not consider itself bound by Section 7a. He told a Senate committee that if the steel industry's right to bargain collectively with its own employees in its own way were not recognized, "the industry is positive in the belief that the intent and purpose of the bill cannot be accomplished." In other words, the steel companies were ready to break the law rather than deal with independent unions.

And steel was not bluffing. On the very day President Roosevelt signed the bill the Associated Press reported from Youngstown that 7,500 employees of the Republic Steel Corporation were being herded into a company union to act for them "in all matters relating to wages, working conditions, welfare, sanitation and general conditions affecting workers and the company." The same dispatch said that "a similar employee-representation plan was announced almost simultaneously by the Carnegie Steel Company in notices posted in its plants here and at Pittsburgh. Both the Carnegie and Republic plans are patterned after a system in effect in the Bethlehem Steel Company and in the Youngstown Sheet and Tube Company since 1918." The Bethlehem and Youngstown employee-representation systems are among the oldest and most notorious company unions in the country.*

Other industries were quick to follow. Those who lacked courage were prompted to take action by statements from outstanding representatives of big business. Henry I. Harriman, of the United States Chamber of Commerce, and W. W. Atterbury, president of the Pennsylvania Railroad, virtually invited violation of the law by declaring that Section 7a did not require employers to deal with unions or their employees to join unions.[62] The National Association of Manufacturers asserted that closed-shop agreements were specifically outlawed by the Recovery Act. "The Association," according to a dispatch from Washington, "also informed employers that under the law they could advise workers against joining a labor union, or, within limits, offer special inducements, such as group insurance, to employees who would join and bargain through a company union."

Before the Recovery Act was many days old several million workers in at least thirty large industries had been forced into company-controlled unions. Those who refused to come in quietly, or who sought to join or organize independent unions, were subjected to threats of various kinds. Thousands were summarily dismissed from their employment. At the end of the first month the American Federation of Labor had assembled huge stacks of evidence pertaining to these wholesale violations of Section 7a. Much of this evidence was turned over to the Labor Advisory Board of the NRA, but nothing

* That the spokesmen for the steel industry were as good as their word is indicated by the survey published in *Steel Facts* for July, 1935, showing that in the company-union elections held in June 90.13 per cent of the employees of the steel industry participated. In the 1934 elections 85.39 per cent of the steel workers cast ballots under the various employee-representation schemes.

seems to have come of it. Some time later, in a survey covering the first few months of the life of Section 7a, the National Industrial Conference Board found that of the approximately four million workers included in the study, 45 per cent had been induced to join company unions, 9 per cent belonged to or had affiliated themselves with independent unions, while the remainder were still unorganized.

It was not only through company unionism that the employing class fought back. In the first rush of the American Federation of Labor to organize the workers a few employers, perhaps good Democrats, perhaps sincere patriots, or perhaps merely men who were afraid that the Roosevelt Administration would really use its tremendous power in behalf of the labor movement, willingly complied with both the spirit and the letter of the law. But the majority resisted. They had recourse to all of the violent and brutal methods known to industrial history. They flaunted their defiance in public meetings and public statements and in full-page advertisements in the metropolitan press. They called up the police and the militia, as well as their own strike-breakers, to aid them. The workers had to fight every inch of the way. More than half of the strikes that took place in 1933–34 were called to compel compliance with Section 7a on the part of employers. Most of the strikes were lost. The workers succeeded in some cases where labor was already strong, but failed where the capitalist-entrepreneur class had managed to preserve the open shop in times past and was determined to crush this newest drive of organized labor.

Employers, however, were not alone in sabotaging Section 7a. Hugh Johnson waited only a few days after taking office to join the employers in scuttling labor's " magna carta." The National Association of Manufacturers and other employer groups were contending that they should be in no way restricted in their age-old privilege of entering into wage agreements with individual workers. This practice would naturally continue, law or no law, where no sentiment or demand for collective agreements existed among the workers. What the employers wanted was the right to deal with workers individually in cases where their employees were seeking to compel them to enter into collective agreements. To recognize individual agreements under such circumstances would obviously reduce the principle of collective bargaining to a farce. Nevertheless, General Johnson obliged the employers by ruling on July 7 that the law " recognizes the right of individual workers to bargain for their own conditions of employment."

One such interpretation after another tumbled from the prolific minds of Messrs. Richberg and Johnson.* Within six weeks the situation had become so confused by their various orders and decrees that they were moved to publish what purported to be a formal clarifying opinion. Actually their opinion of August 23 cut the heart out of Section 7a. Buried in the fifth paragraph of this statement appeared the following sentence: " Neither employers nor employees are required by law to agree to any particular contract, whether proposed as an individual or collective agreement." Stated otherwise, the workers could have all the collective bargaining they desired, but their bosses could not be compelled to accept the bargains arrived at.

* Johnson and Richberg resorted as well to other means, too numerous to recount here, of sabotaging the labor provisions of the Recovery Act. Indeed, the former had no hesitancy in revealing his anti-labor bias whenever the occasion seemed propitious. The failure to enforce Section 7a resulted in a wave of strikes in 1933 and 1934. In October, 1933, General Johnson warned organized labor that the right to strike would be outlawed if the strike movement was not checked, though this would have closed to the working class the last possible means of securing the collective bargaining promised in the Recovery Act. The following summer he personally intervened on the side of the employers in the San Francisco strike, frankly approving their efforts to crush with brute force what he called " a civil war." Richberg was more subtle and indirect in his methods, but he, too, favored direct action upon occasion. This he showed notably in his handling of the automobile code and in the Jennings-Newspaper Guild case.

Johnson and Richberg were responsible neither to the people nor to Congress, but only to the President. He had appointed them. He could remove them at his pleasure. In the last analysis he was responsible for their activities. If their attitudes or policies displeased him, he could readily have called for their resignation. That he did not do so suggests he was in full agreement with them in their handling of the labor problem.

On August 5, 1933, he himself announced " the creation of a distinguished tribunal to pass promptly on any case of hardship or dispute that may arise from interpretation or application of the President's Reemployment Agreement." To his "distinguished tribunal" he appointed a liberal United States Senator, a conservative labor economist, a " golden rule " business man from Boston, two of the three most reactionary labor leaders in the country, and two industrialists who had long sponsored employee-representation plans and similar schemes designed to prevent labor from organizing itself. The tribunal — first known as the National Board of Arbitration and later called the National Labor Board — was soon found dealing with all types of labor disputes arising under the NRA code system.

The President called the creation of the labor board " an act of economic statesmanship." He said it was necessary as a measure for the preservation of " industrial peace." But labor history shows only too well that by " industrial peace " is meant suppression of strikes and other forms of labor militancy in the interest of the employers. The President's action implied that he intended to deal with the problem of enforcing Section 7a according to the old and deceptive theory of " the neutral state." That is to say, there would be no effort to enforce this law as a law, but if controversies should arise under it, " the neutral state " would step in and try to conciliate or arbitrate such disputes. But the question would obviously arise only when an employer had sought to withhold the rights extended to the workers under Section 7a. If upon proper judicial inquiry it was determined that the employer had actually violated the law in this respect, he was then subject to the penalties laid down in the law. Under the Constitution the executive branch of the Government could have no choice in the matter. It could not legally submit the fact of the violation to a labor board for " adjustment." It would be just as logical and lawful to arbitrate the guilt of a convicted thief instead of packing him off to jail.

The President elected, however, to follow the theory of " the neutral state," although the capitalist state obviously cannot be neutral in any conflict between the interests of the capitalist class and those of the working class. In any case, the labor board was left to do what it could to " adjust " violations of Section 7a. While it was apparently successful in a number of cases of lesser consequence, at least to the extent of preventing or settling strikes in certain instances, adequate enforcement of Section 7a remained as distant as ever. Employers continued to defy or ignore the law. Strikes for union recognition kept piling up faster than the board could settle them with its promises and compromises.

The President and his advisers attributed the weakness of the board, not to the fallacious principle upon which it was founded, but to its lack of sufficient authority. They did not seem to consider that the law itself was sufficient authority for its own enforcement, that it was neither possible nor necessary to reach out elsewhere for this power. On December 19, 1933, the President clothed the National Labor Board " with the full legal power it had lacked." In the same order its duties were minutely defined. Apparently this was not enough, for on February 1 he issued another order " designed to clear away all doubt as to the board's authority in disputes over company unions." Still something was amiss, for exactly four weeks later a third executive order came from the White House again defining and adding to the board's duties and powers. In this third order the President at last appears to have recognized that it might be well to consider violators of Section 7a in the same light as other law-breakers, though he took care not to give the labor board mandatory power to proceed against them. He decreed that

. . . whenever the National Labor Board shall find that an employer has interfered with the board's conduct of an election or has declined to recognize or to bargain collectively with a representative or representatives of the employees adjudged by the board to have been selected in accordance with Section 7a, or has otherwise violated or is refusing to comply with Section 7a, the board, *in its discretion, may* report such findings and make appropriate recommendations to the Attorney General or to the Compliance Division of the National Recovery Administration. (Italics mine.)

This was like telling a policeman, who had caught a criminal in the act, that he might use his own discretion in deciding whether or not to hale the culprit before a court of justice.

In the following month the President had another opportunity to aid and abet the employers in their efforts to checkmate the labor movement. With a major strike in the automobile industry threatening his recovery program, as he believed, he was confronted with a dispute in which no real compromise was possible. The automobile manufacturers were determined to tolerate no bargaining with the American Federation of Labor. They said so frankly in their talks with General Johnson, Donald Richberg and the National Labor Board, and even more frankly in a series of newspaper advertisements. The American Federation of Labor, on the other hand, being still hopeful that the President meant to enforce Section 7a, was no less insistent that the manufacturers recognize and deal with its new union in the automobile field. It was plain that the President would either have to stand by the manufacturers and their company unions, or else throw his support to the independent labor movement. There was no middle ground.

He met the situation, and averted the strike, by what appeared at first glance to be a shrewd compromise. Actually his " compromise " was nothing more than a rephrasing of a scheme brought to Washington by lawyers for the industry. The President yielded to the latter on every point but one. Summed up, the settlement seemed to promise that the question of whether the workers preferred to bargain through an independent union or through company unions would be inquired into by a board made up of one member from the industry, one from the ranks of the workers, and one, to act as chairman, representing the Government. (The manufacturers had urged that the inqury be undertaken by an " impartial " board to be named by the code authority for the industry, that is, by the board of directors of the National Automobile Association of Commerce. This was the only point at which they were defeated.) But this promise was offset by another section of the settlement. The President informed the American Federation of Labor that " the Government favors no particular union or particular form of employee organization or representation," and at the same time he pointed out that Section 7a, as he saw it, gave the employees the right to organize into more than one group, if they so desired, with each group entitled to be represented in whatever bargaining ensued. " If there is more than one group," he said, " each bargaining committee shall have total membership pro rata to the number of men each member represents." [63]

The only effect of this compromise could have been to legalize and strengthen the company unions at the expense of the independent union. It would, it is true, place the two on the same basis in theory. In practice, however, this hypothetical equality would give the company unions a decisive advantage.

As matters turned out, there was no thorough inquiry into the preferences of the automobile workers. Instead, after a delay of some months, the Automobile Labor Board created by the President proceeded to hold elections to " bargaining committees " in " districts " within the industry. These committees had no independent or unified organizations behind them. They had no indisputable mandate regarding wages or other conditions from the workers they were supposed to represent. Under the circumstances, since the workers were not being permitted to organize for the purpose and since they were being deliberately divided into their separate and unrelated districts, it would not be possible for them to settle their own differences in advance or to present a common program of demands. Moreover, the committee members themselves were in no sense free to undertake negotiations on an independent basis. They were all employees of the companies with whom they were to bargain. This made it possible, as William Leiserson has put it, " for employers to discipline, transfer, discharge or otherwise punish the bargaining agents of the employees." Even though the Automobile Labor Board might conceivably prevent outright coercion or intimidation, yet the knowledge that the employers had this power would inevitably influence the attitudes and decisions of the bargaining committees.[64] The only difference between this scheme and the ordinary company union is that by the former arrangement Government appointees rather than company officials supervise the election of employee representatives. It is an interesting fact that under the Fascist Charter of Labor, adopted in 1926, the Italian Government follows precisely the same formula in regulating relations between workers and employers.

When the automobile settlement plan of March 25, 1934, was made public by the President, it was universally acclaimed by employers, by public officials, and even by a few labor leaders. General Johnson announced that the works-council idea embodied in this plan would be introduced into other industries by the NRA. Senator Wagner promised to have it written into law. William Green, head of the American Federation of Labor, accepted the settlement with a cheer, though it was a patent betrayal of his followers. And Franklin Roosevelt himself looked upon his handiwork as a wondrous piece of "social engineering."

Later, when the Automobile Labor Board had put the bargaining-committee or works-council plan into effect, he signified his approval in no uncertain way. He commended the board for its success and prolonged its life in face of the demands of the American Federation of Labor that it be abolished.[65] Organized labor had by that time come to appreciate what "works councils" really mean. At the same time the President renewed the automobile code, against which organized labor also had many grievances, particularly because of the inclusion in the code of a "merit" clause that would have made collective bargaining in the automobile industry meaningless had such bargaining ever been introduced. He let it be known through his subordinate, Donald Richberg, that labor had been consulted in connection with his decision to renew the code. This was untrue. Labor was in no way consulted or given a voice in the matter. The President did not even seek the opinion or advice of his own Secretary of Labor.[66]

Again in the Jennings case he was successful in hamstringing Section 7a. In this case an employee of the San Francisco *Call-Bulletin*, a Hearst publication, was discharged for his activity in connection with the Newspaper Guild, a union of reporters and editorial workers. This was a flagrant violation of Section 7a. The Guild demanded that at the very least the National Labor Board order Jennings reinstated. The board indicated that it was so disposed, but at this point Donald Richberg, carrying out instructions from the White House, removed the case from the jurisdiction of the labor board and turned it over to the Newspaper Industrial Board, which meant, in effect, since the latter agency was controlled by the employers, that they would sit in judgment upon one of their number in a case involving his action against an employee. This done, President Roosevelt ordered the National Labor Board to keep its hands off such cases in the future.[67]

The Weirton case was allowed to drag along for months before the Roosevelt Administration took definite action. The independent steel union, which was trying to organize the workers in the Weirton plant in West Virginia, sent several delegations to Washington to complain of the unlawful activities of the Weirton Steel Corporation. The delegations declared that not only was the company preventing its employees from joining the independent union, but was forcing them to join its newly created company union. The complaints went unheeded until a strike was threatened and thereupon the President's Labor Board suddenly deemed it expedient to arrange for an election among the Weirton workers to determine which union they wanted to represent them. The company, however, refused to permit the referendum to be held.

Two courses of action lay open to the Administration. It could proceed against the steel company under Section 3f of the Recovery Act, which provided specific penalties for violations of any NRA code, including its labor provisions; or it could act under Section 3c, which merely authorized Federal District Attorneys " to institute proceedings in equity to prevent and restrain such violations." The Administration elected the latter, which was seemingly the easier course. The hearing on its petition for an injunction against the company was not finally ended until February 27, 1935, eighteen months after the independent union had first asked the National Labor Board to intervene. Federal Judge Nields ruled, *inter alia*, that " by a clear preponderance of evidence this court finds that the plan of employee representation in effect among the em-

ployees of the defendant affords a lawful and effective organization . . . that in all respects complies with the provisions of Section 7a . . . in all respects it is satisfactory to the
great majority of the defendant's employees." [68] It would have
been surprising, indeed, had this steel corporation not been
able to whip a presentable company union into shape in the
time which the National Labor Board allowed it.

It may be held that in the Weirton case the labor board
rather than the White House was to blame. This would be
mere logic-chopping, for the board was created by the President and was responsible to him alone. In the Houde case,
moreover, even this excuse did not apply. The Houde Corporation, a Buffalo, New York, concern, was one of the many
violators of Section 7a. The reconstructed National Labor
Relations Board, successor to the former labor board, was
anxious to bring the Houde company into court. It believed
its violation of the law afforded the strongest possible test
case. First Chairman Lloyd Garrison, and then his successor,
Francis Biddle, sought to prevail upon the Department of
Justice to take action, but the Attorney General refused to
move. That official declared that the evidence was insufficient
to justify a court test. Chairman Biddle raised a storm, showed
that the Attorney General was mistaken, and intimated that
the Administration lacked the courage — or the desire — to
take a defiant employer into court. The White House immediately let it be known that it had recanted and the Attorney General found that the evidence in hand was sufficient
after all.

The Houde case, however, was allowed to drag along until,
finally, the Supreme Court threw out the whole Recovery
Act, including Section 7a. Thereupon all court action under
this law was dropped. But practically all of the pending cases
had to do with other sections of the Recovery Act. Indeed, of
the hundreds of violations of Section 7a that were reported,

only two ever found their way into the courts, and of these only one was finally decided, the Weirton case, and that went against the working class.

Even after two years of this sad experience with labor's "new charter of rights" the self-designated friends of labor in Congress, as well as the bureaucrats of the American Federation of Labor, remained convinced that the law rather than President Roosevelt was to blame. They did not seem to perceive that every time he had had to come to an unequivocal decision as between the working class and the employing class he had simply ignored the law in order to side with the employers. True, he had continued to pay lip service to the rights of the workers, and he had succeeded in maintaining an appearance of impartiality, largely by letting all-too-willing subordinates bear the immediate responsibility for the execution of his labor policies and by postponing critical decisions whenever that was at all feasible. But not once had he lifted a finger of his own accord to give meaning to labor's " charter of rights." Not once had he sought to safeguard the principle of collective bargaining when it was opposed by any employer or group of employers.

Nevertheless, Senator Wagner and his colleagues felt that another and stronger law would remedy the situation. They offered a bill to this end in 1934, only to be defeated by the opposition of the employers and the refusal of the President to lend his support. They tried again in 1935 and this time were successful.* It was doubtful, however, that the new law

* The new Labor Disputes Act is also based on the theory of "the neutral state." Indeed, it even goes further in implementing this theory than did the Roosevelt executive orders creating the old labor board. A new Labor Board is to have the power not only to "adjust" disputes concerning collective bargaining, but also (Section 9b) to decide for itself in any given case whether "the unit appropriate for the purposes of collective bargaining shall be the employer unit, craft unit, plant unit or other unit." Obviously, under this clause a state agency is being authorized to determine what form labor organization shall take. It may even turn the whole labor movement over to company unionism. Thus, the "neutral

would fare better than had Section 7a. No amount of legislation would suffice so long as the chief executive officer of the Government had not the will to enforce it.

---

state" not only intervenes in disputes between capital and labor, but takes charge of the collective bargaining of the workers. This is indicated, too, in the provision which makes the decisions of the Labor Board binding upon the parties to such disputes. In short, though it pretends to protect the right to strike, the new law actually seeks to substitute compulsory arbitration for the right to strike.

9

RESTORING THE ANCIENT TRUTHS

ᔓ

IN his inaugural address Franklin Roosevelt said:

. . . the rulers of the exchange of mankind's goods have failed through their own stubbornness and their own incompetence, have admitted their failure and abdicated. Practices of the unscrupulous money changers stand indicted in the court of public opinion, rejected by the hearts and minds of men.

True, they have tried, but their efforts have been cast in the pattern of an outworn tradition. Faced by failure of credit they have proposed only the lending of more money. Stripped of the lure of profit by which to induce our people to follow their false leadership they have resorted to exhortations, pleading tearfully for restored confidence. They know only the rules of a generation of self-seekers. They have no vision, and when there is no vision the people perish.

The money changers have fled from their high seats in the temple of our civilization. We may now restore that temple to the ancient truths.

This was no new attitude for Franklin Roosevelt to take. While he was Governor of New York, it must be conceded, he had refrained from interfering in any way with the practices of the money changers. His moral indignation was none the less aroused by the events of October, 1929, and seemed to increase, indeed, as the ever-widening depression brought him closer to the White House. Immediately after the stock market crash he had referred to " the improper schemes and questionable methods" used " in some cases " in the stock market, though he also felt that "many investors" were to blame for having " lost sight of the real purpose of the Exchange in a fever of old-fashioned speculation." By January, 1932, he was questioning both the wisdom and the ethics of the money changers and their business and political henchmen, though he believed that " nothing is to be gained by making them the scapegoats," for they are "heartily sorry for their sins " and " appreciate the errors of their teaching." However, by May of that year, speaking in Atlanta, he was convinced that "we cannot allow our economic life to be controlled by that small group of men whose chief outlook upon the social welfare is tinctured by the fact that they can make huge profits from the lending of money and the marketing of securities."

And now that he was in the White House, with the banking system seemingly in ruins all about him, he put the money changers in their place with an outpouring of pietistic scorn. The people applauded. This was what they wanted to hear. They had been swindled by the sharpers of Wall Street, or so they believed. They needed to be reassured, and they were reassured by these words from the man to whom they had entrusted the enormous powers of the presidency. Yet the same words seemed to satisfy the money changers as well. At least they showed no outward sign of perturbation. The new President had named no names, had not sought to identify their unscrupulous practices with the ruthless methods of modern capitalism. The finance capitalists knew that so far as they were concerned, the man was dealing in demagogic platitudes. They knew that at that very time he was consulting and advising with some of their number regarding a plan for reopening the banks. The plan he adopted was their plan. And the soundness of their judgment was further revealed three months later when several of their " good friends " were found occupying high places in the Roosevelt Administration.[69]

For it was a sham battle from the beginning. Franklin Roosevelt might call loudly for "honest dealing in securities." He might denounce the "fetishes" of the "so-called" international bankers. He might send a personal emissary, Jesse H. Jones, to a convention of bankers to tell them to "be smart for once." He might let his party subordinates on the Senate Banking and Currency Committee continue to pillory the bankers, including the almighty J. P. Morgan, through a whole summer to the greater glory of his own reputation as an archenemy of the money changers. He might insinuate that the bankers were holding up the recovery parade by refusing to lend money to business men willing to gamble on the sorcery of the blue eagle. He might threaten the bankers with government competition as punishment for their misbehavior. He might praise the British bankers with just enough extravagance to suggest to the people that American bankers were lacking in patriotism. This was all a part of the game. So long as the people were in the mood to hold the bankers to account for the ills that had fallen upon the country, the White House was encouraged to play deftly though with guarded subtlety upon the same theme.

But at no time did he do more than question the wisdom and the ethics of the money changers. He was not concerned with the roots of the evil. In fact, he had let it be known during the campaign that he was "not prepared to say that the system which produces them is wrong." He wanted to reform, not the system, but the men directing it. In his own words:

I propose an orderly, explicit and practical group of fundamental remedies. These will protect not the few but the great mass of average American men and women who, I am not ashamed to repeat, have been forgotten by those in power. These measures, like my own whole theory of the conduct of government, are based on telling the truth.

Government cannot prevent some individuals from making errors of judgment. But government can prevent to a very great degree the fooling of sensible people through misstatements and through the withholding of information on the part of private organizations great and small which seek to sell investments to the people.[70]

His remedies were: Federal regulation of the sale of securities — " to inspire truth telling "; more rigid supervision of the national banks; discouragement and prevention of speculation; separation of investment and commercial banking; restriction of the Federal Reserve Banks; an executive policy under which it would " no longer be possible for international bankers or others to sell to the investing public in America foreign securities on the implied understanding that these securities have been passed on or approved by the State Department or any other agency of the Federal Government "; and a promise " that high public officials in the new administration will neither by word nor deed seek to influence the prices of stocks and bonds." [71]

It is not that the President had no inkling of the fundamentals involved. In the same statement he pointed out that:

Two-thirds of American industry is concentrated in a few hundred corporations, and actually managed by not more than five thousand men. More than half of the savings of the country are invested in corporation stock and bonds, which have been made the sport of the American stock markets. Fewer than three dozen private banking houses, and stock-selling adjuncts in the commercial banks, have directed the flow of capital within the country and outside it. Economic power is concentrated in a few hands.[72]

Marx, Lenin and other scholars had pointed to this evil long before and almost precisely in the same language. Lenin, for example, had said: "In proportion as banking develops and becomes concentrated in a small number of institutions, the banks grow from modest intermediaries into all-powerful monopolists having at their command almost all the money capital of all the capitalists and small business men, as well as the greater part of the means of production of a given country or in a number of countries. . . . A handful of monopolists controls all the operations, both commercial and financial, of capitalist society." [73] But whereas Marx and Lenin had quite another solution to offer, Franklin Roosevelt thought the evil might be overcome by making honest men of the finance capitalists.

But would it? There can be little doubt that the world would then be a better place to live in. Fewer suckers would be hooked, fewer widows and orphans would be fleeced of their legacies, fewer petit-bourgeois souls would be robbed of their savings, fewer bankers would resort to outright stealing. But the central problem would be left untouched. The effective economic power would remain concentrated in a few hands. The finance capitalists would still be in a position to " direct the flow of capital within the country and outside it." They would still be able to dictate the terms upon which the country's business might be done. And they would still have to find profitable employment for surplus capital and profitable markets for surplus goods.

One school of liberal economic thought would have the state exercise its taxing power to eliminate these embarrassing surpluses and at the same time break the stranglehold of the finance capitalists upon the national economy. Surplus profits would be levied upon to an extent sufficient to balance savings against spendings. The revenues thus accruing would be used to develop social services such as unemployment insurance and old-age pensions for the benefit of the lower classes. This school overlooks the fact that surplus capital also arises from the savings of the petit bourgeoisie. It overlooks the more im-

portant fact that any levy upon surplus profits would constitute an added burden upon the *rate* of profit. The monopoly
capitalists would undoubtedly endeavor to meet the added
cost by still more wage cuts, more labor-saving machinery,
and by redoubling their efforts to extend their control over
production and markets. Without the exercise of a social or
state control over all income, the surplus-profits tax would
merely accentuate existing capitalist contradictions and not
disturb the power of the finance capitalists in the least.

A kindred school would, therefore, go further and have the
state take over the active direction of "the flow of capital."
This plan has certain plausibility, but it could not be made to
work unless the state were to take over complete control of
all the elements that enter into income. It would have to regulate, not only capital investments, but wages, salaries, savings
accounts, bank deposits, insurance funds and the like, as well
as profits and prices, for to leave any one of these elements
unregulated would obviously jeopardize the balance between
savings and spendings which would be the goal of this state
intervention. Such rigid control would mean that the effective economic power had been transferred from the private
capitalists to the state, but it would also mean that the backbone of the profit system had been broken.

Franklin Roosevelt was not inclined, however, to favor a
tax on surplus capital or surplus profits.* And he was to at-

* The President's tax program of June, 1935, which is discussed below,
was ostensibly designed to take away a larger part of the income of a few
of the wealthiest capitalists of the country and to make it more difficult for
huge family fortunes to perpetuate themselves. It would also provide for an
increase in corporation taxes graduated according to the size of individual
corporations. But nothing was said in the President's message of June 19
with respect to surplus profits, though the President did add that ultimately
"unwieldy and unnecessary corporate surpluses" should be "discouraged."
In any event, his plan would in no real sense affect the economic power of
the finance capitalists, for that power rests, not upon their own incomes,
nor yet upon family fortunes, but upon their control of the production
and credit machinery. Nor would it affect the accumulation of surplus
capital to any important extent, for that surplus grows, not out of the
excess income of a few wealthy individuals, but out of the profits of the

tempt nothing by way of state regulation with a view to balancing savings against spendings — unless his manipulation of the currency can be said to fall into that category. In his NRA and AAA experiments he was actually to move in the other direction, to levy upon consumption income in order to protect production income. His banking measures did not even come close to the central problem. The Glass-Steagall Act of 1933 sought in the main only to separate commercial from investment banking and in no sense set up a control over the flow of investments. Another part of his program provided for Government insurance of bank deposits, which placed a premium on bad banking, but did nothing to govern the uses to which the deposits might be put.

For the rest, the President strove to establish a higher ethical standard for the money changers by legislative compulsion. In asking Congress to empower the Federal Government to regulate the securities business, for example, he said:

> This proposal adds to the ancient rule of caveat emptor the further doctrine: "Let the seller also beware." It puts the burden of telling the whole truth on the seller. It should give impetus to honest dealing in securities and thereby bring back public confidence.[74]

Certainly no one, except perhaps the crooked bankers and brokers themselves, will quarrel with Franklin Roosevelt's modest and highly moral efforts to reform the money changers. Had it been feasible to implement these efforts in a positive and concrete way, it would have represented a distinct social gain. But even this was not to follow. Writing of one of the Roosevelt reform laws, the National Securities Exchange Act

---

entire business and financial community, as well as out of the savings of the lower middle class. In short, the President's plan, far from even approaching that complete scientific control which is necessary to the attainment of a balance between savings and spendings, barely touched the surface of the problem.

of 1934, John T. Flynn has told of " that amazing and un-paralleled storm of propaganda unloosed by the wounded beast in Broad Street " against this attempt to inject a little common decency into the stock market. In time " this terror succeeded in penetrating the President's official family, and the order came to revise the bill." Mr. Flynn continues:

Then the President directed the Secretary of the Treasury and the Governor of the Federal Reserve Board to collaborate with the framers of the bill in a revision. Mr. Thomas Smith, assistant secretary of the Treasury, Mr. Eugene Black, governor of the Reserve Board, Messrs. Pecora, Corcoran, and Cohen and a few others went into conference about this revision. It was at this point that Mr. Smith and Mr. Black did their work of emasculation on this bill while the President was talking for public consumption about a bill " with teeth in it." The chief fruit of these labors was to take out of the bill itself almost all of its teeth and lodge the almost complete discretionary control in a commission. The bill subsequently introduced followed this pattern. . . . The bill had degenerated to a collection of regulations to govern the game of speculation as between the speculators, with the United States sitting in as umpire. . . . It is perfectly clear to me that a bill with real teeth in it could have been enacted if the President had been willing to make a fight for such a bill.[75]

And the Securities and Exchange Commission, which was to exercise this discretionary control over stock-market operations, was promptly delivered into the hands of a Wall Street operator. Only a short time after his designation to the chairmanship of the commission by the President, Joseph P. Kennedy was revealed by the Senate Banking and Currency Committee, in a report severely condemning such activities, to have been a participant in a stock-gambling pool of the very sort that had led to the demand for government control of the stock market.[76] It was stated on Mr. Kennedy's behalf, to be sure, that he was thoroughly honest and would exercise his powers in a very conscientious manner. It was likewise stated that President Roosevelt deemed it more sensible to entrust this task to a man who was intimately acquainted with the inner workings of Wall Street than to give the job over to someone who knew the stock market only in theory. This capacity for neat rationalization has always come to the rescue of the President when he has had to explain away prior promises in the face of awkward and stubborn facts.

While the appointment of Mr. Kennedy was well received in Wall Street, neither the finance nor the industrial capitalists were content to let it go at that. They seemingly did not appreciate President Roosevelt's moral efforts on their behalf. They insisted that the restrictions placed upon the securities business were hampering the normal flow of capital funds and retarding recovery. For example, the Durable Goods Industries Committee of the National Association of Manufacturers demanded that the Securities Act be amended and liberalized "so that durable goods industries can immediately secure new and needed capital and permanently reemploy many skilled men heretofore engaged in this work." [77] It is true that capital funds were not moving, but this was not because of the Securities Act. The capital market was stagnant solely because the continued depression was keeping the demand for funds at a minimum. Nevertheless, Mr. Kennedy's commission responded in time to this pressure by "simplifying" its requirements. On January 13, 1935, dispatches from Washington announced:

In a move to speed reopening of the capital market and give impetus to recovery, the Securities and Exchange Commission today issued a simplified form, A2, for registration of securities by established and seasoned corporations. The commission has been working on the new form for the last four months. . . .

Simplification of registration has been accomplished not by wiping out any of the requirements set down in the Securities Act, but by the revision of the forms and regulations issued thereunder, in the shaping of which the act gives the commission a large measure of discretion as to just what information corporations and other issuers must file before being permitted to market securities.

Of course, it was hardly necessary to wipe out any of the requirements of the law in view of the fact that the law itself gave the commission such a large measure of discretion " as to just what information corporations and other issuers must file." The President had promised to put " the burden of telling the whole truth on the seller." But the commission, set up to judge such matters, was steering away from the whole truth and requiring " established and seasoned corporations " to do no more than tell the simplified truth.

Franklin Roosevelt was to favor the money changers in another and no less important way, and for this he was to receive the applause of two large sections of the lower middle class, the farmers and small home owners who were laden with mortgages. During the campaign he had promised to save their homes from foreclosure. At about the same time President Hoover had also reached the conclusion that foreclosure sales would have to be stopped. Franklin Roosevelt intimated that Herbert Hoover was inspired by political considerations. He declared that the home owners " are no longer forgotten, because, in the midst of the campaign, the Federal Administration has finally considered their difficulties." One cannot say whether or to what extent President Hoover had the political campaign in mind. It is conceivable that he hoped to pick up votes by promising relief to home owners.* Yet there was a more urgent reason for taking this step at this time. The inability of the small property owners to meet the service on their indebtedness was beginning to embarrass holders of farm and home mortgages. Many of these were large financial institutions whose collapse might result in a general debacle.

* Nor is it to be supposed, of course, that Franklin Roosevelt was promising the same sort of relief as an inducement to these people *not* to vote for him. He was fishing for votes just as Herbert Hoover was.

The Government had already intervened through the Reconstruction Finance Corporation to save them from their own debts. Now it had to save them from those who were indebted to them.

When Franklin Roosevelt's relief plan was finally brought out, it was found to differ in no essential respect from that of his predecessor. The objectives of both were the same, the motives were identical. Both men were concerned with the deflation in the realty mortgage field and wanted to check it before it became a serious menace to the capital structure as a whole. Both endeavored to do this by underwriting the claims of the creditors. That such relief might simultaneously help the debtors, or a few of them, was obvious, although only incidental to the main purpose. However, Herbert Hoover failed to make much of this opportunity because he lacked his successor's superior talent for turning necessity into political virtue. Franklin Roosevelt had little difficulty in making it appear that while protecting the interests of the money changers, he was really doing the lower middle class an unprecedented favor.

In a special message to Congress on April 13, 1933, he declared that "the broad interests of the nation require that special safeguards should be thrown around home ownership as a guaranty of social and economic stability . . . to protect home owners from inequitable enforced liquidation, in a time of general distress, is a proper concern of the Government." But the bill accompanying this message provided that relief should be extended only with the consent of the mortgage holder. If the debtor was still good for the full amount of the debt, the creditor was privileged to insist upon full payment, even though that might mean "inequitable enforced liquidation." On the other hand, if the debtor was in such straitened circumstances that he could neither meet the service on the mortgage nor through foreclosure fully satisfy the claim, the creditor was lawfully entitled to throw the bad debt upon the Government, for which he received in return tax-exempt bonds guaranteed by the Treasury both as to principal and interest. The Home Owners Loan Corporation then, and only then, refinanced the mortgage and reduced the interest rate to 5 per cent.

The Roosevelt Administration was actually putting up more money to "safeguard" a few hundred thousand home owners and farmers than it was spending directly on the ten to fourteen million jobless workers. Yet it must not be forgotten that the main purpose, despite the President's reference to a social guaranty in his message of April 13, was to guarantee economic stability. The unemployed had only to be fed and sheltered, but in the case of the home owners it was necessary to protect the mortgage system, one of the main columns of capitalism. In this the President may be said to have done well. The money lenders were fully protected, while the home owners were helped only as and when the money changers gave their consent. Thus Franklin Roosevelt proceeded to restore the temple to the ancient truths.*

The battle of the bankers was not entirely a matter of jousting with rhetorical phantoms. Upon one issue the President and the finance capitalists seemed seriously divided. This was

* From June 1, 1933, to October 10, 1934, mortgage loans totaling $1,217,000,000 were granted to farmers by the Farm Credit Administration. Of this amount, according to a reckoning which the FCA has made, 26.3 per cent went to liquidate indebtedness with commercial banks, 12.3 per cent went to insurance companies, 7.1 per cent to joint stock land banks, 3 per cent toward payment of taxes, 40.9 per cent was used to satisfy debts of unclassified creditors, and 4.9 per cent was used to redeem or repurchase land previously foreclosed, etc., while only $66,966,000, or 5.5 per cent, was used for such purposes as the buying of new land and equipment, construction and improvement of buildings and "general agricultural capital." So it can be seen that the money lenders were getting their due, while the farmers, though they received a slight reduction in interest, remained in debt as before.

Nor, incidentally, did this relief plan halt the wave of foreclosures. In the first quarter of 1934 as many as 15,160 farm mortgages were foreclosed, while in the same quarter of 1935 the total went to 16,826. (Washington Post, June 2, 1935.)

the question of providing commercial credits for business as a means of supporting the recovery program. The President intimated that the bankers were deliberately withholding their support. In a message to the American Bankers Association convention on September 5, 1933, he insisted that:

> Loans can and will be made. I want you to know that we rely on your organization for its cooperation in furthering the free flow of credit so essential to business enterprises, whether they be large or small. Only if this is done can employers do their full part in the great recovery program now under way.

It was to the same meeting that the President sent Jesse H. Jones to " present my compliments," which Jones did with his "be smart for once." He harangued the bankers for an hour, trying to convince them that they could adopt more generous credit policies and still remain safely liquid.

The bankers believed they knew better, and they doubtless did. They had been severely burned in the panic only a half year before and they were in no mood, even if sound banking practice had permitted it, to step too far out in front. They were more than dubious about the President's currency policy and, not knowing what might happen to the dollar, they were anxious to avoid undertaking any but the most secure commitments. Moreover, inspection of the banks had tightened up considerably after the panic. The care-free days of the Hoover regime, when Government officials permitted banks to falsify their records by carrying assets on their books at figures higher than prevailing market values, were definitely gone. But most important was the fact that the business situation did not justify the granting of more commercial credit than was then being extended. Sound banking practice requires reasonable assurance of repayment of credits. The applicant for a loan must show orders actually in hand or must give other proof that his prospect of making money on the loan is based on something more substantial than eager hope or personal optimism. What Messrs. Roosevelt and Jones were asking was that the bankers gamble on the success of the NRA program. The bankers had previously promised to do what they could, but they had also declared that " such loans should be granted, of course, only where the credit of the borrowers justifies it, and each loan must be considered on its own merits." [78] In other words, NRA or no NRA, the banks would still lend only on definite business prospects.

But the President seems to have believed that this was another one of those economic laws that could be set aside at will. When the bankers refused the generous support he believed ought to be forthcoming, he not only threatened but tried to put the Government into the commercial banking business in competition with the private houses. In the latter part of August, 1933, he directed the Reconstruction Finance Corporation to consider ways and means of making direct loans to NRA members. This apparently did not have the expected result, for in the following April he was found approving a bill to enable Federal Reserve Banks to make direct loans to any " established industrial or commercial business." In May two other and similar schemes were before Congress, one of which authorized the Reconstruction Finance Corporation to lend $250,000,000 " to promote activity in hard-pressed smaller and medium-sized industries." On June 19 the President signed two of the bills, one putting the RFC and the other the Federal Reserve Banks into the commercial banking business. A total of $580,000,000 was made available by Congress for this purpose.

The Roosevelt effort was bound to fail unless business activity warranted an increase in commercial credit. In that case, of course, the commercial banks could meet the demand. In the first two months of this particular prime-the-pump experiment, however, the Federal Reserve Banks paid out only $298,000 in business loans. By December 12 they had made advances totaling approximately $11,000,000 and had agreed to make other loans of the same character in the amount of $7,000,000. The RFC did no better. By December 1 it had authorized commercial loans in the sum of $23,666,100; but of this amount $1,938,700 had been withdrawn or canceled, $17,471,018 remained at the call of borrowers, and only $4,256,000 had actually been distributed.[79]

In the meantime the commercial banks were fully satisfying all the real needs of business. Their "loans to others" ran into the billions of dollars. In seven months of 1934, for example, the banks in the Chicago Reserve district alone made "loans to others" totaling $629,000,000.[80] This did not represent an increase in commercial credits outstanding, for simultaneously other loans were being paid as they fell due. What it meant was that practically all of the commercial banking business was going to the regular banks as usual.

Indeed, the vaults of these institutions were literally choking with funds. The total deposits of all the Federal Reserve member banks in the country increased from $23,646,000,000 in December, 1933, to $28,538,000,000 in the following December.[81] Nor can it be held that the banks did not want to lend this money. The average banker would much rather take the 4 to 6 per cent he would ordinarily get from business loans than put his money into Government bonds yielding only 2¾ to 3 per cent or into other paper yielding even less. But the demand for business loans seemingly would not expand despite the wish-thinking of the President and other politicians in Washington. Instead it even decreased in 1934. The total of "loans to others" fell from $11,315,000,000 in December, 1933, to $10,486,000,000 in December, 1934.[82] Even so, the outstanding $10,000,000,000 in commercial loans by private banks made rather an impressive showing compared with the approximately $20,000,000 President Roosevelt's rival Government banks had outstanding at that time.

Toward the end of 1934 Franklin Roosevelt was apparently beginning to tire of his shadow-boxing with the money changers. But his followers in Congress were still under the impression that all that was needed to revive business was to lend money. Several bills to this end were prepared for the 1935 session of Congress. One would have created a new Government credit agency and would have authorized it to make loans up to a total amount of $1,000,000,000, the loans to be secured by " mortgages, warehouse receipts, shipping documents," or " other evidences of probability of repayment of the loan when due." Needless to say the commercial banks are always ready to make advances upon equally good security. Another measure, written by Marriner S. Eccles, President Roosevelt's " liberal " Governor of the Federal Reserve Board, would have modified the rules regarding collateral required to secure commercial loans. This bill would also have extended the Government's control over the credit policies of the Federal Reserve System, supposedly on the theory that if politicians instead of bankers were to exercise this control, business men would be found more eager to borrow to finance business prospects that did not exist, or existed only in the imagination of the Government. But the President's heart was obviously no longer in the job. He casually approved one or two of these proposals, but he did not get out and fight for them.

More pertinent evidence of his change in heart came during the convention of the American Bankers Association in Washington in October, 1934. It was at this meeting that he arranged a public reconciliation with the bankers. After a private peace conference in the White House, he addressed the convention on October 24. He could not quite divest himself of his crusading pose, but instead of lecturing the delegates as he had done in his message to the Chicago convention of the bankers the year before, instead of holding them to answer for the possible failure of his recovery program, he praised them highly and asked only that they join with him in a cooperative effort to restore prosperity. The bankers, speaking through Jackson E. Reynolds of New York, repaid him in kind. Reynolds declared that for his " service to us, and through us to our country, he deserves our sympathetic and helpful response."

The " country " bankers at the convention, who far outnumbered the powerful New York delegates, sought to spoil the pre-arranged love feast. They were under the impression, as were most Americans at the time, that Franklin Roosevelt really meant to drive out the money changers. One after another these provincial delegates arose to criticize or denounce him and his works. But the finance capitalists from New York had little difficulty in suppressing the revolt. They could afford to take a magnanimous stand in dealing with the President. They knew that they were still in control of the economic machinery of the country. They knew, too, that despite his extraordinary expenditures on unemployment and other forms of relief, which they were willing to agree was a necessary evil, and despite his gestures of defiance and opposition, he was not really bent on disturbing their control.

✵ 10 ✵

FOOLS' LUCK

∾

IN September, 1931, it will be recalled, Franklin Roosevelt had taken President Hoover severely to task for having borrowed money to meet the Federal deficit. He went on to say:

I don't believe in banking on fools' luck as applied to the public finances in spite of the fact that it has come to the rescue of some communities and some divisions of government in this nation in times past. . . . This depression is today's problem . . . we cannot and must not borrow against the future to meet it. We must share now out of what we have, not out of what we expect to have some day in the future. We must distribute fairly among those who are able to pay, the burden of aiding those who cannot exist without help. The funds that we must have for unemployment relief should be raised by the speediest possible method of current taxation that will result in such an equitable assessment.

Of course, Franklin Roosevelt, then Governor of New York, was under constitutional compulsion to balance the State budget. Moreover, it must have seemed politically expedient for him to stress his own balanced budget as a contrast to the growing Federal deficit under Herbert Hoover, against whom in all likelihood he would soon be contending for election to the presidency. Doubtless his attitude toward the budget problem was not solely a matter of expediency. It was upon careful and orthodox financial management that the family fortune had been built. And it is certain that the accounts at Hyde Park were always kept in good order. He would have been untrue to his heritage and early training had he taken any other attitude.

Again and again during the 1932 campaign he emphasized his faith in orthodox public financing. The Democratic platform, which he accepted " 100 per cent," called for " maintenance of the national credit by a Federal budget annually balanced on the basis of accurate executive estimates within revenues, raised by a system of taxation levied on the principle of ability to pay." In his Pittsburgh speech of October 19 he again vigorously denounced the Hoover fiscal policies. He condemned Herbert Hoover for not taking immediate action to stem the crisis. " Although six weeks had elapsed since the worst economic crash in history," he said, " the Federal budget of December, 1929, did not even refer to it." * Thereafter, he asserted, the Hoover Administration seemed merely to be drifting along until revenues had fallen more than a billion dollars behind expenditures. And then, " instead of financing the billion-dollar deficit in the regular way, our government simply absorbed that much of the lending capacity of the banks, and, by so much, impaired the credit available for business." † He summed up his criticism in the following words:

* Franklin Roosevelt himself had been woefully slow in awakening to the significance and extent of the crisis. In his own roseate report on New York State finances in January, 1930, ten weeks after the Wall Street collapse, he took no more cognizance of "the worst economic crash in history" than President Hoover had done.

† The inference here is that business was deprived of credit it might otherwise have obtained. This was by no means true. There was still more than enough credit available for business. The bankers would have been only too happy to put their idle funds to work in business, had this been feasible, for the returns from commercial loans are always higher than the yields to be had from Government bonds. But business prospects did not justify an expansion of commercial credit. It was just about this time that the Hoover Administration sought through the open-market operations of the Federal Reserve Banks to pump an additional billion dollars of credit into business channels. It was no more successful in this experiment than the Roosevelt Administration was in its subsequent efforts to compel the banks to expand commercial credit or in any of its attempts to " prime the pump " by other and no less artificial methods.

Our Federal extravagance and improvidence bears a double evil; first, our people and our business cannot carry its excessive burdens of taxation; second, our credit structure is impaired by the unorthodox Federal financing made necessary by the unprecedented magnitude of these deficits. . . .

All this is highly undesirable and wholly unnecessary. It arises from one cause only, and that is the unbalanced budget and the continued failure of this administration to take effective steps to balance it. If that budget had been fully and honestly balanced in 1930, as it could have been, some of the 1931 collapse would have been avoided. Even if it had been balanced in 1931, as it could have been, much of the extreme dip in 1932 would have been obviated. . . .

Would it not be infinitely better to clear this whole subject of obscurity — to present the facts squarely to the Congress and the people of the United States and secure the one sound foundation of permanent economic recovery — a complete and honest balance of the Federal budget?

It must be added that Franklin Roosevelt recognized the probability that the demand for unemployment relief would continue for some time. He said that "if starvation and dire need on the part of any of our citizens makes necessary the appropriation of additional funds which would keep the budget out of balance, I shall not hesitate to tell the American people the full truth and recommend to them the expenditure of this additional amount." He also said, elsewhere in the same speech, that "if men or women or children are starving in the United States, I regard it as a positive duty of government *to raise by taxes* whatever sum may be necessary to keep them from starvation."

President Roosevelt began by adopting an economy program the like of which Washington had never experienced. This was to carry out his Pittsburgh pledge of a 25 per cent reduction in governmental costs. Within five weeks of his taking office it was reported that he had reduced, or soon would reduce, benefits to the war veterans by about $400,-

000,000 annually, would trim the army and navy budgets by more than $125,000,000, would save as much as $250,000,000 through reorganization of existing departments and bureaus, and would subtract another $100,000,000 a year by cutting the pay of Federal employees by 15 per cent.* The total reduction in annual expenditures would come to no less than $1,020,000,000, which fully met his economy promise.

This was an impressive beginning. It helped to restore confidence in the business community. As it turned out, however, much of this economy was illusory and more of it was to fall by the wayside before the end of the first two years. It is to be doubted that anything like $250,000,000 was saved as the result of "department reorganization." In fact, President Roosevelt later admitted that little could be done in that direction.[83] And the small sum that was ultimately saved was more than offset by the multitude of new agencies and bureaus created by the President and financed largely out of "emergency" funds. In addition, the Federal pay cut and a part of the reduction in veterans' benefits were restored, while the army and navy were not only given about $400,000,000 of public-works money to make up for the $125,000,000 they were supposed to have lost from their regular budgets, but in 1935 they had their direct appropriations boosted beyond anything they had received before in peace time.

But even while these initial economies were reaching the front pages of the newspapers, the President and his advisers were planning vast "emergency" expenditures, which, it was announced, "may reach $8,000,000,000." [84] Thus the Roosevelt economies, actual or merely advertised, quickly faded into insignificance. And once this spending began the deficit naturally expanded beyond even the "unprecedented magnitude" that Franklin Roosevelt had found so "highly unde-

* In a campaign speech in Boston Franklin Roosevelt had urged the employers to provide better living standards for their help by increasing their pay. He had emphatically added that "government must set an example in the case of its own employees."

sirable and wholly unnecessary " in October, 1932. At the
close of the fiscal year 1932–33, the last year of the Hoover
Administration, but including also the first four months of
the Roosevelt regime, the total deficit stood at $5,799,000,000.
The following year it jumped to $9,429,000,000, and in 1935
to $13,004,000,000. The President himself forecast a further
loss of $4,528,000,000 in the succeeding fiscal year, which
would have brought the total deficit on June 30, 1936, to no
less than $17,532,000,000.

There were two ways in which the deficit could be financed.
The cost could be shared "now out of what we have," as
Franklin Roosevelt had previously insisted it should be; or it
could be taken out of "what we expect to have some day in
the future." That is, it could be financed by taxation or by
borrowing. At the President's direction a few minor and for
the most part temporary taxes were voted early in his regime,
but the revenues thus produced were far from enough to
bridge the ever widening gap. Not once during his first two
years in office did he propose a general increase in income,
estate or corporation taxes. True, in January, 1933, he had
agreed with Democratic leaders in Congress to support a program looking toward a broadening of the income-tax base and
toward an increase in the normal rates.[85] But this program
came to naught. Later, when Senator La Follette offered a
similar proposal as an amendment to a then pending tax bill,
the President's aides in the Senate moved quickly to kill it.* [86]
Not until virtually the whole of his recovery program had
collapsed did he finally suggest (in the summer of 1935) that
Congress increase tax rates to meet the deficit.

Through the first two years he continued to borrow from
the banks as Herbert Hoover had done. He explained to the

* The New York *Times* reported from Washington that "in rejecting
the La Follette amendment for higher income taxes, the Senate accepted
the assurances of Chairman Harrison of the Finance Committee that the
extra revenue sought thereby was not needed for President Roosevelt's
fiscal program."

press on March 24, 1933, that he expected to " end the next fiscal year with a balanced budget on *ordinary* government expenses " — which was to be done by the simple expedient of keeping two sets of books, one for the regular budget, the other for "emergency " expenses. He took the position, said the dispatches from Washington, that "some of the expenditures to be made to aid farmers and construct public buildings and for reforestation should be considered permanent improvements of benefit to the future, and as such . . . can be amortized without saddling the debt on the present generation of taxpayers."

No genuine effort was made, or probably could be made, to break down the spending of the Roosevelt Administration into its two general categories — " normal " and " emergency." Except in the case of agencies authorized to do their own borrowing, it was not possible to say just which expenditures came out of current income and which were financed by loans. Nothing resembling a " capital budget " was set up. The Treasury simply borrowed as it needed funds, that is, borrowed to meet the whole of the deficit without stopping to draw any distinction between " normal " or " emergency " issues. It deviated not in the slightest from the course it had been following under the Hoover Administration. As a result, the gross public debt, which stood at $19,487,000,000 on June 30, 1932, and at $22,537,000,000 a year later, had by December 31, 1934, climbed to $28,478,664,000, while President Roosevelt predicted in his 1935 budget message that it would go to $34,-239,000,000 by the end of the fiscal year 1935–36. This would put it nine billion dollars above the war-time peak of $25,315,-000,000.

At Pittsburgh Franklin Roosevelt had said that he would permit but a single exception to his promise to maintain " a complete and honest balance of the Federal budget," and that would be in the event that "starvation and dire need on the part of any of our citizens makes necessary the appropriation of additional funds which would keep the budget out of balance." However, not all of his extra-budgetary spending went into direct relief of the starving and needy. A large part went into interest charges, contractors' fees, manufacturers' profits and the like. In some instances no doubt these charges were essential to the permanent improvements he had in mind; but in other instances, as in the case of the CWA and most of the work-relief projects, there were few improvements of positive or enduring social value. In such cases capitalist charges ate up anywhere from 30 to 70 per cent of the relief money that might otherwise have gone to the unemployed. Another part, notably that poured into agriculture and business by various Government agencies to check the deflation, support the debt structure and safeguard the profit mechanism, might be considered relief of a sort, but it was hardly designed to aid the starving. Another part went to finance some of the Roosevelt experiments such as the subsistence homesteads and the Tennessee Valley scheme, while a number of minor expense items, ordinarily paid for out of current income, were met by the " emergency " funds.

Some members of the Roosevelt Administration held that generous Government spending was just what was needed to restore prosperity. The more outspoken opponents of this school, including Lewis Douglas and O. M. W. Sprague, soon found that they were fighting a losing battle and retired, while the advocates of spending, mainly Harold L. Ickes and Harry Hopkins, not only remained but were reenforced by the appointment of Marriner S. Eccles to the governorship of the Federal Reserve Board. Governor Eccles was a frank champion of the theory that an unbalanced budget is essential to recovery. It was reported that President Roosevelt himself had espoused the cause of the spenders after a conference with Maynard Keynes, the British economist. Keynes held that " if America spends approximately $400,000,000 a month from now until recovery sets in, it makes no difference how or for what purpose the Government spends its money, and it makes no difference how large the national debt will be when recovery finally does set in." [87] Six months after his visit to the White House the Administration brought out its plan to spend the sum of $4,880,000,000 for " relief " during the next fiscal year. This works out at the rate of $400,000,000 a month.

While the advocates of " recovery by spending " were given a fairly free hand in putting their theory to the test, there is no evidence that the President, in the beginning at any rate, was enthusiastic about the idea. In Albany he had favored work relief as against the hated dole, not as an instrument of recovery, but to save the morale of the workers. He carried this sentiment with him into the White House. In his 1935 message, in which he outlined his $4,880,000,000 spending program, he talked at length of the moral need of providing work for the jobless. He said that " continued dependence upon relief induces a spiritual and moral disintegration fundamentally destructive to the national fiber. To dole out relief in this way is to administer a narcotic, a subtle destroyer of the human spirit. It is inimical to the dictates of sound policy. It is in violation of the traditions of America. Work must be found for ablebodied but destitute workers."

But nowhere was there a suggestion that he looked upon this contemplated spending as offering a certain road to recovery. His other recovery experiments having failed to yield the anticipated results, it may be that he was willing to give the theory a wider test than it had theretofore received. His adoption of the $400,000,000-a-month formula would suggest as much. Yet he was evidently not willing to commit himself publicly to the theory. In his bonus-veto message, indeed, he seemed to take a firm stand against the notion that purposeless public spending holds the magic key to prosperity.*

* Public spending offers, of course, no solution of the basic problem of capitalism. It creates no new wealth, no new goods to be exchanged in the market at a profit. It creates no new or permanent markets, but at best

He sought in other ways to reassure the capitalist-entrepreneur class. In his 1934 budget message he said that "we should plan to have a definitely balanced budget for the third year of recovery (1935–36) and from that time on seek a continuing reduction of the national debt." In his 1935 budget message he frankly acknowledged "that we have not yet reached a point at which a complete balance of the budget can be obtained"; but he insisted that "except for expenditures to give work to the unemployed . . . every current expenditure of whatever nature will be fully covered by our estimates of current receipts. Such deficit as occurs will be due solely to this cause, and it may be expected to decline as rapidly as private industry is able to reemploy those who now are without work." He added that "I do not consider it advisable at this time to propose any new or additional taxes for the fiscal year 1936." And in discussing his work-relief program in his annual message three days before he said: "Preference should be given to those projects which are self-liquidating in the sense that there is a reasonable expectation that the government will get its money back at some future time."

Obviously he was living in the hope that prosperity would soon be restored. Although the more timid-minded capitalists could only see future taxes piling up as the government spending went on, from the standpoint of their own best interests the President was undoubtedly following the wisest course. If he were to stop spending and lending, consumption would

---

represents no more than a temporary transfer of buying power from one class to another. As an artificial stimulant to domestic buying, its effect lasts only so long as the spending goes on. Moreover, spending of this nature is specifically designed to inflate rather than deflate prices and it results in an enlargement rather than a reduction of the debt structure, thereby prolonging and intensifying two of the chief causes of capitalist depression. True, public spending adds to public and not to private debt, but the economic effect is the same, for all capital claims must be met out of productive capital. Inevitably, therefore, the spending tends to increase the pressure on the rate of profit and so to prolong the stagnation in the capital market.

quickly decline and it is conceivable that the deflation would set in again. Business and the creditor class would be among the first to be hurt. Besides, he was distributing his largess judiciously. Business, industry and the banks, as well as the farmers and the jobless, were direct beneficiaries. Nor did he pass the cost of this charity on immediately to the capitalist-entrepreneur class in the form of higher taxes. By borrowing instead of taxing, incidentally, he also gave the banks a chance to put some of their idle funds to work at a modest profit. Considering all of the objective factors in the situation, the capitalist-entrepreneur class would seem to have had little real cause for complaint.

It was possible, of course, that the promised prosperity might not appear, that the rate of profit might remain depressed even while industrial activity was returning to " normal." It was possible, too, that unemployment might continue upon a large scale because of technological improvements or for other reasons. In either event the Government unquestionably would have to continue spending. If this went on until the idle funds in the banks were entirely absorbed and the bond market began to break, the Government's credit would be endangered. It would then have to resort to the printing press to pay its bills. While this possibility appeared to be still quite remote in the summer of 1935, for the banks at that time were heavily laden with unemployed deposits which they were glad to lend to the Government, the Roosevelt Administration nevertheless sought to prepare itself against the day when this fount of plenty should be exhausted.

Through the Eccles plan it stood ready to take over virtually complete control of the Federal Reserve Banks — as much control as though it actually owned the banks, according to Governor Eccles — and so to place itself in a position to command the Reserve Banks to buy its bonds at any time and whatever the state of the bond market and to pay for them with their own notes. That would be printing-press inflation and nothing else. It would doubtless help to wipe out many of the capital claims now clogging the productive machinery of capitalism. It would also reduce costs by deflating real wages still further. It would expedite the transfer of tangible property holdings to the capitalist class, for no other class would be in a position to buy the property of firms and individuals forced into bankruptcy by inflation. But the basic problem of capitalism would remain unsolved. German capitalism went on a wild printing-press spree after the World War. Ten years later it had to resort to the most brutal and violent tactics of fascism to save itself from a proletarian revolution.

In his message to Congress of June 19, 1935, the President appeared to be taking a step away from disastrous inflation and toward a balanced budget. But upon examination it is revealed that this appearance was misleading. He did not propose that public spending be limited. He did not suggest that the budget be brought into balance. He went no further than to " strongly urge that the proceeds " of the new inheritance, succession and legacy tax he was asking for " be specifically segregated and applied, as they accrue, to the reduction of the national debt." He added that " by so doing we shall progressively lighten the tax burden of the average taxpayer, and, incidentally, assist in our approach to a balanced budget."

Since the President did not include them among the taxes to be applied to reduction of the national debt, it may be presumed that the other increases he proposed could justifiably be used as the basis for new spending. However, even if all of the new taxes were to be included, the total would hardly make a dent either in the budgetary deficit or the public debt. The schedules adopted call for an excess-profits tax (which the President had not asked for) and a general increase in surtaxes on incomes above $50,000. Altogether, it was estimated, the new taxes would yield no more than a total of $250,000,000 annually. With the deficit growing at the rate of $3,500,000,-000 a year and with no limitation upon spending in sight, it can readily be seen that the increased revenues would not begin to keep pace with the deficit and the national debt. Since, moreover, the tax plan would take up to 79 per cent of the biggest incomes and up to 70 per cent of the largest estates (to say nothing of State taxes and other charges upon incomes and legacies), it is apparent that even if the rates were raised higher little more than $250,000,000 a year could be hoped for.

It could not have been the real purpose of the Roosevelt proposals, therefore, to use higher taxes as a means of balancing the budget and averting inflation. Nor, as has been noted above, could this plan be used to break or limit the power of finance capitalism. The existing financial and corporate combinations would not be disturbed. The shares of almost all of the larger banking institutions and industrial corporations are widely held. In some instances — for example, in the case of the American Telephone and Telegraph — no individual holds more than 1 per cent of the shares. Even if the largest single stockholder were to die and his holdings had to be dumped on the market to meet the Federal death tax, the affairs of the corporation would not be affected in the slightest.

A somewhat heavier burden would fall on family units such as the Ford Company, but family units are rare among the giant corporations of the country. Moreover, if Henry Ford were to die, his heirs would be given a number of years in which to pay the death tax. In the meantime they would have several ways of raising the necessary funds. They could introduce still more wage-saving machinery into the Ford plants. They could cut their variable costs, i.e., wages. They could raise the prices of their products, though, of course, they could not go very far in that direction without playing into the hands of their competitors, General Motors. But let us suppose that they failed of their objective and the Ford Company had to be sold. Who would buy it? Who, indeed, but the finance monopolists standing behind General Motors, or perhaps some rival group of finance capitalists. No one else would have the means of undertaking such an extensive transaction. Obviously, the Ford Company could be scrapped, but that would simply give General Motors practically complete control of the automobile industry.

Lesser family units would fare worse, for they have not the many resources that are available to the Ford family. The pressure of even a small death tax, say 25 per cent, would be enough in most instances to send these companies into bankruptcy, for a large majority of them, to judge by the Treasury Department's corporation-tax returns, have for years been earning little or no profit. When a small company is wiped out, its business does not disappear. Instead it is taken over by the larger and stronger survivors in the field. To the extent, therefore, that the Roosevelt death tax proved a drain upon these intermediate enterprises, it would tend to strengthen monopolism.

Nevertheless, the President took the opposite view in his message of June 19. He held that the existing taxation system operated " to the unfair advantage of the few." He declared that " social unrest and a deepening sense of unfairness are dangers to our national life which we must minimize by rigorous methods." He suggested that his proposals would tend to " prevent an unjust concentration of wealth and economic power " and would, indeed, constitute " a very sound policy of encouraging a wider distribution of wealth." It should be clear, however, that no real or substantial redistribution of wealth would be effected. The causes of the present maldistribution would not be touched. Secondly, while the Roosevelt plan might embarrass and annoy and possibly impoverish a few wealthy individuals, it would add practically nothing to the wealth of the remainder of the population. The sum of $250,000,000 spread over the thirty million families of the country would give each family about $8.33 a year. If distributed among the 20,000,000 persons on relief, it would give each of these public wards $12.50. If spent wholly upon the ten million jobless, it would amount to $25 per unemployed worker per year.

The real, though unstated, purpose of the Roosevelt message was to offset the gains being made by Huey Long and other reactionary demagogues of the petit-bourgeois right who were advocating share-the-wealth schemes on their own account and so were making deep inroads among the original followers of the President who had not been helped by his reform program. His message of June 19 seemed not only to steal the thunder but to appropriate the very language of Huey Long. Like the Senator from Louisiana, the President promised to touch only the very richest people. He went even so far as to imply, through an illustration he presented, that the increase in taxes "upon very great individual net incomes" he was proposing would apply only to persons with incomes in excess of $1,000,000 a year. Huey Long was also promising that under his scheme only those persons who were making more than $1,000,000 a year would have to share their wealth. Whether the President's political gesture would win the support of the Long adherents remained to be seen. It is worth noting, however, that Huey Long was promising his followers a "guaranteed" income of $2,500 a year. The unguaranteed $8.33 a year under the Roosevelt scheme could hardly be considered an attractive counter-offer. To be sure, the limitations of the profit system would never permit Huey Long to make good his promise — it would cost $75,000,000,000 a year — but most of his followers might not understand that.

In any case, whether the President brought his plan forward with real sincerity or merely as a political gesture, it is clear that his plan would not and could not achieve any of its avowed objectives. It would not result in a balanced and more equitable economy. It would not even balance the budget. The President would have to continue to bank on that fools' luck he had once so strongly denounced.

✲ I I ✲

A KISS FOR CINDERELLA

⟿

FRANKLIN ROOSEVELT remained hopeful, if not always so sweet of temper, in the face of these stubborn realities. He was convinced that soon or late the desired recovery would somehow be produced. If he was not to restore prosperity by destruction, nor yet by spending, there were certainly other ways that could be tried.

Yet he was also to admit, though only by reluctant implication, that even if his experiments were to meet with success, there would be a vast surplus population still to be cared for. He was to confess, by implication again, that with all the good will and all the earnest planning of which its most progressive and enlightened advocates are capable, capitalism cannot solve its basic problem, cannot provide for anything like an equitable distribution of the wealth produced among those who produce it, cannot, indeed, meet even the simplest wants of many of its workers. Why else would there arise a demand for " economic security "? Why else would President Roosevelt seek to have the state guarantee at least a bare livelihood for a large number of its citizens?

Not that Franklin Roosevelt ever saw the problem in this light. To him it was a moral rather than an economic problem. He was originally " sold," as he has said, on old-age " pensions " by the touching sight of the suffering of a family of old neighbors. He quite obviously did not stop to consider why the existing industrial system was accustomed to discard workers

251

still in their prime as being " too old," or why it was becoming increasingly difficult for workers to put away a part of their earnings against old age. His attitude was ever that of the kindly and somewhat sentimental lord of the manor. One could not imagine him beating his horse. No more could one picture him starving one of his employees at Hyde Park or Warm Springs or turning a servant out to fend for himself without good cause. And it is just in this benevolent manner that he looked upon the unfortunate servants of industry who are turned out to shift for themselves for reasons beyond their control.

As Governor of New York, he sponsored a mild program of social reforms, though his program was far behind that which had already been put into effect years before in Prussia and England and was not as advanced as that advocated by the Progressives in his own country in 1912. His old-age pensions plan was at best no more than a modification of the existing pauper-relief law. And he was not to begin talking of unemployment insurance until after the depression had set in, and then he was to consider it a matter of no particular urgency.

In a special message to Congress on June 8, 1934, he declared:

This security for the individual and the family concerns itself primarily with three factors. People want decent homes to live in; they want to locate them where they can engage in productive work; and they want some safeguard against misfortunes which cannot be wholly eliminated in this man-made world of ours. . . .

The third factor relates to security against the hazards and vicissitudes of life. Fear and worry based on unknown danger contribute to social unrest and economic demoralization. . . .

Next winter we may well undertake the great task of furthering the security of the citizen and his family through social insurance.

This is not an untried experiment. Lessons of experience are available from States, from industries and from many nations of the civilized world. The various types of social insurance are interrelated; and I think it is difficult to attempt to solve them piecemeal. Hence, I am looking for a sound means which I can recommend to provide at once security against several of the great disturbing factors in life — especially those which relate to unemployment and old age. . . .

These three great objectives — the security of the home, the security of livelihood and the security of social insurance — are, it seems to me, a minimum of the promise that we can offer to the American people. They constitute a right which belongs to every individual and every family willing to work. They are the essential fulfillment of measures already taken toward relief, recovery and reconstruction.

This seeking of a greater measure of welfare and happiness does not indicate a change in values. It is rather a return to values lost in the course of our economic development and expansion.

The argument here is wholly moral both in tone and in basis. The President stressed the need of security as a means of preserving social morality, of preventing " social unrest and economic demoralization." He spoke of " rights " and " values." Those alone are entitled to these rights and values who are " willing to work." He pointed to his social-security program as an " essential fulfillment of measures already taken toward relief, recovery and reconstruction." In other words, even with the attainment of recovery and reconstruction, even when the Roosevelt economic reforms had triumphed, the workers would still be subject to the hazards of unemployment and want. To guard against this the President proposed the adoption of measures having nothing to do with the normal functioning of the economic system, but which were of a purely moral character.

Nor did he stop anywhere to explain why or how the " values " he prizes so highly had been " lost in the course of our economic development and expansion." He did not bother about causes. He merely suggested that whereas " security was attained in the earlier days through the interdependence of members of families upon each other and of the families within a small community upon each other," today "the complexities of great communities and of organized industry make less real these simple means of security." But why has this happened? Why has Hyde Park been thus betrayed? Why has "organized industry" made "less real these simple means of security"? Franklin Roosevelt was sure, at least, that the fault did not lie with the profit economy. Elsewhere in the same message he declared:

Ample scope is left for the exercise of private initiative. In fact, in the process of recovery, I am greatly hoping that repeated promises that private investment and private initiative to relieve the government in the immediate future of much of the burden it has assumed will be fulfilled. We have not imposed undue restrictions upon business. We have not opposed the incentive of reasonable and legitimate private profit. We have sought rather to enable certain aspects of business to regain the confidence of the public. We have sought to put forward the rule of fair play in finance and industry.

The cost of social security would have to come out of income, that is, out of profits and wages. If the former were levied upon, the rate of profit would suffer. This would not follow, however, if the cost were to be taken entirely out of wages. Living standards would fall, for the gainfully employed workers would be sharing their income with the jobless and the destitute. But the total wage income would be unchanged and buying power would in the aggregate remain the same. Thus, from the standpoint of the profit system it would seem advisable to throw as much of the burden as possible upon the wage-earners. President Roosevelt was to move far in that direction.

To help draw up his program he called to Washington a number of distinguished social reformers, welfare workers, economists and other experts. These advisers were all without exception committed to the existing social order. They would recommend nothing likely to jeopardize that order, though they might seek to have the cost distributed equitably between profits and wages. Eventually they drew up a 30,000-word report, which was essentially conservative, but which recommended that the social-security program be financed largely by means of higher income taxes and inheritance taxes. The President had previously declared, however, that " we must not allow this type of insurance to become a dole through the mingling of insurance and relief. It is not charity. It must be financed by contributions, not taxes." [88] So he simply ignored the recommendations of the experts and allowed his political subordinates to prepare a bill guaranteed to result in less pressure either directly or through taxation upon the rate of profit. The measure was subsequently enacted into law without substantial change.

The bill had three main sections. That purporting to deal with unemployment insurance in fact did nothing more than invite the State Governments to set up insurance systems on their own account. It also left to the States the question of dividing the costs as between employers and employees. However, it was stipulated that all payments into a State insurance fund be turned over promptly to the Secretary of the Treasury for safe-keeping. He in his turn was to be required to invest this money in Federal Government bonds or in other securities guaranteed both as to principal and interest by the Federal Government. In addition, a 3 per cent tax would be levied against the pay rolls of all employers with an average of ten or more full or part-time employees. But the revenues from this tax would not be applied in any way toward unemployment insurance. Instead such revenues would pass directly into the general fund of the Treasury. It would appear that this section of the bill was conceived mainly as a new method of meeting the Federal deficit rather than as a means of caring for the jobless.

However, employers in States that created insurance systems would be permitted to deduct from their Federal tax all amounts paid into a State insurance fund up to 90 per cent of the Federal tax. It was supposed that this would inspire employers to support unemployment-insurance legislation in their States on the ground that they would rather help their employees in this manner than pay a penalty tax to the Federal Treasury. The flaw in this reasoning is that the employer would be required in any case to pay at least 3 per cent no matter what his State Government did about insurance. If the State adopted no plan at all, or levied an insurance tax upon him of less than 3 per cent, he would still have to make up the difference in his payments to the Federal Government. And there would always be a danger that the State tax might be higher. It would be cheaper, simpler and less hazardous for him to pay the Treasury its 3 per cent and let it go at that. As the *New Republic* has suggested, " he is then saved the trouble of wrestling with two sets of taxes and the annoyance of keeping extra books and of being visited by extra sets of inspectors," while " he also avoids the risk that his State, once it has set up unemployment insurance, may increase the rate." [89]

A second section of the bill provided for " old-age assistance." Here again effective action was left to the States, the Federal Government merely promising to help as and when the States took proper action. It agreed to match, dollar for dollar, payments made to aged persons by the States up to a maximum of $15 a month for any one beneficiary. This would tend to limit to $30 a month the amount any one person would receive. Only those persons 65 years of age or older who could prove that they were without other means of maintaining " a reasonable subsistence compatible with decency and health " would be eligible to receive such benefits. This was not insurance, of course, but pauper relief. It bore a striking resemblance to the New York " old-age pensions " plan adopted under Governor Roosevelt in 1930 and which President Roosevelt in 1934 regarded as still "the most liberal in the country." [90]

Under the third major section of the bill pauper relief would within seven years or so give way to a system of pensions financed out of contributions from employers and workers alike. Only in this one instance was anything even remotely approaching social insurance on a national scale provided for. Contributions were to begin at once with a view to building up a reserve fund, but the payment of pensions would not begin until the year 1942. No pensioner would be entitled to more than $85 a month, but to earn this maximum he would have had to be employed steadily from the age of 20 to the retirement age of 65 at an average wage or salary of $250 a month, out of which he would have made regular contributions to the pension fund. Since the average earnings of American workers are hardly more than $100 a month, it is readily seen that few workers would be eligible for a maximum pension. It has been estimated that most of them, if the plan were to work out as anticipated, would get between $40 and $50 a month and then only after having been steadily employed for a period of 35 to 40 years. But a little arithmetic would show that the average pension would probably be less than $30 a month.

It is only by refraining from being too meticulous about definitions that this pension plan can be called *social* insurance. The state would contribute nothing except its services as bookkeeper. While half the cost would come ostensibly out of profit income, this half would in the last analysis come largely out of wage income. There are occasional employers making comfortable profits who might, out of the goodness of their hearts, willingly pay their share out of their own pockets. But the average employer would not voluntarily meet this cost himself. He would seek to pass it on either indirectly to the wage-earners, i.e., consumers, in the form of higher prices, or directly in the form of lower wages.

The remaining half of the cost would come straight out of the current income of the working class. It would, in effect, constitute compulsory saving. Since, however, the workers on the whole do not earn enough to enable them to lay away money against old age — a fact to which even conservative economists such as Irving Fisher have subscribed — it is difficult to understand how compulsory saving could be made to overcome this deficiency. It could be done if real wage income were to be increased, but otherwise only by lowering the already low living standards of the mass of the workers. That was precisely what the Roosevelt pension plan envisaged. Instead of being *social* insurance, it was essentially a scheme to compel the workers to insure themselves at the expense of their own living standards.

No doubt the Roosevelt program seemed daringly radical in the light of American history, but it was certainly a timid proposal compared with the existing need. It could hardly be held that the objective economic situation did not justify a bolder attack. If the President needed factual support, visible evidence of widespread want, he had only to look about him. If he needed the support of public opinion, he had only to study the Congressional elections of 1934, in which the lower classes had overwhelmingly and unmistakably expressed themselves in favor of further Government spending and further Government intervention on behalf of the victims of modern capitalism. These victims had his sympathy without question, but he dared not go too far in trying to help them.

To his mind, moreover, social insurance was not enough, no matter who paid the bill. There would still be danger in enforced idleness. Work was the only proper solution. And there was plenty of work to be done. His virile imagination roamed the national landscape and conjured up visions of vast reclamation projects. There were great stretches of submarginal farm lands to be taken out of production and turned into forests. There were deserts to be irrigated and made to bloom. There was an immeasurable amount of water power to be harnessed. There were natural resources crying out for intelligent social utilization. And there were countless workers living in enforced idleness in the congested industrial centers who had only to be moved elsewhere to bring these worthy projects into being.

Redistribution of the population had early been one of the chief objectives of his social philosophy. When he was Governor of New York, he had discussed this idea in newspaper interviews, though not very lucidly. He had urged the State Assembly to " adopt a farreaching policy of land utilization and of population distribution," though he confessed that " we cannot tell, until we try to find out, how many urban families in this State would be glad to return to the smaller communities even with the full understanding that in so doing they would in all probability never become millionaires." [91] He returned to the theme in his campaign speeches and in his inaugural address.

In his social-security message to Congress on June 8, 1934, he declared:

People want decent homes to live in; they want to locate them where they can engage in productive work . . . economic circumstances and the forces of nature dictate the need of constant thought as to the means by which a wise government may help the necessary readjustment of the population. We cannot fail to act when hundreds of thousands of families live where there is no reasonable prospect of a living in the years to come. This is especially a national problem. Unlike most of the leading nations of the world, we have so far failed to create a national policy for the development of our land and water resources and for their better use by those people who cannot make a living in their present positions. Only thus can we permanently eliminate many millions of people from the relief rolls on which their names are now found.

The task the President was setting for himself was no petty one. How many families now " live where there is no reasonable prospect of a living in the years to come "? It is hard to say. The number of permanently unemployed, not including agricultural workers, has been variously estimated at between four and ten million. Most authorities, including some in the pay of the Roosevelt Administration, have placed the total in the neighborhood of five or six millions. Before the crash there were at least three million, perhaps four million, jobless in the country, despite the fabulous prosperity of that period. Let us presume that there are no fewer than three million workers " who cannot make a living in their present positions."

To these must be added probably another three million farmers — owners, tenants, share-croppers, hired hands, including the more than 300,000 share-croppers who have already been forced off the land and onto relief rolls as a result of the Roosevelt cotton program. Still others, owners and tenants, have been losing out because of the drought and the dust storms. The crop-reduction scheme must, at least to the degree that it results in permanent loss of foreign markets, lead to a general reduction in real farm income. Thus, the number of farm families operating at or below a bare-subsistence level, a number already running into the hundreds of thousands, if not into the millions, will be increased. These families certainly are eligible for " redistribution." Indeed, though for the nonce the Roosevelt Administration has continued to subsidize them, one of its avowed objectives is to take the submarginal farms and submarginal farmers, perhaps a million of them, out of production. And what of the workers in the hauling and processing industries? With less wheat and cotton and hogs to haul and process there are fewer jobs for them. They, too, will have to be cared for.

How could these millions be persuaded to abandon their familiar environments and move to the new sites designated for them by an altruistic government? In a liberal democracy it would not be possible for the authorities simply to command them to move. Tangible inducements would have to be held out. The families to be transported would hardly respond to a plan which amounted to nothing more than swapping relief in one place for relief in another. At the very least a decent living wage would have to be offered as compensation for breaking sentimental and other ties with their home environments. Even then the task would be far from easy, as the Roosevelt Administration might have reason to know from its experience in trying to induce a few Middle Western farmers to migrate to Alaska and in trying to persuade a few Ozark mountaineers to give up their " ridge " farms for better farming land down the valley.

What new " productive work " would or could be provided for six million or more workers who were eligible for " redistribution "? Could they be employed on the reclamation or other public projects envisaged in the President's land-utilization program? Perhaps, though it would be ridiculous to move whole families, whole communities, out into the sparsely settled areas of the country to undertake such jobs. The task would seem more suitable to the $1-a-day laborers enrolled in the Civilian Conservation Corps. Moreover, the cost would be enormous. If all of the six million were to be paid a minimum living wage, say $1,200 a year, their labor alone would come to $7,200,000,000 annually. The Public Works Administration has found that the average cost of materials on such projects runs about twice that of the pay roll. This would bring the bill for materials and wages to $21,600,000,000 a year, which is equal to almost half of the total national income in 1934.

Doubtless a public-works program on such a lavish scale would prove a great boon to private enterprise, at least while the spending went on. But in the end, for these public projects would produce no profits to be reinvested in capital goods, private enterprise would be no better off. It would have to meet the cost out of its own profits — or in any case out of wages, though that would so drastically deflate buying power as to more than offset the original benefits of the public-works boom. Obviously the national income could not long stand the strain of keeping six million workers and their families on such a basis so long as they were contributing nothing toward the accumulation of capital. Even the National Resources Board, which President Roosevelt had set up to study this problem, could do no more than recommend an expenditure of about $105,000,000,000 over a period of twenty to thirty years, and then deemed it expedient to suggest that " the cost seems a heavy charge upon the national income." [92]

Nor does it appear that the President ever had any real intention of bodily transporting entire communities for this purpose. Although something like $6,000,000,000 was spent on public works and similar relief projects during the first two years of his term and an additional $5,000,000,000 was made available in the third year, none of this money was used to redistribute any of the submerged families for the sake of putting them to work on a comprehensive " land utilization " program. In fact, when in 1935 he asked Congress for $4,880,000,000 to carry on his work-relief program, the President specifically declared that " effort should be made to locate projects where they will serve the greatest unemployment needs as shown by present relief rolls." So it was to be a matter of bringing the jobs to the jobless and not the other way about.

What, then, did Franklin Roosevelt really mean when he talked about redistributing the population? Would he put these millions to farming? But there were already too many farmers. Would he arrange new industrial occupations for them? He was finding it hard enough to provide jobs in the established industries. An indication of what he was driving at may be garnered from the following passage in his last annual message to the New York State Assembly:

. . . the fact remains that in the smaller cities and in the villages and the country districts, even though the shoe pinches in many households, the actual suffering and destitution is far less severe than in the big cities.

In other words, we seem to have established that the distribution of population during recent years has got out of balance, and that there is a definite over-population of the larger communities in the sense that there are too many people in them to maintain a decent living for all.

Great problems of distribution of the necessities of life are involved, but we have sufficient studies to know that an immediate gain can occur if as many people as possible can *return closer to the sources of agricultural food supply*.

This is not a mere " back-to-the-farm " movement. It is based on the fact that the pendulum has swung too far in the direction of the cities and that a readjustment must take place to restore the economic and the sociological balance.

I am a great believer in the larger aspects of regional planning and in my judgment the time has come for this State to adopt a farreaching policy of land utilization and of population distribution.

Let me illustrate from two extremes. At one end of the scale we are actually solving the problem of the unprofitable farming operation conducted on land unsuited to agriculture. This land, representing perhaps 20 per cent of the area of the State, will be gradually returned to its most profitable use — forestry, hunting or recreation.

At the other extreme lie the industries in great metropolitan centers, where land values, taxes and living costs are so high as to make the cost of production too high to compete with areas where the overhead is far lower. In between these two extremes lie tens of thousands of square miles and thousands of communities where agriculture may be made profitable enough to sustain life on a reasonable basis and where industries may *with proper relationship to agriculture* itself thrive more soundly than in the metropolitan areas.

To which, in his book, *Looking Forward*, he appended the following:

For example, in a valley in Vermont a woodturning factory for the making of knobs for the lids of kettles has already been so successful that the trend of the rural population to the city has been definitely stopped and the population of the valley finds that *it can profitably engage in agriculture during the summer with a definite wage-earning capacity in the local factory in the winter months.* (Italics mine.) [93]

Here we have the substance of the Roosevelt idea. Farmers do not make enough to live on. Let them add to their earnings by working in factories in the winter. Factory hands do not earn enough. Let them raise their own food in the summer. This is the principle underlying the subsistence-homestead communities being created in various sections of the country by the Roosevelt Administration. This is what the President meant by redistributing the population. He would move the farmers off their submarginal lands and into artificially-organized communities. He would move groups of stranded miners, and presumably other disinherited industrial groups and families, into similar or the same communities. Then he would induce industrial corporations to establish shops and factories in these pastoral villages. And so everyone would have work and " decent " wages.

The purpose would be to make the homesteaders self-sustaining, or as nearly so as possible. " Only thus," to quote Franklin Roosevelt, " can we permanently eliminate many millions of people from the relief rolls on which their names now appear." These sheltered villagers would not only raise their own food, but to a considerable extent would be expected to fashion their own tools, build their own furniture and make their own clothes. In fact, some of the advocates of this undoubtedly noble experiment would have the homesteaders " grow their own flax and weave their own linen, card their own wool and make their own homespun, tan their own hides and put together their own shoes." Nor, since these people would be removed from the orbit of the prevailing national economy and yet would have to meet many of their own needs, would it be inappropriate for them to return to ways of an earlier handicraft economy.

This would mean, of course, a corresponding decrease in the domestic demand for farm and industrial goods. There would be six million fewer families for the remaining farmers of the country to feed. There would be six million fewer families for the factories of the country to clothe and equip. It may be argued that in as much as these millions are now virtually destitute, and so, apparently, represent no effective demand in the domestic market, there would be no important loss if they were to feed and clothe themselves. This would be to ignore the fact that many of these families are now on relief and are spending their relief wages in buying goods for sale in the domestic market. Even the submarginal farmers who are not on relief must manage somehow to scrape together enough cash or credit for essential tools, clothing and the like. While the total number of families in the country runs between twenty-five and thirty million, the removal of six million families in the lowest-income group from the domestic market would not necessarily result in a 20 to 25 per cent reduction in the demand for all kinds of goods. Yet it should be obvious that to take one-fifth of the consumers out of the domestic market, low though their buying power might be at the moment, would have a serious deflationary effect upon the national economy as a whole.

Secondly, the goods produced in the factories in which the homesteaders were to find part-time employment would inevitably come into competition with goods produced in other factories. If this were to develop on an extensive scale, it would naturally result in growing disemployment among the workers remaining in the urban industrial centers. To be sure, industries would not locate in these communities unless the terms held out to them were sufficiently attractive. Virtually all industrial establishments are located where they are now for sound and substantial economic reasons, that is, because of access to sources of raw materials, presence of a dependable labor supply, proximity to the markets for their goods, available transportation facilities and so forth. They will not "decentralize" at the suggestion of the Government unless it is made worth their while. Nor will they be found inclined to expand plant capacity, at least not without sufficient inducement, at a time when industrial plant is already greatly overbuilt throughout the country.*

What might be considered sufficient inducement? Not cheaper land, for that could be obtained in suburban areas where the industries would still be close to markets and good transportation. Indeed, a recent survey shows that such decentralization of industry as has taken place in the last few years has reflected a trend toward the suburbs adjacent to industrial centers rather than to the open country. Cheap capital might help, if industries were ready to expand their plant; but even if they were, they could get all the capital they needed at rates as low as any the Government could offer in the regular investment market. Cheap labor would certainly be an inducement, though the Roosevelt Administration could not consistently promise cheap labor in the subsistence communities at the same time that it was insisting upon payment of minimum-wage rates under the NRA code system (though even the NRA pay rates were cheap enough). Nothing else would seem to remain but for the Government to subsidize these factories.

An example is cited by Harold M. Ware and Webster

* In trying to give the Reedsville, West Virginia, project a good send-off the Roosevelt Administration proposed that the Government build a $500,000 factory there to make equipment for the Post Office Department. The furniture industry complained, however, that it was operating at only 20 per cent of capacity and that many factories capable of making such equipment were standing idle. Though the Public Works office was ready to supply the money to build the factory, Congress, heeding the furniture industry's plaint, refused to appropriate the money needed to keep the factory running. And so the plan was dropped.

Powell in connection with the establishment of a factory for the Electric Vacuum Cleaning Company, a General Electric subsidiary, in the Arthurdale, West Virginia, community. According to Messrs. Ware and Powell:

> The planned cost of the factory is $25,000, for the use of which the company contracts to pay 5 per cent of its cost annually. The company also agrees to supply plans for the factory, install its own equipment and management, keep up the insurance and pay taxes if there are any on government property, and to guarantee 36 weeks' employment for 40 homesteaders at 36 hours a week, paying code wages which are approximately 35 cents per hour for general labor.
>
> The company plays safe all the way. If the vacuum-cleaner market fails to absorb its products, it may cancel its lease in two years. The Government builds the factory and prorates its cost among the homesteaders. If business is good, the lease can be extended at the option of the company for ten years. Its products will be advertised as a partnership with the Government. The homesteader will continue to get 35 cents an hour, some of which he must pay back in his monthly amortization payments, which include his prorated share of the factory in which he labors. This arithmetic is of vital importance to the homesteaders, since it means that the subsistence worker has to help pay for the factory in which he works to get a subsistence wage.[94]

There can be little doubt that if offered such generous terms many industries would be found willing to establish branch factories in the homestead villages. Ordinarily under capitalism industry finances the building of its factories indirectly out of surplus labor value, but under the Roosevelt homestead plan it would seemingly be possible for industry to get its required capital by making the workers supply it directly out of their wages. Never before has the principle upon which capitalist production operates been so frankly revealed.

This would not be the only cost the supposedly impoverished homesteader would have to meet. He would have to pay for his homestead — over a period of twenty years and on generous terms, of course. Messrs. Ware and Powell say it has been estimated " that the average homestead costing from $2500 to $3500 will require a $15 monthly payment to amortize the debt." Actually most of the homesteads to date have been costing nearly $5,000 each. The average at the Reedsville, West Virginia, project, according to Secretary of the Interior Ickes, has been $4,880, while the lowest-priced homestead in that community cost no less than $4,396.34.[95] Hence the monthly amortization payment would be likely to run over $25. This would not be all, for the homestead cost does not include furniture or farm tools. It does not provide for roads, schools, churches, stores, movie houses, medical and sanitary services, fire and police protection, or other community necessities. Someone would have to meet these additional expenses, and since it is the purpose of the Roosevelt Administration to establish these communities with a view to making their inhabitants self-sustaining, thus relieving the Federal Government of the expense of keeping them on relief, it would follow that this extra load would also fall upon the homesteaders.

How would the redistributed farmer or worker pay these bills? He would need at least $25 monthly to amortize his debt, $35 cash " to make up a minimum living standard," as Messrs. Ware and Powell estimate, and in addition whatever else it would be necessary for him to contribute toward maintenance of the community. He would be fortunate if his cash expenses ran to less than $80 a month. It is doubtful whether he could earn that much working part-time in a factory. Indeed, the average earnings of full-time industrial employees in the country have been running only slightly higher than $80 a month. It is hardly likely that an industrial corporation, which would have to be lured by special inducements into the homestead community in any case, would be willing to pay as much as that for part-time work. In connection with the Arthurdale project, for example, the company's contract stipulates a maximum annual wage of $420, which is only $35 a month. In short, the subsistence-homesteader must either be given full-time employment — if the Government can induce enough industries to come to its assistance — or else he must "look abroad for subsistence."

The whole experiment might conceivably end by the Government's meeting the deficit of these communities, which would mean that it was not escaping the relief burden after all. In any case, the Government would have to undertake the initial financing of the experiment. Granting that at least six million families would have to be provided for, the initial cost of building and outfitting their homesteads (but not including furniture or tools) would come to approximately $30,000,-000,000. And it must be remembered that six million represents but a minimum estimate of the number of submerged families eligible for redistribution.

And then, as Louis Hacker has suggested, something would also

have to be done about the many service activities which, in the course of time, have grown up about the settlements to be wiped out: the local hay and feed establishments, the grocery shops, the professional men's offices, the schools and court houses. To the bill, obviously, will have to be added the cost of compensating all those humbler members of the middle class who once served the farmers and who, in turn, will be doomed now that these farmers are to be transported to happier seats; to the bill, also, will have to be added the cost of financial assistance to be rendered those townships and counties which will become crippled as a result of the departure of so many of their property-owners and taxpayers.[96]

So it might turn out that the cost, in the beginning at any rate, would be greatly in excess of $30,000,000,000.

It is a curious fact that while this particular security plan drew little enthusiasm or support from among the workers and farmers, it met with considerable approbation from busi-

ness men and notably from those who are sometimes called
"enlightened" capitalists. For instance, when asked whether
he favored the subsistence-homestead idea, Henry I. Harriman, then president of the United States Chamber of Commerce, emphatically replied: "Of course I do." He went on
to call it the "most fundamental and farreaching movement
under way today. . . . Social security has got to be given
the people of this country. The subsistence homestead projects
will show us the way to the necessary decentralization of industry; the relief of mass congestion in the cities; provision
for workers to own their own homes *and contribute to their
own support.*" [97]

Even before Mr. Harriman, however, Henry Ford and the
United States Steel Corporation had in their own ways expressed similar approval. The latter had developed an extensive "garden" project for its employees in Gary, Indiana,
with the help of social workers and the University of Indiana,
for the sake of enabling these employees to raise their own
food when wages are cut or employment reduced. Mr. Ford
had tried to sell the idea early in the depression to President
Hoover. He had also taken space in the newspapers to adver-
tise his own success in this field. One such advertisement said:

Ten years ago we started seven village industries on small
water power sites, all within twenty miles of Dearborn, our purpose being to combine the advantages of city wages with country
living. The experiment has been a continuous success. Overhead
cost has been less than in the big factory, and the workers would
not hear of going back to the city shops. As they are free to till
land in the growing season, throughout these trying times they
have all remained self-sustaining. Their security is produced by
machine *and* farm, not by one alone.[98]

What the Roosevelt-Ford-Chamber-of-Commerce-Steel-
Trust scheme would come down to would be the establishment of a benevolent feudalism. A peasant-labor class would

be developed. It would be bound to the soil, not only by reason of its indebtedness, which the Roosevelt plan would saddle upon it from the start, but also because its income from other sources would be kept insufficient to meet its fundamental economic needs. At the same time it would — eventually — provide a cheap and docile supply of labor for industry. And without question it would help to relieve the taxpayers of the cost of maintaining the country's surplus population.

Mr. Hacker suggests that the American Government, " hard driven by the contradictions of its own position, may even (as in Italy and Germany) seek to build up exactly such a sheltered peasant group as a rural reactionary bloc to withstand the revolutionary demands of the organized industrial workers." [99] Messrs. Ware and Powell assert that the intention is " to decentralize both discontent and industry and so diffuse the social risks of revolt during the period when wage standards are being reduced to coolie levels." [100]

Even if we take a more charitable view, if we agree with Mrs. Franklin Roosevelt that the President has had nothing of this sort in mind but has only been trying " to make poverty more endurable," it still is obvious that he would throw the cost squarely upon the workers. This is equally true whether we look to his social-insurance plan or to his subsistence home-steads. He will not, and within the limits of the existing social system cannot, eliminate poverty or the surplus population. But he is at least willing to let the superfluous workers and farmers secure themselves against want — at their own expense. He has said, in effect, that Cinderella must remain content with her station in life. But he is willing to give Cinderella a well-deserved kiss — if she'll pay for it.

PART FOUR

THEY CALLED IT REVOLUTION

✍

UPON his arrival in Washington Franklin Roosevelt found the stage set for action and himself the principal actor. Through three years of crisis Herbert Hoover had done little more than to attempt to stem the tide of petit-bourgeois unrest, to hold the field a while longer for *laissez faire*. This condemned him to inaction, for political inertia is of the essence of *laissez faire*. The capitalist-entrepreneur class was satisfied to have such privileged assistance as came to it from the Reconstruction Finance Corporation and similar agencies, and it would no doubt have been pleased had the anti-trust laws been repealed. But further than that it did not want the state to go. Above all, it wanted no social legislation. Herbert Hoover performed his appointed task as best he could. His reward was to bring down upon himself the bitterest denunciation heaped upon any President in recent times, for he was doing nothing for the masses of the people. On November 8, 1932, they registered their demand for change, for action. During the interregnum their anxiety increased. Popular pressure was brought to bear on Congress to clothe the President with extraordinary authority so that he might move swiftly and surely toward a solution of the crisis.

More than that, on March 4 the bank panic was at its height. The immediate future was dark, unpredictable. Congress was ready to abdicate. Only the White House seemed to hold forth a promise of deliverance. The people wanted to trust the new President, to believe in his every word and deed. They would have followed wherever he was willing to lead. When, five days later, he sent his emergency banking bill to Congress, that body whipped the bill through to enactment with reckless speed, without even a pretense of adequate consideration or debate. Not more than a half-dozen members in the lower House had had time to read the bill and hardly more than that in the Senate. So great was the popular pressure for action.

Franklin Roosevelt had to move, and move quickly and vigorously. Had he followed the course of the retiring President and ignored the public demand for "leadership," he would have promptly destroyed his prestige — and his political future. It remained to be seen, of course, whether the action he was to take would be really fundamental, or would consist mostly in sweeping surface gestures, benevolent in word and purpose, but barren of basic or permanent accomplishment. In any event, the surface activity that followed was almost without parallel. It electrified the country and led many otherwise sober students into believing that a revolution was literally taking place before their eyes. One of the chroniclers of this period declared:

It was a bloodless revolution, to be sure. In fact, a completely peaceful revolution accomplished without an ounce of armed force, or the threat of its use, without a black shirt, a brown shirt, an underground organization. On the contrary, it was effected with the most scrupulous observance of the recognized processes of lawmaking and meticulous regard for the historic rights of free speech and free assemblage. Yet the word "revolution" sprang naturally to the lips. No other word seems strong enough to describe a change so swift and so fundamental. The United States had embarked on an experiment in new economic relationships of revolutionary audacity and magnitude. As an incident to this, President Roosevelt had been endowed with greater power than any American had possessed in peace-time since the adoption of the Constitution. Probably never before had a change so abrupt and far-reaching been wrought peaceably within the framework of democratic institutions.[1]

But it was not revolution. Certain superficial changes and reforms were effected, certain concessions were made to the working class, and certain vested interests were threatened, or seemed to be threatened. That was all. The rest, so far as revolution was concerned, was sheer ballyhoo, whether it issued in dulcet tones over the radio from the White House or was formally and solemnly inscribed upon the statute books of the Federal Government.

What is revolution? Simply stated, it is the transference of power from one class to another. A certain group or class, with definite economic interests and prejudices, controls the state today; tomorrow another group, with very different interests and prejudices, arises to seize the state machinery. It does so not without reason, but because at a given stage in the development of human society a political revolution becomes essential to the further economic and social progress of mankind. When the class interests of the ruling group begin to impede that progress, it becomes necessary to substitute another group or class whose interests will more effectively meet the requirements of society.

Thus, the bourgeois revolution that attended the rise of capitalism represented a transfer of power from the feudal aristocracy to the " middle " class — that is, to the class of middlemen, the merchants, bankers and manufacturers. But the bourgeois revolution was not merely the substitution of one ruling class for another; it was the outward and inevitable expression of fundamental economic change. The era of invention and discovery laid the groundwork for capitalism. The rigid political forms of feudalism, the absolutism of church and prince, stood in the way of the development of a free market, and without a free market primitive capitalism could not survive, let alone prosper. Absolutism was forced to give way to a political system that could guarantee freedom of action to the new economic forces. That system was liberal democracy. The basic change was evolutionary, the political transition revolutionary, for the feudal lords resisted the change. Except in a few rare instances where they became capitalists on their own account and so passed automatically into the new ruling class, they were in no way disposed to surrender their feudal privileges. They had to be deprived of them by force.

We have come now to a new stage in the evolution of human society. There is no longer need for a free market to encourage and facilitate the accumulation of capital. The productivity of existing capital has reached the point where it can create abundance. But abundance must in the end destroy the rate of profit. Capitalism's answer is to choke off the free market by trade barriers, price fixing, "planned" production and similar monopolistic devices. Yet these devices in their turn, though they may temporarily hold up prices and profits, must also add to the surplus of capital, lead to disemployment and diminishing buying power, and eventually result in crisis. There was a time when the capitalist crisis tended to cure itself, but that time is no more. Today a thorough deflation would wreck the capitalist structure. In self-defense, therefore, both monopolism and the state must seek to check deflation before it goes too far, and in this they must resort to the very devices which are the causes of crisis. They must throttle abundance and endeavor to perpetuate that scarcity which alone ensures profits.

This course is plainly suicidal, not only or not even necessarily because the hungry masses, the victims of scarcity, may rise up in revolt, but because artificial scarcity is itself destructive of profits. Capitalism is compelled, therefore, to move still further along the same road. Living standards fall ever lower, society begins to turn backward. The retrogression is not only economic. It is also political and cultural. Witness the medievalism, the anti-intellectualism and the abandonment of political freedom in countries where the capitalist crisis has reached its most acute stage, notably Nazi Germany. Scientific progress must likewise be checked. As yet enterprising industries and corporations may turn to new inventions and methods designed to lessen the burden of human labor because the costs thus saved give them an advantage over competitors. But competition is already being restricted in wholesale fashion, not only by private monopolism, but by the state itself, and as this continues the necessity for seeking competitive advantage through labor-saving machinery must also decrease.* Moreover, there has arisen a tendency to halt the flow of new inventions which cut into buying power and increase the productivity of capital. This tendency is discernible in many patent pools, which are used deliberately to prevent the employment of new inventions, and in the provisions of a number of NRA codes, which forbade the introduction of new machinery except with the consent of the dominant groups within the industries concerned.

Society can move forward to more abundant living, but not upon the present economic and political bases. It cannot have both abundance and profits. If it chooses to cling to the latter,

* Some finance and industrial capitalists have already seriously proposed that the flood of new inventions be curbed before it wrecks the economic order. Thus, Sir Josiah Stamp, head of the London, Midland & Scottish Railway Company and a director of the Bank of England, declared before the British Association for the Advancement of Science at Aberdeen, Scotland, on September 6, 1934, that "in all quarters one sees scientists trembling with enthusiasm on the threshold of great discoveries, but I tremble with dread as to what is going to happen to any kind of economic organism which is trying to keep in balance, particularly under an individualistic form of society. . . . I feel inclined to say to all of you scientific pundits from other sections: There would not be a problem at all if you were not so chaotic in your discoveries — if you would only introduce them into the body politic *under conditions that we could control.*" In other words, humanity should not be deprived altogether of the benefits of labor-saving inventions, but such benefits should be conferred upon humanity only to the extent that they do not disturb the existing economy.

it must turn backward. If it wants abundance, it must dispense with profits. And that means, of course, that it must dispense with a ruling class whose sole economic interest is based upon maintenance of the profit mechanism. If social progress is to continue, political power must pass to a class whose interests are bound up with the present interests of society. In brief, it must pass to the real producers, the workers and farmers, who produce for use and not for profit. Obviously the transition would have to be complete. Socialization of the distributive machinery alone (by consumers' cooperatives, for example) would not touch the root of the problem. That root is the private ownership of the means of production. Privately-owned capital will produce only so long as profits are assured. Hence the means of production would also have to be socialized.

Much of the confusion over the Roosevelt position has been due to the conflict of interest between the upper and lower strata of the middle class. Historically, the upper bourgeoisie have already won. Yet because the lower middle class is numerically superior and still possesses the franchise, it remains possible for this group to challenge the victory of the monopolists. It has done so upon several occasions in the past. But whenever leaders or movements have arisen to defend or promote the interests of the petit bourgeoisie, the political agents and journalistic apologists of the ruling class have promptly denounced them as " demagogues " and " radicals." Even as early as the 1880's legislation designed to benefit this class was labeled " communistic," a tag that Senator Hawley applied to the Funding Bill in Congress on the day before Franklin Roosevelt was born. Again and again the Populists, the Progressives, the Free Silver Democrats, the Weavers, Sockless Jerry Simpsons, Bryans and La Follettes were scathingly condemned as dangerous enemies of the existing order. Had the Soviet Union then been in existence, they would unquestionably have been called "tools of Moscow," as some of them actually were called after the war.

The lower middle class was — and still is — anything but revolutionary. It is not even progressive in an historic sense. What it wants is to turn back, not go forward. It wants to halt the spread of monopolism, the relentless advance of modern capitalism that is undermining its economic status. When it demands anti-trust laws, regulation of the railroads and other utilities, state control of shipping rates, central banking, income-tax laws, it is because it wants to check the steady encroachment of the gigantic combinations of financial and industrial capital upon its own economic security and its own income. Essentially the conflict with the upper bourgeoisie is a quarrel over the division of the spoils of the profit system. As monopoly grows, the lesser bourgeoisie are getting a relatively smaller and smaller share, which tends to deprive them of their class basis and drive them, economically speaking, into the proletariat.* In the words of the Communist Manifesto:

The lower middle class, the small manufacturer, the shop-keeper, the artisan, the farmer, all these fight against the bourgeoisie, to save from extinction their existence as fractions of the middle class. They are, therefore, not revolutionary, but conservative. Nay, more, they are reactionary, for they try to roll

---

* It is a strange fact that some political students, especially those who consider themselves "progressives," contend that the lower middle class is not facing extinction, but is actually growing. They point to the increase in what they call the "new" middle class, made up primarily of service and other white-collar workers. This is somehow thought to prove that the Marxian theory is wrong and that, therefore, the predicted collapse of capitalism and eventual revolution is quite impossible. But economically these "new" members of the lower middle class are really proletarians. They do not own their tools. They do not derive their main source of income from profit, interest or rent. They are wage earners, though they may seek to hide this fact by calling their wage a salary. It is true, however, that since they identify themselves emotionally with the lower middle class, they are apt to be as reactionary in their political views as are the real members of that class.

back the wheel of history. If by chance they are revolutionary, they are so only in view of their impending transfer into the proletariat.

Until the present depression began these reactionary radicals made no appreciable progress, though they succeeded in getting some of their views written into law. For the petit bourgeoisie on the whole were not generally aware of the predicament of their class and so were not disposed to follow "progressive" leadership. Under the influence of the "American dream" they thought they were going forward with capitalism, and so long as capitalism was expanding this appeared to be true. Hence most of them associated themselves with the Republican Party or with its weaker twin, the Democratic Party, owned and controlled though these parties were by the bankers and industrialists. That their interests and those of the monopolists were not identical first became apparent to many of the petit bourgeoisie during the Hoover regime. Every act of the Republicans in Washington during the first three years of crisis showed that they were in office to protect the capitalist-entrepreneur class and no other. Government relief, with a few minor exceptions, was poured into the economic structure from the top, it being implied that at least some of this largess would in time trickle down to the lower grades, to the real victims of the crisis.

But this, alas, did not happen to any measurable extent, and the real victims of the crisis, the petit bourgeoisie, began to awaken. For they felt the full impact of the crisis. The propertiless proletarians had little to lose but their jobs and meager wages. The upper bourgeoisie found their wealth marked down in terms of stock-exchange values, but their tangible holdings were actually increased. In between stood the lesser bourgeoisie, who lost not only their employment, but their businesses, their homes, their personal possessions, their savings and insurance policies. The ceaseless process of monopolization, which went on unchecked through the depression, wiped out many of them. The collapse of the suburban real-estate booms, the foreign-bond fiasco, the Kreuger, Insull and similar catastrophes ruined many others. Every bank crash took heavy toll among them. Many fell from a comfortable standard of living all the way to the bottom.

And so fifteen million petit-bourgeois voters, to judge by the 1932 election returns, also lost their faith in the Republican Party — " the party in power." That these dissenters should have turned to the Democratic Party and not to a third capitalist party, to a distinctively petit-bourgeois party, was perhaps accidental. Had a third party been in existence, it would doubtless have attracted a goodly number of them. Without organization and without funds, the La Follette-Wheeler ticket drew almost five million votes from the petit bourgeoisie in 1924, when only the farmers and a few white-collar workers in the cities were restive. Eight years later this whole class was in ferment. Another La Follette-Wheeler ticket might easily have drawn many more than five million votes, might, indeed, have proved victorious. At that time, however, none of the potential leaders among the progressives had the wit or the courage to undertake a third party; and so, having nowhere else to go, the petit-bourgeois voters turned *en masse* to the Democratic nominee, Franklin Roosevelt.

It was doubtful, of course, that he or his party could give them the satisfaction and security they were seeking. The Democratic Party was little more than a hybrid aggregation of sectional and local machines, further apart in their social and economic views than were the two Republican factions. Nor was there much in Franklin Roosevelt's experience or record to indicate that he was especially fitted to cope with the problems of the petit bourgeoisie or genuinely in sympathy with their class interests. His attitude had been that of the righteous conformist, the benevolent paternalist, not that of the ardently sincere progressive. He was himself of the *rentier* class. As such, he could not have wanted to tear apart the great combinations of financial and industrial capital, to kill the geese that were laying the golden eggs, though he might have wanted to make them efficient and honest so as to enable them the more certainly and readily to meet their just obligations to those who held their bonds and securities.

Even if he had so desired, he would have found it impossible to break monopolism and at the same time preserve the profit system. For today they are one and the same. The petit bourgeoisie have already lost the battle. No amount of economic planning, no amount of Tugwellian discipline, could restore them to their former privileged position. The planning board or control administration would serve but to disguise and simultaneously to promote the spread of monopoly — which is precisely what happened under the NRA. The ruthless elimination of the "small enterprises," for which President Roosevelt was to show such great rhetorical solicitude, would go on just the same. Those in possession of the effective economic power would continue to hold it and to exercise it to their own profit.

Nevertheless, Franklin Roosevelt could meet the lower middle class on common ground. By 1932 "trust busting" had lost favor with this group. Instead talk was increasingly heard of the necessity for what the elder La Follette called " scientific regulation " of the monopolies and the younger La Follette dubbed "economic planning." This latter phrase had caught the fancy of the petit bourgeoisie. It seemed to offer both an intelligent way out of the depression and a permanent check upon monopoly. Franklin Roosevelt also was a " planner." He also believed in "scientific regulation." He also wanted to increase the power of the state to deal with economic and social problems. And he, no less than the petit bourgeoisie, was anxious to hold the state's intervention within the bounds set by the profit system. While his objective was different, he could go a long way with the lower middle class in phraseology.

In seeming to identify himself with this class, in ostensibly clasping " the forgotten man " to his bosom, he won the applause of the progressives and social liberals. He spoke their language, included a few of them among his most intimate advisers, and adopted some of their political measures for his own. They were convinced that he was working toward that " social state " which is the goal of social democracy in Europe and of progressivism and social liberalism in the United States. He was welcomed as a fellow revolutionary of the gradualist school. Hence, and not stopping to distinguish between word and deed, they hailed his every concession to the submerged classes, his every gesture in their direction, as " a move to the left."

The individualists of " the right " had no doubt, of course, that this was true. They brought out and applied to him all of the old labels that had in the past invariably been used to discredit anyone and everyone who dared to challenge, or even to appear to be challenging, the ruling class. He was " a dangerous radical," " a visionary," " a collectivist," " a fascist," " a communist " — the critics of " the right " used these terms interchangeably, as synonyms. Not all of the monopolists joined in the chorus of denunciation and abuse, nor even, perhaps, a majority of them, but enough of their more articulate defenders in journalism and politics took part to make it seem as though the capitalist-entrepreneur class was united against the President.

The conservative opposition to his program can be traced to other causes as well. At the start more than one banker and industrialist with an uneasy conscience was mortally afraid that he actually meant to drive them from the temple. Later they took fright at his tinkering with the currency, and still later they were alarmed by his prodigious spending, not because they did not see the necessity for making concessions to the submerged classes, but because they did not want the cost passed on to them. There were other conservatives whose personal connection with the Republican Party kept them in the opposition, or who, looking back over the history of the country since the Civil War, were certain that no Democratic Administration could possibly serve the capitalist-entrepreneur class as faithfully as had the Republicans. Still others clung to their faith in *laissez faire* and could see little good coming from state intervention in economic or financial affairs. But there were also conservatives who saw clearly enough that, whether they wished it or not, the state was destined to play an ever larger role in such matters, but who nevertheless disagreed with Franklin Roosevelt on questions of method and were suspicious of his occasional excursions into demagogism.

To point out, however, that the beneficiaries of the profit system have not been united in supporting President Roosevelt in everything he has done is not to prove that he is an enemy of the profit system, but is merely to emphasize that, like the workers, the capitalists can rarely agree upon what may be in their best interest. In fact, as the record so clearly shows, the American bourgeoisie could have searched far and wide before finding a more devoted and effective champion of their cause. He had no desire to disturb the bases of the existing order, but wanted only to preserve and strengthen them. His major recovery experiment, the NRA, at one and the same time strengthened monopoly and sought to check the ruthless price-cutting that was prolonging a deflation already gone ominously far. His efforts to make honest men out of employers and bankers and stock-market operators actually represented no more than an attempt to save capitalism from its own excessive greed. His crusade against holding companies — a particularly sore point with some of his tory opponents — was designed to rid the capitalist body of a parasite that was sucking out precious quantities of its life's blood — profits — and giving nothing in return.

Even in his concessions to the lower classes he was to keep the needs of capitalism ever in mind. His subsidies to the farmers were needed to make farming "profitable" again. They had to take the place of the profits that could no longer be earned in the market, for it would never have done to admit that abundance is incompatible with the making of profits. His mortgage-relief plan was of greater benefit to the capital-claims structure, which he was seeking to save from the ravages of deflation, than it was to the debt-laden property owners. His minimum-wage proposals were designed as much, if not more, to revive the domestic market as to help the lowest-paid workers. His insistence that the jobless be spared the iniquitous dole and be compelled to work for their relief was based, as he himself said, upon a desire to save the morale of the workers, that is, to keep them loyal to the capitalist state.

It should be obvious that Franklin Roosevelt has been and is no revolutionary, nor yet a reactionary radical of the Bryan or La Follette or Villard school. He has not only been sincerely desirous of preserving the economic system upon which his income as a *rentier* depends, but he has had the courage and the will, despite strong vocal opposition, to point out to the bourgeoisie what he considers, in the light of his experiences and prejudices, some of the shortcomings of that system. He has attempted to correct these weaknesses. And he has believed it wise to keep the submerged classes satisfied with a modicum of bread and an unusually spectacular and noisy circus.

DARK PROPHECY

ဢ

THERE are critics and commentators who believe that the American problem is so vast and complex and popular motives and emotions so mixed that it would be futile to attempt to trace any definite political or social trend in the United States today. To suggest and offer proof that the country is moving toward fascism (or in some other direction), say these critics, is simply to apply selected facts to preconceived theories or personal prejudices, for the available facts are so many and so diverse than no one can properly interpret them.[2] There are other critics who would hold the contention that the country is moving in one direction or another to be demonstrably false unless it is supported by concrete evidence of subjective intent on the part of those individuals and groups who may be affected by the movement. For example, when I suggested that the lower middle class, in turning against the *laissez-faire* Republicans in 1932, was really laying upon their Democratic successors the duty of enlarging the power of the state to deal with economic matters, it was argued that this had not been proved because the petit-bourgeois voters had not formally got together and said in so many words that that was the mission with which they were charging Franklin Roosevelt.[3]

Both of these views, alas, disregard the importance of objective factors in political economy. They consider subjective influences to be the determinant factor in shaping the course of society, though this runs counter to all historic experience.

A thousand men may want to proceed in a thousand different ways in providing bread for themselves, but if the objective conditions are such that they can produce bread in only one way, they must perforce choose that way or starve. They may cling to their own subjective ideas and may even quarrel among themselves as to whether each of their ideas would not be better than the one method of producing bread which is open to them. And they may never sit down and formally and solemnly agree to follow this method. Yet they must follow it if they would eat. It is the objective factor that shapes their action, whatever the subjective influences that might be at work among them. Their subjective inclinations may modify their action but cannot fundamentally alter it.

Society itself must obey the dictates of objective factors. In a capitalist society the primary economic determinant is the rate of profit. The production of goods depends upon the assurance of profit. As this assurance diminishes, production diminishes. If it were to be wiped out altogether, capitalist production would cease. But even a capitalist society must continue to produce the goods it needs, for otherwise it cannot survive. Hence it seeks in every way to protect the rate of profit. This it can do only by a ceaseless extension of monopoly. Here, then, is an objective factor that is forcing capitalism to move in a single direction. Subjectively, any number of capitalists may want to move off in another direction, back to the free market with its potentially unlimited abundance, for example; but the economic determinant will not permit them to do so.

This economic determinant has an equally marked reaction upon the political structure of capitalist society. As monopolism spreads, competition decreases, economic opportunities dwindle, real wages fall and disemployment grows, those who suffer seek to protect themselves. To what means or what agency can they turn for protection? Certainly not to any economic means, for the economic power rests with the sur-

vivors in the capitalist struggle, with the monopolists. The
only other agency to which they can turn is the state, for the
state, at least in a representative democracy, remains the sole
means through which any of the less fortunately circumstanced classes can collectively press their economic demands.
As their position becomes worse, they tend more and more to
do so. Until 1932 this process had gone much further in the
advanced industrial powers of Europe than it had in the United
States. Even in Cobden's England the state was and long had
been intervening in economic matters. The 1932 election reflected a sharp turn in that direction on the part of the American lower middle class. The election was a rebellion against the
laissez faire of the Republicans. The voters did not want the
Hoover policy of inaction continued and certainly they did
not want less action on the part of the government. What they
wanted was more action. The successor to Herbert Hoover,
whoever he might have been, had to increase the power of the
state to deal with economic questions.

There is another objective factor that leads to enlargement
of the state authority. The modern capitalist crisis has become
one in which survival is at stake. The capitalist state would
itself come down if the capital structure were to be toppled
over by a deflation carried to its logical conclusion. As a matter of self-defense as well, then, the state must step in and attempt to check the deflation by whatever means it may devise.

Hence, the rate of profit also shapes the political course of
capitalist society. Just as it forces the growth of monopoly in
capitalist production, so must it compel the capitalist state to
move ever closer to absolutism. It might be argued that this
is not true so long as representative institutions are retained,
and in practice, indeed, elective legislative bodies do continue
to function, for a time at any rate, while the movement toward absolutism goes on. But the state's action is rendered
increasingly ineffective if it must wait upon legislative delib-
eration. In the words of Harold Laski, "the leisurely processes

of parliamentary debate are far too slow for the requirements of economic decision." [4] The tendency is to transfer the real power to the executive branch of government. As the German crisis deepened, the Reichstag was permitted to remain in being, but the divisions within that body were such as to prevent agreement on important economic questions. In consequence Chancellor Brüning deemed it necessary to assume more and more authority for himself under the emergency clause of the Weimar Constitution.

And so long as representative institutions are retained there will remain the danger that the submerged classes might use them to force reforms upon the state that are unacceptable to the capitalist-entrepreneur class. When that is threatened, the latter must in self-defense seek some means of abolishing the popular legislature. While the Nazis could be set off against the Social Democrats and Communists, the German ruling class was content to let the Reichstag live and to let Brüning use his extended powers under Article 48 in endeavoring to save German capitalism. But when toward the end of 1932 the Nazi vote showed a marked decline and the Communist vote an equally marked increase, the overlords of German capitalism promptly deposed Brüning and then von Papen and von Schleicher. Finally they called in the leader of the Nazis, who, though a fanatic, was a petit bourgeois and so was loyal to capitalism. This served the double purpose of checking the alarming desertion of petit-bourgeois Nazis to the Communist ranks and of bringing into the Government the leaders of a mass party who were committed not only to capitalism, but to totalitarianism, that is, to the abolition of all representative institutions.

As a capitalist state approaching exhaustion, Germany could no longer afford to throw sops to the working class and the impoverished sections of the lower middle class as a means of keeping them subdued. It had become dangerous, therefore, to let them retain the franchise. A capitalist state with fairly substantial reserves still on hand — and the United States is in that position — can concede a few apparently generous but relatively harmless demands for the sake of restraining the lower classes. So long as this policy can be followed and remains effective, there is no need to suppress Congress. Nevertheless, though the capitalist crisis in America had not gone nearly so far as in other countries, Franklin Roosevelt believed it necessary in the first two years of his regime to restrain Congress and assume more and more authority for himself in the name of the "emergency." At the same time he was extending to the lower classes those concessions which the objective situation seemed to require, but which, had these classes been permitted to express their unrestrained will through their representatives in Congress, might have taken a form far more detrimental to the best interests of the capitalist-entrepreneur class.

He had said in his inaugural address that he regarded the Constitution as "so simple and practical that it is possible always to meet extraordinary needs by changes in emphasis and arrangement without loss of essential form." Thereafter he and his associates were careful to follow the outward forms of the basic law. They conceded that Congress was the legislative arm of the Government, but they argued that in the exercise of its legislative duties it could delegate the broadest authority to the President to carry out its general mandates. Proceeding upon this theory, the President asked and was given power which, in practical effect, permitted him to write his own laws. In brief, much of the legislative power was actually transferred to the White House. It was held, of course, that this was only for the period of the "emergency" and that, in any case, the President would exercise these legislative functions only in the best interest of the people as a whole.

That the emergency powers would tend to become permanent was soon made clear by the President himself. As some of the temporary laws automatically expired, he sought to have them extended. With regard to the most important of them, the National Industrial Recovery Act, he insisted in a message to Congress that it was intended not to meet an emergency but to enable the state to help industry make itself over and that this could not be done in a day or a year. Secondly, it must be asked, if Congress may delegate such a large part of its legislative power to the President, what would there be to prevent it from delegating a still larger part, or the whole of it, to the Chief Executive or some other agency? And if the emergency of 1933–35, such as it was, provided sufficient justification for this transfer of power, would it not be logical to transfer a still larger part in the event the crisis continued or became acute? Lastly, if the President could be depended upon to exercise a part of this power in the best interest of the people, would it not follow that he would serve the people even better if he were to take over the whole of it?

It should be obvious that Congress might, upon the basis of this reasoning, abdicate altogether in favor of the President. That this step, given the proper stage setting and ballyhoo, might be enthusiastically welcomed is suggested by the unprecedented applause Franklin Roosevelt received when he blithely assumed the extraordinary powers given him in his " emergency " legislation. True, this would not of itself make a dictatorship, for there still would be the constitutional provisions for popular elections to be gotten around. Yet it must not be overlooked that it was not until he had regularly been appointed Premier and had taken over the duties of his office that Mussolini's march on Rome took place and he began building his corporative state; and it was not until Adolf Hitler had been lawfully and formally inducted into office that he went about the business of tearing up the Weimar Constitution.

This is not to suggest that Franklin Roosevelt has ever consciously contemplated the assumption of outright dictatorial powers or ever dreamed of destroying the Federal Constitution by deliberate intent. Temperamentally, indeed, it might be said that he is not fitted for the part. Rather does it seem that he has played Heinrich Brüning's role in American affairs. He has managed to be far more generous in his concessions, for American capitalism was and still is in a much healthier condition than was German capitalism in 1930–32. On the other hand, at least until he was checked by the Supreme Court, he also went much further than did his German model in breaking down the Constitution (after all, Dr. Brüning had Article 48 to rely upon) and in creating a gigantic bureaucracy such as American tradition holds to be the antithesis of liberal democratic government and which, in fact, absolutism cannot do without.

Despite his pledges given in campaign speeches at Pittsburgh and elsewhere, he was before the end of two years to create some three score and ten new bureaus and agencies and to add greatly to the number of employees on the Federal pay roll. A vast majority of the new bureaucrats were political appointees. Democrats in Congress insisted upon this to provide jobs for constituents, and the President acquiesced in the arrangement, though it meant the establishment of a great bureaucratic machine made up of persons not necessarily qualified for their jobs and not protected by the civil service laws, but whose tenure of office depended upon their conducting themselves and ordering their work to comply with the political views and objectives of the administration in power. As early as May, 1933, Professor Laski saw that this was likely to result in the erection of " a highly centralized political machine more apt to the development of industrial feudalism than the world has seen in modern times." [5]

Subjectively, of course, a majority or an influential minority of the members of the capitalist state, though clinging to their faith in capitalist production, might not want to travel the Roosevelt road to absolutism or fascism. It is possible, too, that antiquated political machinery might impede, though only temporarily, the movement toward state capitalism. This happened in May, 1935, when the Supreme Court found the Recovery Act unconstitutional. The court ruled again, as it had previously done with respect to the section of the Recovery Act dealing with the petroleum industry, that Congress may not lawfully delegate to the President more authority than is absolutely necessary to carry out its policies and mandates. The effect was to wipe out the NRA, with its various restraints upon competition, and to jeopardize other sections of the Roosevelt program. Jeffersonian Democrat and tory Republican alike hailed the ruling as signalizing a return to economic freedom. And, in truth, it did seem to be pointing American capitalism back to the free market.

Yet, in a larger sense, this was not true, for the court did not, and could not, check the force of the primary economic determinant of a capitalist society, the falling rate of profit. This would, on the one hand, continue to compel capitalist production to seek protection in the suppression of competition and, on the other hand, would continue to force the victims of monopolism to turn to the state for protection. Indeed, the monopolists themselves would want to continue to use the state machinery to assist them in " regulating " competition precisely as they had been doing under the NRA. The moment the restraints of the Recovery Act were removed many business men, both big and little, demanded, first, that the NRA code restrictions be voluntarily kept in force, and, second, that the Roosevelt Administration quickly find some effective substitute for the illegal NRA.

While the Supreme Court's decision temporarily blocked the movement toward state capitalism, in its ultimate effect it must strengthen the forces behind that movement. The longer they are held back, the stronger they will become. Eventually they must break through the bounds of the present rigid constitutionalism. This might be done by a broad amendment to the Constitution which would destroy the balance between legislative and executive and greatly enlarge the latter's authority. But if there were to be a sharp downward turn in the economic situation before the long and laborious task of changing the basic law could be completed, it might be that these forces would not wait upon correct legal procedure but simply overleap the constitutional bounds. Thus, while the Supreme Court may be said to have halted the Rooseveltian drift toward state capitalism, it may turn out that it has really invited fascism via the man on horseback.

But the Roosevelt program has not only been the outward political expression of a gradual movement toward fascism. It has also intensified American imperialism, which, in essence, is but another facet of the same phenomenon. Imperialism is the exploitation of foreign markets by surplus domestic capital seeking profitable employment. As these markets have tended to be preempted by rival imperialist powers, or have in growing measure closed their own doors to foreign exploitation, the struggle for markets among all imperialist powers has grown sharper. In 1914 the struggle reached a critical stage and the World War followed. The war provided no solution and the economic conflict was immediately resumed.

After 1929 the imperialist powers redoubled their efforts, for the capitalist struggle had begun to wreck home markets as well as foreign markets. Tariffs were boosted still higher and new quota systems and other protective schemes that choked off trade were devised. Wages and similar variable costs were slashed, both directly and by monetary devaluation, in the hope of restoring the margin of profit in foreign and domestic trade. Surplus goods were dumped abroad at any price they would fetch – or wantonly destroyed while the workers who produced them went without. Every capitalist state was adopting policies injurious to the vital interests of its neighbors and rivals. Witness only the disaster that followed the wrecking of the Creditanstalt by the French and the tremendous repercussions, in the United States and elsewhere, of Great Britain's abandonment of the gold standard. Witness, too, the sudden Japanese invasion of England's, Germany's and America's markets after the yen was debased.

And every capitalist power began building up its armaments, for this economic struggle could not long go on without precipitating another political crisis like that of 1914. By 1935 it had become abundantly plain that the world-wide conflict would soon again pass into its military phase. Indeed, military hostilities had already begun in the Far East, the Italian dictator was reaching out for new colonies in Africa, while the rise of a reckless, swaggering, defiant Hitlerism signified that the position of Germany, finally at the end of its resources, had become so desperate that German capitalism was preparing to conquer by violence the markets it had to have in order to live.

Feeding upon its fat reserves and separated from the bitter national antagonisms of Europe and Asia by two broad oceans, American capitalism might have felt that it could look askance at the preparations for war going on elsewhere. But it was participating in the economic war as much as ever was British or German or Japanese capitalism. The Smoot-Hawley Tariff, the Hoover moratorium, the Stimson Doctrine were evidence enough of that. As the crisis deepened, American capitalism would inevitably take a more active and aggressive part, would, finally and despite the childish faith of the American people in isolation and self-determination, be drawn into armed strife.

Only by lessening the necessity for seeking new markets, only by relieving the pressure of surplus capital upon the national economy, could American capitalism be turned back from this course. President Roosevelt would either have had to resort to such thorough deflation that it would probably have wrecked the capital structure, or else to such rigid regulation of the flow of income that it would have broken the backbone of capitalism. He chose to do neither. He sought to halt the deflation before it had achieved a thorough cure. He did resort to regulation, but his regulatory efforts were designed to strengthen the flow of profit income, not to check it or to balance it against consumption income. In other words, he was strengthening and stimulating the causes of imperialism.

He did not purpose, it will be remembered, to adjust consumption to production. That would have meant increasing the abundance which is the deadly enemy of profits. Rather did he endeavor to make the adjustment the other way about, to limit production to consumption. The results are obvious. Unemployment has not been appreciably reduced. Real wages, the only accurate measure of consumer buying power, have not increased, but have actually declined. Farm buying power has been stimulated, but by artificial means, through manipulation of the currency and the payment of direct subsidies. The Roosevelt policy, in the words of John Strachey, has been one that " only impoverishes the internal market still more." [6] This means, of course, that a proportionately larger part of the productive capacity of American capital cannot be put to profitable employment at home.

Through other sections of the Roosevelt program this surplus capital has even been augmented. Prices were raised by restricting competition, limiting production and debasing the dollar. The price rise reflected no genuine increase in consuming demand. Indeed, its effect was to impoverish the internal market still more. Yet, for the time being, the rise in prices has enabled some businesses to add considerably to their earnings. The Roosevelt spending program has also helped them to put money in the bank. Ordinarily, a large part of this profit income would go into new investment, into new capital plant. But the domestic market is not expanding, at least not in relation to the normal rate of expansion of productive capacity, which means that capital is again accumulating faster than buying power. Hence the opportunities for earning new or increased profits from new investments remain few and far between. Bank deposits and bank reserves have steadily expanded, commercial loans have shown no comparable growth, and the capital market has remained stagnant. In sum, not only has the Roosevelt program tended to keep a large part of the capital plant of the country idle, but it has served to pile up still more idle capital in the banks.

What can be done with this surplus capital which cannot be put to work producing goods for the domestic market without further impairing the rate of profit? Can it be destroyed? President Roosevelt has chosen rather to protect it through the Reconstruction Finance Corporation, the Federal Deposit Insurance Corporation and other agencies. Can it be used in stock market speculation? Obviously it could, though that would offer no real or enduring solution, as was shown by the events of 1929. The only alternative is to use it in exploiting foreign markets. Such exploitation takes place either through the direct sale of goods abroad or through their indirect sale by means of foreign loans. Direct sales are increasingly difficult, however, since imperialist and colonial powers everywhere have raised their tariff barriers ever higher to protect their own trade and markets. Foreign loans are also difficult to place because potential borrowers either lack the means of ensuring a fair and safe return on such investments or are burdened with a surfeit of capital on their own account. Franklin Roosevelt vehemently denounced the foreign-loan policy of the preceding Administration as one of the most ruinous of Herbert Hoover's " economic heresies." Nevertheless, he has sought to follow the same policy even more directly than his predecessor. Two Export-Import Banks were created with a view to facilitating the extension of credit to foreign customers. Thus, while the Republican Presidents were content to let the capitalists take care of their own loan operations and asked only that the loans be such as not to conflict with national policies, President Roosevelt has used the power of the state in attempting directly to stimulate trade through the granting of credit. But the Export-Import Banks have accomplished very little.

One weapon, however, has proved effective – devaluation of the dollar. This automatically increased American tariff rates by approximately 69 per cent, so affording additional protection to the domestic market, and at the same time it reduced the gold prices of American goods in the world market by about 41 per cent. The advantage over American trade that the British had gained by abandoning gold in September, 1931, was soon wiped out. American exports of manufactured goods increased steadily but slowly through 1934 and the early part of 1935. But by the middle of 1935 the impetus of the cut in the dollar had about spent itself. The export trade had again turned downward. The Administration would have to redouble its efforts to capture foreign markets.

It was about then, too, that the Administration seemed once more to be turning toward internationalism. Secretary of the Treasury Morgenthau hinted in a radio speech at the desirability of currency stabilization and a general international trade conference. The Bureau of Foreign and Domestic Commerce took up the same theme a few days later. And in the first week of June Secretary of State Hull, the only confirmed internationalist in the Roosevelt Cabinet, was for the first time given a free hand in promoting reciprocal trade agreements when George N. Peek, an ardent advocate of a closed economy, was dismissed from his post of " Special Adviser to the President on Foreign Trade."

Actually this did not mean that economic nationalism was being abandoned or diluted, for the Administration continued to seek to develop an ever firmer control over the domestic market despite the hindrances being placed before it by the courts. Indeed, a closed economy was becoming increasingly essential to success in the struggle for foreign markets, since only thus can prices and wages be regulated in such a way as to make it possible to earn profits on exports of surplus goods and capital. The change of front merely signified a growing realization on the part of the President and his associates that the problem of putting surplus capital to work could not be solved exclusively within a closed economy. It heralded a determined renewal of American participation in the fight for markets. But meantime, alas, the basic crisis was running on unchecked and the world-wide economic conflict was growing more tense. One after the other of the remaining gold-standard countries was being caught up in currency difficulties, that is, they were losing trade to rivals who had already cheapened their own currencies. So one by one these countries were taking up the same weapon, adding meanwhile, along with the rest of the world, to their military armaments.

Nor were the stronger imperialist powers disposed to compromise or sue for peace. The British were refusing to listen to any talk of currency stabilization. They hesitated to drive the pound sterling down still further in order to regain the advantage they had lost to the United States — for currency depreciation is a two-edged sword that cuts into domestic buying power as well as into the trade of rivals — but they insisted on keeping this formidable weapon close at hand as the economic war grew more bitter. Nor, in its rediscovered internationalism, was the Roosevelt Administration taking any other attitude. Secretary Morgenthau certainly was not suing for peace in his radio speech. Rather was he laying down terms upon which other powers might have peace. He was seeking, in effect, to consolidate the victory of the dollar over the pound sterling. He warned the British that " we are no longer at a disadvantage. We revalued our currency no more than was necessary and we can go either way. Our hands are untied." [7] No petition for peace was this, but an ultimatum, a challenge to the enemy to yield or take the consequences.

But whatever new economic measures he may take in the future to strengthen the United States in this world-wide struggle, it has long been plain that Franklin Roosevelt is getting ready in a military way for the ultimate outcome of the economic war. Here is a role for which he is eminently fitted by tradition, training and temperament. His is the blood of the seafaring Aspinwalls and Delanos and of the earnestly patriotic Roosevelts. As a boy, his mother has said, " he always thrilled to tales of the sea. . . . Franklin's wanderlust, confined though it was at first to mythical excursions, can be attributed directly to my own love of ships and distant horizons. The Delanos have always been associated with the sea. My grandfather, who owned a fleet of rugged sailing vessels, became his own best sea captain, and my father, like his father before him, had a great affection for the sea. . . . [Franklin] loved history in any form and used to pore over Admiral Mahan's ' History of Sea Power ' until he had practically memorized the whole book." [8]

The authors of one of the biographies of Franklin Roosevelt tell of his " passionate interest in the lives of naval heroes. He read everything of the kind he could find: the life of Perry, of Bainbridge, John Paul Jones, Decatur, Farragut. . . . Eventually his dreams took definite form. He wanted to go to sea. This idea he confided to his parents. They smiled and considered sending him to Annapolis." [9] In his 'teens he was given a ship of his own to sail in the neighborhood of Campobello. Earlier he had begun collecting naval mementoes. He used to bring home for safe-keeping, according to his mother, " a button ripped off an officer's coat in action, a miniature brass cannon, or a tarnished bit of braid torn off a battered cap." [10] While at Harvard he began to assemble a naval library, which contained almost ten thousand volumes by the time he had become Assistant Secretary of the Navy at 31, and which today is doubtless one of the finest and most extensive collections of its kind to be found anywhere.

His navalism exhibited itself again in his jumping at the chance to become chief assistant to Secretary Daniels in the

Wilson Administration after he had rejected posts offered him in other branches of the Government. Here his sense of leadership, the streak of righteous rebellion that was in him, and his profound devotion to the navy caused him to upset admirals, bureaucrats and red tape in his efforts to improve the personnel and fighting quality of the fleet. He was always quick to reward personal efficiency and valor, even in connection with the drive of American imperialism in the Caribbean. Thus, he was instrumental in obtaining a Congressional Medal of Honor for Smedley D. Butler, then a major in the Marine Corps, for the latter's exploit in taking Fort Reviere and wiping out a force of three hundred natives during the American occupation of Haiti in 1915.

When the World War began, Franklin Roosevelt was among the first to assert that the United States needed a powerful navy, a fleet second only to that of England. He delivered numerous public speeches to urge support for his program. He wrote many newspaper and magazine articles to the same end. His biographers report that " he joined General Leonard Wood and Colonel Theodore Roosevelt in the declaration that ' a big navy inspires respect rather than active antagonism.' " [11] He appeared before Congressional committees to insist that the Government build more ships. Before the House Committee on Naval Affairs on March 28, 1916, he expressed the opinion that " in a naval building race the United States could outbuild Germany," though such references to Germany would seem to have been in violation of the spirit, if not the letter, of President Wilson's neutrality proclamation. When the little-navy group in Washington, for reasons of economy, began to criticize the naval-expansion plans, he replied that " not one dollar, not one ship, not one man " must be taken from the building program. " Although we have in the past few years increased our navy faster than ever before," he declared, " other powers have increased theirs even faster." He was not only willing but eager to press forward in that mad race.

He remained the navalist and expansionist after the war. He wanted a big fleet maintained and a huge naval reserve created. He even favored universal training for both the army and navy, as he suggested in a speech before the New York State Convention of the American Legion at Rochester on October 11, 1919. With the passing of time he apparently felt it necessary to make concessions to the peace movement. Thus, in another talk to the Legion, at Saratoga Springs on September 5, 1930, he said: " We should all work against war, but if it should come we should be better prepared than we were before. . . . I am not militaristic by any means. I do not believe in a large standing army, as you know, nor in a large navy, but I am 100 per cent for having this country ready for an emergency." Such, of course, is the language of every militarist.

When he entered the White House he showed almost at once that he meant to have the country get ready for an emergency, that is, for war. His appointment of Senator Claude Swanson to be Secretary of the Navy was significant. Swanson was even more popular with the admirals than his predecessor had been, though Secretary Adams had gone so far as to quarrel publicly with President Hoover on the big-navy issue in order to curry favor with the admirals. Swanson had attended the Geneva Disarmament Conference the year before and had come away with the unshakable conviction that the other naval powers were actively preparing for war and that, therefore, it behooved the United States to do likewise.

No less significant is the blessing President Roosevelt has heaped upon the elaborate construction program for which the admirals had long been agitating. Even Presidents Coolidge and Hoover thought these plans too extravagant to be considered. Franklin Roosevelt was to show no hesitation in accepting them, though his action meant the launching of what — with one exception — was the biggest and costliest peace-time preparedness program in the country's history. The exception was the 1916 program, and it will be remembered that it was the same Franklin Roosevelt who had taken the lead in that year in persuading Congress and the country that the United States ought to have a navy "second to none."

His economy pledge appeared for a while to stand in the way of the new program. The President sought to redeem this pledge by cutting the army and navy budgets by about $100,-000,000. But then he turned to the Public Works fund and from this handed the Navy Department approximately $290,-000,000 and the War Department about $100,000,000. (The Engineer Corps of the army was also given $353,000,000 of Public Works money for rivers and harbors projects and similar improvements usually included in the War Department budget.) The Hearst press and the Navy League were jubilant. They had bitterly criticized the naval policies of the Republican Presidents, but they met the Roosevelt policy with loud acclaim. "For the first time in twelve years," declared the Navy League's president, Nelson Macy, " the Navy League, in paying this tribute to President Roosevelt, has the satisfaction of congratulating the American people upon the attainment of an adequate and reasonably assured program of naval construction. The forceful leadership of the President, with the cooperation of Congress, has accomplished all that could have been accomplished to redeem the neglect of naval construction since the Washington Treaty of 1922." [12]

Since then the President has dumped his economy pledge overboard and has approved, not only extensive additions to the naval establishment along the Pacific Coast, not only a series of army and navy war games on the largest scale the country has even known, and not only an " adequate " merchant marine to serve as a naval auxiliary (for which he won the "warm approval" of the Navy League), but also the largest naval and military appropriations in American peacetime history.

William T. Stone, of the Foreign Policy Association, has looked into the question of devising legal means of keeping the

United States out of the approaching imperialist war. He has found both the State Department and the Senate, in response to growing popular pressure, at work on legislation to achieve this end. But the White House has proved a stumbling block.* Writing in August, 1935, Mr. Stone declared:

A few months ago there were hopeful indications that the Roosevelt Administration was about to make up its mind on this paramount issue. Our State Department experts, it was revealed, had been making an exhaustive study of neutrality, with a view to revising our traditional neutrality policy. Their studies were shrouded in secrecy, but there seemed reason to believe that something tangible might emerge. Mr. Roosevelt, at one of his press conferences last December, went so far as to suggest that he might have something to say about this matter very soon. Before he left for his Florida fishing trip in March the President ordered Secretary Hull to complete his survey with all possible speed. Senator Nye, whose munitions committee had been pursuing the trail of American bankers through the maze of wartime financing, was led to believe that a program to keep us out of war might actually be pressed at this session of Congress.

But nothing happened. In April Mr. Roosevelt returned from Florida with a fresh coat of tan and promptly called for Secretary Hull to submit his completed report. Mr. Hull complied, though what his report contained and what the President proposed to do

* Shortly after Mr. Stone's article appeared the Italo-Ethiopian crisis became acute. The isolationists in the Senate, frightened by this development, sought to force through Congress an ill-considered " neutrality " resolution that would, in effect, have automatically cut off American economic relations with most of the world in the event of another major war abroad. While the Senate resolution left it to the President to say what actually constituted a war, legally the resolution tied his hands. President Roosevelt did not relish being thus limited in his freedom to deal with foreign affairs. Through his lieutenants in the House he was able to have the terms of the Senate resolution liberalized and its life limited to a period of six months. This action left the whole question of neutrality legislation open to further consideration and debate. The President's attitude indicated anew, as pointed out below, that he does not intend, in the event of another war, to abandon foreign trade and foreign markets without a struggle. Were he inclined to abandon this trade, he would, of course, have had no good reason for opposing the plan offered by the isolationists in the Senate.

about it remained a mystery. Repeated queries merely brought the reply that the Department's survey had revealed appalling difficulties and enormous complications. About the only tangible thing that emerged was a report that the navy, with professional interest in the freedom of the seas, had lodged strenuous objections with the State Department and the White House to any modification in our traditional doctrines of neutrality. When Senators Nye and Clark called at the White House a few days later, they encountered a vague uncertainty on the whole subject. . . .[13]

On the one hand, then, the Roosevelt economic policies, shaped to conform with the objective needs of the profit system, have been forcing the country ever further along the road of imperialism; on the other, the Roosevelt military and naval policies have been preparing the country for the inevitable outcome of that imperialist struggle. When the question arises as to whether the United States can stay out of the coming war, " appalling difficulties and enormous complications " are discovered — which can only mean that a policy of isolated neutrality, if rigidly adhered to, would cause such a great loss of trade and thereby cut so deeply into the rate of profit as to bring about a domestic depression of truly menacing proportions. And when Senators who feel that even this is not too much to pay for peace approach the President on the question, they encounter " a vague uncertainty on the whole subject."

In truth, there is no vague uncertainty about it. The President made it plain in his special message to Congress on March 4, 1935, that he has no intention of giving up American foreign trade because other countries go to war. In this message he specifically requested the construction of an " adequate merchant marine " to enable the United States to carry on a " neutral peaceful foreign trade . . . in the event of a major war in which the United States is not involved." But the experience of 1914–17 has clearly indicated that in the event of another major war there will be no such thing as a " neutral peaceful foreign trade." In all human probability the world will then be divided into two rival camps and the only trade of consequence that could be carried on would be that with one or the other of the two groups of belligerents. This would place the country in the very position in which it found itself in 1916 and 1917. Through his naval-expansion program, moreover, the President has made it equally plain that he has no intention of meekly abandoning foreign trade or foreign markets when the imperialist war arrives — one does not build warships to protect trade if one plans to withdraw that trade the moment the need for such protection arises. The President may be wholly sincere in his oft-expressed desire for peace, but the course he is following — and is compelled to follow, for the objective needs of a profit economy give him no alternative — is one that leads directly to war.

☼ 3 ☼

NOBLESSE OBLIGE

~

HISTORY will in time, of course, render its own verdict as to
the social worth and significance of Franklin Roosevelt. His
contemporaries must base their judgment on contemporary
values and standards. And in this shorter view many have found
him wanting in certain apparently essential respects. He has
seemed purposeless, confused, unstable. He has yielded to pressure and has frequently contradicted and repudiated himself.
He has wavered between what the popular journalists have
lately learned to call " the right " and " the left." Early in 1932
Walter Lippmann wrote of him that he " is a highly impres-
sionable person without a firm grasp of public affairs and without very strong convictions . . . an amiable man with many
philanthropic impulses, but he is not the dangerous enemy of
anything. He is too eager to please." [14] After he had been two
years in the White House the editors of the *New Republic*
reported that

the weakness of his method and of the forces behind him, apparent to some from the first, has been growing more obvious
month by month. There has never been a very clear idea, in his
mind or anyone else's, of what sort of new order he was bent on
creating. His program was improvised from suggestions arising in
dozens of sources, many of which were mutually incompatible.
In political terms, it seemed to be built up by attempting to satisfy
everyone, by yielding to this pressure or that. He threw a bone
to labor and a piece of meat to employers, arranged higher prices

309

for farmers, and also higher prices for industry, whose products farmers buy; he called for regulation of abuses, but refrained from demanding regulation stringent enough to accomplish his purpose, or failed to enforce it though he had the authority, whenever someone powerful raised an objection.[15]

He has revealed himself as well through his choice of associates and advisers. They have represented every shade of political thought and economic opinion to be found within the broad confines of capitalism. They have included agents of the monopolists and spokesmen of the lower middle class, high protectionists and Manchester liberals, advocates of *laissez faire* and industrial disciplinarians, classical economists and worshippers at the shrine of Maynard Keynes, internationalists and isolationists, Republicans and Democrats, confessed Fascists and ardent Social Democrats. Their presence in his entourage has reflected both his eagerness to please and the amazing confusion existing in his mind.

To be sure, his confidence in himself is almost beyond compare. He has a sense of *noblesse oblige* such as few, if any, American Presidents have had. He feels that persons of his kind and social standing owe it to their fellow men to take over positions of responsibility in public life. He believes that such persons, when entrusted with public office, can really do no wrong. They may make mistakes, but they will be mistakes of the head and not of the heart. His own mistakes have been of this kind. He has erred, not because he has not meant well, not because he has not tried to do right, but largely because of his economic illiteracy and his class prejudices. His emotions run deep, but his thinking skips lightly over the surface, affected only by the more concrete experiences and more obvious facts of life. In 1929 he did not even suspect that anything might be amiss with the underlying economic situation. Only a few months before the Wall Street crash he had found industry in New York State "in a very healthy and prosperous condition." When the storm broke, its meaning wholly escaped him. Even later, in his Atlanta speech in 1932, he was to confess, though only by implication, that he did not know why the economic system had run amok or how to set it right again. But he yearned to do something to the end that it might be set right again. He wanted also to do something for the unfortunate victims of modern capitalism, but here again he was moved by moral considerations and visual evidence of suffering and not by profound knowledge of economic causes.

Yet he has not been without purpose. What he has been trying to do — subjectively and, perhaps, subconsciously — is to recreate in the modern and complex industrial society which is America the pleasant human relationships that exist in the manorial community of Hyde Park, or that may once have existed in the agrarian community of Jefferson's time. He has wanted to make men moral, to teach them to be honest in their dealings with their fellows and fair in their treatment of their inferiors. He has wanted to teach the leaders of the community that leadership consists in responsibility as well as authority, and to teach the workers that it is their place to toil faithfully for their own betterment and that of the community. He has wanted, in his own words, "to try to increase the security and the happiness of a larger number of people in all occupations of life and in all parts of the country." *Noblesse oblige* could go no further.

Objectively, his task has been to tide American capitalism over a particularly critical period, and to achieve this he has had to deal with hard realities that have forced him to shift and maneuver with a frequency disturbing both to " business confidence " and to the liberal intellectuals who would make America over into something they call " the social state." Various factors, not the least among them being the subjective influence of his prejudices as a member of the *rentier* class, have compelled him to yield to superior forces in the national economy. Thus, he has found it impossible to reconcile " a fair reward " for honest toil with " fair profits " for the owners and managers of his " everlasting American system." He has found it impossible to carry through any of his grandiose reform schemes, much to the bewilderment of his liberal and progressive supporters. To a certain extent, it may be said, his confusion, his apparent planlessness, has but mirrored the irreconcilable confusions of modern capitalism. Men must be fed, or they may revolt; work must be provided, or the whole machine may break down; but when means of providing work and wages are sought, it is promptly discovered that the only available means are those which threaten the rate of profit, the mainspring of modern capitalism.

Nevertheless, Franklin Roosevelt's presence in the White House has been of benefit to the profit system, not only because he has strengthened the forces of industrial and finance monopolism, but because of his influence upon the masses of the people. His air of friendly and confident leadership has served to check the fears of the petit bourgeoisie and to allay, if only for the time being, the unrest of the workers. He has induced the capitalist state to yield a number of purely defensive concessions to the lower classes. There can be little doubt as to his sincerity in wanting to help them; yet, objectively, these concessions have come just at a time when American capitalism would seem to need the continued support of the masses.* If American capitalism were less affluent, somewhat nearer the final crisis, President Roosevelt's true role would be more readily apparent than it is today. For if its reserves were ex-

* History shows that a ruling class whose social usefulness has passed invariably finds it expedient to throw defensive concessions to the submerged classes, though these sops, as a rule, prove futile. They do not strengthen the ruling class, nor do they restore its social usefulness, but serve merely as a confession of weakness and so tend to encourage the class which is to succeed to the state power. The French feudal lords gave the rising bourgeoisie the Estates-General. The Russian aristocracy gave the peasants and workers the Duma and the Stolypin "reforms." The American ruling class (though not without opposition from the bourbons among its members) is giving the workers the Roosevelt "reforms" and the empty promise of "social security."

hausted, or nearly so, the state could not afford the luxury of the concessions the President has been making to the lower classes. Then it would be obvious that his objective mission is really to keep these classes loyal to the state. But in such event Franklin Roosevelt, so plainly a representative of the upper classes, would probably not be President. Then it would be found necessary (again in a purely objective sense, of course) to elevate to the presidency someone bearing a working-class or radical label so as to hold the support of the workers by giving them the pretense of a share of political power in place of the more substantial concessions Franklin Roosevelt has promised.

In the process of winning and retaining the loyalty of the masses President Roosevelt has inevitably made enemies of those who have not understood the importance of keeping them content. He has wandered quite often into demagogism, which some people have mistaken for " collectivism " or even " socialism." He has frightened a number of capitalists and many old-fashioned Americans. After all, the " enlightenment " of American capitalism is only skin-deep. Below the surface still lies the restless, independent spirit of the robber barons. Anything smacking of state interference is instinctively resented and distrusted by the descendants of the rugged individuals of 1880. In all likelihood they will in time have to turn to fascism as a means of self-defense, but so long as there is no real revolutionary threat to their economic power they would as soon do without the noise and the trappings and the deceptive regimentation of " national socialism." Nor can it be overlooked that many lesser Americans still have a deep and abiding faith in the " American dream." *

* Whereas two years before the President had been playing for the most part on popular mistrust of the bankers and business leaders, by 1935 he was changing his tune. He was now addressing his appeals as much to the tories and the business community as to the lower middle class. He was finding that his propaganda was being largely offset by counter-blasts from the Hearst press, which was conducting a relentless campaign against com-

Despite the objections of these groups, the authority of the state has perforce been enlarged under President Roosevelt. This is not only because this has been necessary to satisfy his own sense of leadership, but also and more particularly because the economic and political needs of the American social order have required it. So vast and complex are the problems of the national economy becoming that they can only be dealt with by a powerful state agency. A strong state can curb at least some of the excesses of capitalism and thereby tend to slow down its steady progress toward self-extinction. Secondly, a majority of the petit bourgeoisie have lost their confidence in the " American dream " and their traditional dread of bureaucracy and state tyranny. This " dream " did not save them in

---

munism in Russia and was implying that the Roosevelt Administration was carrying the United States in the same direction, from certain business men, whose hopes had been revived by a minor economic recovery and who were demanding that the Government return to a policy of *laissez faire*, and from the reawakened Republicans, who were seeking to make political capital of the " collectivist " tendencies of the Roosevelt regime and of the business community's demand for less experimentation and less interference in its affairs. The President met the counter-attack with his prearranged exchange of letters with Roy W. Howard, the newspaper publisher, in which he promised to give business the " breathing spell " it wanted, though the President could not have redeemed this promise unless he stood ready to discard virtually the whole of his social and economic philosophy, which he certainly was not prepared to do. At the same time he addressed a sharp note to the Soviet Government, declaring that " serious consequences " would follow unless Communist propaganda in the United States were immediately curbed. This signalized his surrender to the Hearst press. The change of front was made in that spirit of joyous unconcern for its effects that had marked all Rooseveltian ballyhoo from the start. For example, the note to Moscow was plainly a threat to break off relations with the Soviet Union. This threat was launched at a moment when international politics was in a particularly delicate state of balance. An Italian war against Ethiopia was about to begin, the menace of Hitlerism was growing in Europe, Soviet-Japanese affairs in the Far East were still in a critical state. Anything as disturbing as the breaking off of diplomatic relations between two great powers — Russia and America — might easily have upset this balance and plunged the world into that tragic conflict which everybody feared and nobody wanted. That the President should have gone to such dangerous lengths in seeking to prove, for the sake of his own political future, that he was no friend of the Communists was characteristic of the man.

1929. They are now quite willing, nay, anxious, to have the state grow stronger in the hope that they might thereby be quickly and effectively helped. The pressure of their voting power compels the state to move in this one direction. Lastly, it should be obvious that the stronger the capitalist state becomes the better it will be able to defend the interests of the ruling class, especially against the advancing working class. The tories in the Republican and Democratic camps may not like this gradual movement toward authoritarianism, but that is mostly because they do not fully appreciate the value of a strong state from the standpoint of their own selfish interests.

In another and no less important sense it can be said that the bourbon gods were kind to American capitalism when they put this country gentleman in the White House. Franklin Roosevelt's patriotism is unimpeachable. Here, too, he is eager to please. He is ready to do or die (or at least to let millions of young Americans die) to guard the capitalist state and all its interests against attack from without. And as the second imperialist war draws near, American capitalism stands in ever greater need of the services of just such a champion.

Indeed, there are some who believe that precisely because of his failure to reconcile the contradictions of the profit system, President Roosevelt may himself choose war as " the way out." This is not to say, quoting Charles A. Beard, who inclines to this belief, " that President Roosevelt will deliberately plunge the country into . . . war in his efforts to escape the economic crisis. There will be an ' incident,' a ' provocation.' Incidents and provocations are of almost daily occurrence. Any government can quickly magnify one of them into a ' just cause for war.' Confronted by the difficulties of a deepening economic crisis and by the comparative ease of a foreign war, what will President Roosevelt do? " And Mr. Beard answers by saying that in his judgment the President " will choose the latter, or, perhaps it would be more accurate to say, amid powerful conflicting emotions he will ' stumble into ' the latter." [16]

315

Nor need this judgment be based wholly on political history, for who, considering the nature of the growing imperialist crisis as well as the lofty patriotism of Franklin Roosevelt himself, his ardent navalism, his eagerness to please, will say with any confidence that he will not lead the country into war?

BIBLIOGRAPHY, NOTES, AND INDEX

BIBLIOGRAPHY

(Including those works to which reference is made in this study or which otherwise were found useful as sources of information and guidance in its preparation.)

Adamic, Louis, *Dynamite*, New York, 1931.

Adams, Arthur B., *Our Economic Revolution*, Norman, Oklahoma, 1933.

Beard, Charles A. and Mary R., *The Rise of American Civilization*, New York, 1927.

Beard, Charles A., and Smith, George H. E., *The Future Comes*, New York, 1933.

Berle, A. A., Jr., and others, *America's Recovery Program*, New York, 1934.

Bernheim, Alfred L., and Van Doren, Dorothy, editors, *Labor and the Government*, New York, 1935.

Bingham, Alfred M., and Rodman, Selden, editors, *Challenge to the New Deal*, New York, 1934.

Bonn, M. J., *The American Adventure*, New York, 1934.

Brown, Douglass V., and others, *The Economics of the Recovery Program*, New York, 1934.

Bryce, Viscount, James, *Modern Democracies*, New York, 1921.

Chamberlain, John, *Farewell to Reform*, New York, 1932.

Corey, Lewis, *The Decline of American Capitalism*, New York, 1934.

Cummins, E. E., *The Labor Problem in the United States*, New York, 1932.

Dearing, Charles, and others, *The A B C of the N R A*, Washington, 1934.

Doane, Robert R., *The Measurement of American Wealth*, New York, 1933.

Douglas, Lewis W., *The Liberal Tradition*, New York, 1935.

Faÿ, Bernard, *Roosevelt and His America*, Boston, 1933.

Gallagher, Michael F., *Government Rules Industry*, New York, 1934.

Galloway, George B., and others, *Industrial Planning Under Codes*, New York, 1935.

Hacker, Louis M., *A Short History of the New Deal*, New York, 1934.

Hacker, Louis M., and Kendrick, B. B., *The United States Since 1865*, New York, 1934.

Hallgren, Mauritz A., *Seeds of Revolt*, New York, 1933.

Hausleiter, Leo, *The Machine Unchained*, New York, 1933.

Henderson, Fred, *Foundations for the World's New Age of Plenty*, New York, 1933.

Holcombe, Arthur N., *Government in a Planned Democracy*, New York, 1935.

Ickes, Harold L., *The New Democracy*, New York, 1934.

Johnson, Hugh S., *The Blue Eagle, From Egg to Earth*, New York, 1935.

Lindley, Ernest K., *Franklin D. Roosevelt*, Indianapolis, 1931.

Lindley, Ernest K., *The Roosevelt Revolution*, New York, 1933.

Looker, Earle, *This Man Roosevelt*, New York, 1932.

Looker, Earle, *The American Way: Franklin Roosevelt in Action*, New York, 1933.

Lyon, Leverett S., and others, *The National Recovery Administration*, Washington, 1935.

MacDonald, William, *The Menace of Recovery*, New York, 1934.

Mills, Ogden L., *What of Tomorrow?* New York, 1935.

Morgan-Webb, Sir Charles, *The Money Revolution*, New York, 1935.

Pitigliani, Fausto, *The Italian Corporative State*, London, 1933.

Robey, Ralph, *Roosevelt versus Recovery*, New York, 1934.

Roosevelt, Franklin D., *Whither Bound?* Boston, 1926.

Roosevelt, Franklin D., *Looking Forward*, New York, 1933.

Roosevelt, Franklin D., *On Our Way*, New York, 1934.

BIBLIOGRAPHY

Roosevelt, Mrs. James, (as told to Isabelle Leighton and Gabrielle Forbush), *My Boy Franklin*, New York, 1933.

Ross, Leland M., and Grobin, Allen W., *This Democratic Roosevelt*, New York, 1932.

Sait, Edward M., *American Parties and Elections*, New York, 1927.

Shouse, Jouett, *You Are the Government*, Boston, 1935.

Small, Norman J., *Some Presidential Interpretations of the Presidency*, Baltimore, 1932.

Soule, George, *The Coming American Revolution*, New York, 1934.

Stolberg, Benjamin, and Vinton, Warren Jay, *The Economic Consequences of the New Deal*, New York, 1935.

Swain, Joseph Ward, *Beginning the Twentieth Century*, New York, 1933.

Symes, Lillian, and Clement, Travers, *Rebel America*, New York, 1934.

Taylor, Alonzo E., *The New Deal and Foreign Trade*, New York, 1935.

Tugwell, Rexford Guy, *The Battle for Democracy*, New York, 1935.

Valenstein, Lawrence, and Weiss, E. B., *Business under the Recovery Act*, New York, 1933.

Wallace, Henry A., *America Must Choose* (pamphlet), New York, 1934.

Wallace, Schuyler C., *The New Deal in Action*, New York, 1934.

Wharton, Don, editor, *The Roosevelt Omnibus*, New York, 1934.

Whitney, Simon N., *Trade Associations and Industrial Control*, New York, 1934.

Willcox, O. W., *Reshaping Agriculture*, New York, 1934.

NOTES

PART ONE

1. *This Democratic Roosevelt*, pp. 21-2.
2. *My Boy Franklin*, p. 13.
3. New York *Herald Tribune*, January 18, 1935.
4. *My Boy Franklin*, pp. 22-3.
5. *The American Way*, p. 80
6. *This Democratic Roosevelt*, p. 27.
7. *Fortune*, December, 1933.
8. *The American Way*, pp. 78-9.
9. Ibid., p. 74.
10. *My Boy Franklin*, p. 33.
11. *Fortune*, December, 1933.
12. Quoted in *Farewell to Reform*, p. 238.
13. *True Story Magazine* advertisement in New York *Times*, May 7, 1929.
14. New York *Times*, March 15, 1929.
15. Ferdinand Lundberg, "Prophets Without Honor: 1914–1934," *The American Mercury*, October, 1934.
16. Speech at Syracuse, New York, February 2, 1929.

PART TWO

1. New York *Times*, May 15, 1929.
2. Radio speech, New York City, April 17, 1929.

NOTES

3. For fuller discussion see *Seeds of Revolt*, Chapter II, "When We Were Very Prosperous."
4. New York *Times*, November 25, 1929.
5. Ibid., March 6, 1930.
6. Ibid., July 1, 1930.
7. Ibid., August 28, 1930.
8. *Commerce Yearbook, 1932*, Volume I, pp. 3, 52, 68, 86.
9. Ibid., p. 57.
10. *The Nation*, February 11, 1931.
11. *Commerce Yearbook, 1932*, Volume I, pp. 52, 68, 556.
12. A lecture at Milton Academy, May 18, 1926.
13. Quoted in Henry Hazlitt, "These Economic Experiments," *The American Mercury*, February, 1934.
14. *Some Presidential Interpretations of the Presidency*, p. 42.
15. *My Boy Franklin*, p. 34.
16. Ibid., p. 26.
17. New York *Times*, July 4, 1930.
18. *This Democratic Roosevelt*, p. 189.
19. Ibid., p. 189.
20. New York *Times*, January 22, 1911.
21. Quoted in New York *Times*, January 22, 1911.
22. Ibid., January 22, 1911.
23. New York *Times*, April 9, 1932.
24. New York *Herald Tribune*, April 3, 1932.
25. Speech in Cincinnati, Ohio, February 26, 1932.
26. *The New Yorker*, November 28, 1931.
27. New York *Times*, June 28, 1932.
28. *The Coming American Revolution*, pp. 171–2.
29. Joint statement by President Hoover and Premier Laval, October 25, 1931.
30. New York *Times*, Annual Financial Review, January 3, 1933.
31. *Monthly Labor Review*, May, 1935.
32. New York *Times*, May 11, 1933.
33. Associated Press dispatch, June 26, 1933.
34. *Seeds of Revolt*, Chapter VI, "Red Strikes in Detroit."
35. John T. Flynn, "Michigan Magic," *Harper's Magazine*, December, 1933.
36. New York *Herald Tribune*, November 15, 1932.

37. New York *Times*, November 14, 1932.
38. Ibid., December 23, 1932.

PART THREE

1. *Roosevelt versus Recovery*, pp. 50–1.
2. London *Times*, October 6, 1930.
3. William Bennett Munro, " Our President's Increasing Power," *Current History*, March, 1931.
4. Baltimore *Sun*, January 11, 1933.
5. New York *Herald Tribune*, September 25, 1931.
6. Ibid., February 14, 1933.
7. Speech before the American Society of Newspaper Editors, Washington, D. C., April 21, 1934.
8. Speech before the Academy of Political Science, New York City, November 8, 1933.
9. Lionel D. Edie, " Recovery Races Inflation," *Current History*, January, 1935.
10. Benjamin M. Anderson, *The Chase Economic Bulletin*, Volume XII, No. 3.
11. New York *Times*, January 1, 1934; *Monthly Labor Review*, December, 1934.
12. Radio speech, October 22, 1933.
13. New York *Times*, May 7, 1933.
14. Ibid., May 17, 1933.
15. *Looking Forward*, pp. 125–6.
16. *A Short History of the New Deal*, pp. 31–2.
17. *The Decline of American Capitalism*, p. 482.
18. Quoted in the *American Guardian*, October 6, 1933.
19. Press Release, Bureau of Agricultural Economics, February 1, 1935.
20. Monthly Bulletin, Bureau of Agricultural Economics, February 15, 1935.
21. New York *Times*, March 18, 1935.
22. Houston, Texas, *Post*, February 1, 1935.

23. *Reshaping Agriculture*, p. 66.
24. Ibid., p. 76.
25. *A Short History of the New Deal*, p. 33.
26. Associated Press dispatch, September 17, 1931.
27. John T. Flynn, " Whose Child is the NRA? " *Harper's Magazine*, September, 1934.
28. *Trade Associations and Industrial Control*, pp. 53–4.
29. Ibid., p. 55.
30. Ibid., pp. 34–5.
31. New York *Times*, May 23, 1933.
32. New York *Herald Tribune*, June 14, 1933.
33. New York *Times*, August 27, 1933.
34. Ibid., August 26, 1934.
35. Ibid., August 3, 1934.
36. Baltimore *Sun*, August 22, 1934.
37. *The Italian Corporative State*, Part II.
38. *Seeds of Revolt*, pp. 13–28.
39. *Monthly Labor Review*, December, 1934.
40. Ibid., February, 1935.
41. New York *Times*, January 8, 1934.
42. Ibid., May 6, 1934.
43. *Report of the Executive Secretary of the Executive Council to the President*, August 25, 1934.
44. Press Release, National Industrial Conference Board, October 10, 1934.
45. Leo Wolman, " Wages and Hours Under Codes of Fair Competition," Bulletin 54, National Bureau of Economic Research, March 15, 1935.
46. Monthly Bulletin, The National City Bank, April, 1935.
47. Radio speech, May 7, 1933.
48. Press Release, " Five Years of Unemployment," National Industrial Conference Board, March 21, 1935.
49. Press Release, American Federation of Labor, September 27, 1934.
50. " Five Years of Unemployment," *supra*.
51. New York *Times*, August 31, 1934.
52. New York *Herald Tribune*, August 12, 1934.
53. Editorial Research Reports, Volume II, 1934, No. 16, p. 292.

54. *Monthly Labor Review*, December, 1934.
55. Editorial Research Reports, *supra*, p. 288.
56. Baltimore *Sun*, January 23, 1934.
57. Speech before the Commonwealth Club, San Francisco, December 3, 1934.
58. *The Labor Problem in the United States*, pp. 444–5.
59. "Whose Child is the NRA? " *supra*.
60. Ibid.
61. *Congressional Record*, Volume 77, No. 71, p. 5413.
62. New York *Herald Tribune*, September 4, 1933; New York *Times*, September 21, 1933.
63. Ibid., March 25, 26, 27, 1934.
64. *The Nation*, March 13, 1935.
65. New York *Herald Tribune*, February 6, 1935.
66. *The Nation*, February 13, 1935.
67. Ibid., February 6, 1935; New York *Herald Tribune*, January 23, 1935.
68. New York *Times*, February 28, 1935.
69. *The Nation*, June 7, 1933.
70. *Looking Forward*, pp. 225–6.
71. Ibid., pp. 227–8.
72. Ibid., p. 223.
73. Quoted in *The Decline of American Capitalism*, p. 400.
74. Special message to Congress, March 29, 1933.
75. John T. Flynn, " The Marines Land in Wall Street," *Harper's Magazine*, July, 1934.
76. Associated Press dispatch, July 15, 1934.
77. Press Release, National Association of Manufacturers, April 12, 1934.
78. New York *Times*, July 30, 1933.
79. New York *Herald Tribune*, December 23, 1934.
80. Ibid., December 23, 1934.
81. *Federal Reserve Bulletin*, February, 1935.
82. Ibid., February, 1935.
83. New York *Times*, June 3, 1933.
84. Ibid., March 25, 1933.
85. Ibid., January 6, 1933.
86. Ibid., April 6, 1934.

NOTES

87. Quoted by James P. Warburg, New York *Times*, June 5, 1934.
88. Address before the Advisory Council of the National Conference on Economic Security, November 14, 1934.
89. The *New Republic*, May 1, 1935.
90. Address before the Advisory Council, etc., November 14, 1934.
91. Annual message to the New York State Assembly, January 6, 1932.
92. *A Report on National Planning and Public Works*, submitted to the President, November 28, 1934.
93. *Looking Forward*, p. 65.
94. Harold M. Ware and Webster Powell, "Planning for Permanent Poverty," *Harper's Magazine*, April, 1935.
95. New York *Times*, July 15, 1934.
96. *A Short History of the New Deal*, pp. 104-5.
97. Baltimore *Sun*, July 30, 1934.
98. New York *Times*, June 3, 1932.
99. *A Short History of the New Deal*, p. 106.
100. "Planning for Permanent Poverty," *supra*.

PART FOUR

1. *The Roosevelt Revolution*, p. 4.
2. Lewis Gannett, New York *Herald Tribune*, September 11, 1933.
3. Elmer Davis, *The Saturday Review of Literature*, September 23, 1933.
4. *American Political Science Review*, August, 1932, p. 636.
5. London *Daily Herald*, May 6, 1933.
6. *The Nation*, January 10, 1934.
7. New York *Times*, May 14, 1935.
8. *My Boy Franklin*, pp. 7, 15.
9. *This Democratic Roosevelt*, p. 31.
10. *My Boy Franklin*, p. 30.

11. *This Democratic Roosevelt*, p. 95.
12. New York *Times*, July 30, 1934.
13. The *New Republic*, August 7, 1935.
14. New York *Herald Tribune*, January 8, 1932.
15. The *New Republic*, May 22, 1935.
16. Charles A. Beard, "National Politics and War," *Scribner's Magazine*, February, 1935.

✿ ✿

INDEX

INDEX

A Note on the Type in which
this Book is Set

This book was set on the linotype in Janson, a recutting made direct from the type cast from matrices (now in possession of the Stempel foundry, Frankfurt am Main) made by Anton Janson some time between 1660 and 1687.

Of Janson's origin nothing is known. He may have been a relative of Justus Janson, a printer of Danish birth who practised in Leipzig from 1614 to 1635. Some time between 1657 and 1668 Anton Janson, a punch-cutter and type-founder, bought from the Leipzig printer Johann Erich Hahn the type-foundry which had formerly been a part of the printing house of M. Friedrich Lankisch. Janson's types were first shown in a specimen sheet issued at Leipzig about 1675. Janson's successor, and perhaps his son-in-law, Johann Karl Edling, issued a specimen sheet of Janson types in 1689. His heirs sold the Janson matrices in Holland to Wolffgang Dietrich Erhardt, of Leipzig.

Composed, printed, and bound by The Plimpton Press, Norwood, Mass. Paper made by S. D. Warren Co., Boston